UTILITY	DESCRIPTION	PAGE
NCD (Norton Change Directory)	Provides quick access to any directory on the disk—you don't have to specify the directory's path name. You can also use it to make, remove, or rename directories.	87
NDD (Norton Disk Doctor)	Finds and fixes logical and physical floppy-disk or hard-disk problems. It can also make a disk bootable or reformat it.	169
NI (Norton Integrator)	Lets you run any of the Norton Utilities programs from its full-screen menu, displaying help for each utility when you highlight it.	10
NU (Norton Utility)	Allows you to display technical information about your disks, search for text strings, and perform a number of data-recovery operations.	32, 60
QU (Quick UnErase)	Is a shorter version of NU's UnErase feature. Although it is quicker to use, it cannot recover files that have been partially overwritten.	58
SA (Screen Attributes)	This utility has been incorporated into the BE (Batch Enhancer) utility.	226, 242
SD (Speed Disk)	Examines disk files and reorganizes them to eliminate file fragmentation. You can move individual files or directories, groups of files quickly, or unfragment all files on a disk. SD can also provide a fragmentation report without reorganizing the files on the disk.	152
SF (Safe Format)	Formats disks so that their existing data can be recovered, unlike the DOS FORMAT command. In full-screen or command-line mode, you can tailor the format to a particular disk type and format mode. You can also add a volume label.	52
SI (System Information)	Provides a detailed report on your system's hardware and calculates three performance indicators.	135
TM (Time Mark)	Enables you to start and reset up to four different stopwatch timers.	244
TS (Text Search)	Allows you to search for the occurrence of specific text in a file or files.	110
UD (UnRemove Directory)	Restores directories you have removed. If the files that were in the directory before it was removed have not yet been overwritten, they will also be recovered.	73
VL (Volume Label)	Allows you to add or change the volume label on a disk.	197
Wipedisk	Destroys the contents of a disk by overwriting them a specified number of times.	186
Wipefile	Overwrites specified files, preventing their recovery by any means.	189

MASTERING THE NORTON UTILITIES

MASTERING THE NORTON UTILITIES™

PETER DYSON

SAN FRANCISCO • PARIS • DÜSSELDORF • LONDON

Acquisitions Editor: Dianne King
Developmental Editor: Vince Leone
Copy Editor: Nancy O'Donnell
Technical Editor: Robert Campbell
Word Processors: Bob Myren and Scott Campbell
Book Designer: Julie Bilski
Chapter Art: Eleanor Ramos
Technical Art: Jeffrey James Giese
Screen Graphics: Sonja Schenk
Typesetter: Winnie Kelly
Proofreader: Chris Calder
Indexer: Anne Leach
Cover Designer: Thomas Ingalls + Associates
Cover Photographer: Mark Johann
Screen reproductions produced by XenoFont

Bernoulli Box is a trademark of Iomega Corporation.
Compaq and Deskpro are trademarks of Compaq Computer Corporation.
C/PM and Concurrent are trademarks of Digital Research Incorporated.
dBASE II, dBASE III Plus, dBASE IV, and Framework II are trademarks of Ashton-Tate, Inc.
Disk Technician is a trademark of Prime Solutions, Inc.
DOS, IBM PC, PC/AT, PCjr, PC/XT, and TopView are trademarks of International Business Machines Corporation.
Epson is a trademark of Epson America, Inc.
Format Recover, the Norton Utilities, Speed Disk, and UnErase are trademarks of Peter Norton Computing, Inc.
Hercules is a trademark of Hercules Computer Products.
Intel is a trademark of Intel Corporation.
Keyworks is a trademark of Alpha Software Corporation.
Lotus and 1-2-3 are trademarks of Lotus Development Corporation.
Motorola is a trademark of Motorola, Inc.
MS WORD, MS-DOS, Windows, and XENIX are trademarks of Microsoft Corporation.
PFS:Write is a trademark of Software Publishing Corporation.
R:BASE 5000 and R:BASE System V are trademarks of Microrim, Inc.
Reflex and SideKick are trademarks of Borland International, Inc.
SpinRite is a trademark of Gibson Research Corporation.
UNIX is a trademark of AT&T Corporation.
VisiCalc is a trademark of VisiCorp, Inc.
WordPerfect is a trademark of WordPerfect Corporation.
WordStar is a trademark of MicroPro International, Inc.
XenoFont is a trademark of XenoSoft.

SYBEX is a registered trademark of SYBEX, Inc.

SYBEX is not affiliated with any manufacturer.

Library of Congress Card Number: 89-60623
ISBN 0-89588-575-1
Manufactured in the United States of America
10 9 8 7 6 5 4

To Nancy

Everything should be made as simple as possible, but not simpler.
—Albert Einstein

ACKNOWLEDGMENTS

A book is never the sole product of the person whose name appears on the cover. Many people have worked on this project, providing technical assistance, advice, and many other services.

I want to thank everyone at SYBEX, particularly Dianne King, acquisitions editor, who first suggested the project; Eleanor Ramos, chapter layout; Winnie Kelly, typesetting; Chris Calder, proofreading; Bob Myren and Scott Campbell, word processing; and Robert Campbell, technical editor. I also want to thank Vince Leone, Nancy O'Donnell, and Peter Weverka for editing the manuscript and Anne Leach for the index. Any remaining mistakes—as they say—are all mine.

At Peter Norton Computing, Inc., I want to thank Alicia Colin for providing prerelease copies and documentation for the Standard and Advanced Editions of the Norton Utilities Version 4.5, and Kraig Lane and J.J. Schoch of Technical Support for answering my questions.

On a more personal note, I want to thank Nancy for all her encouragement, patience, and support; Stephen Wilson for reading and commenting on the early drafts; and Gene Weisskopf for getting me involved with this endeavor in the first place.

CONTENTS AT A GLANCE

TABLE OF CONTENTS

CHAPTER 5 FINDING AND PRINTING TEXT *109*

APPENDIX B EVOLUTION *299*

INTRODUCTION

The Norton Utilities are a unique collection of small, efficient programs. Each program does one thing and does it well. The Norton Utilities initially became famous for their near-legendary ability to recover erased files, but over time the programs have evolved into the well-rounded package of programs that is available today.

WHY USE THE NORTON UTILITIES?

The Norton Utilities occupy a unique position in the MS-DOS world. They supplement the basic DOS operating system in several ways: they provide techniques for repairing disks and restoring erased files and directories, they extend the capabilities of some DOS commands, and they allow the curious user to look into the dark corners of the PC that cannot normally be seen without complex programming.

PREVENTING AND RECOVERING FROM DISASTERS

Problems with hard and floppy disks are both common and avoidable. The Norton Utilities' NDD (Norton Disk Doctor) utility provides you with the means of checking your disks for potential problems and fixing them before they cost you any data—and hard work.

Even when you make sure your disks are in top condition, you can still lose data by accidentally erasing files or directories that you need. DOS does not offer a viable solution. The Norton Utilities package, however, provides two.

The QU program can rescue files after they have been erased by the DOS DEL or ERASE command if you haven't saved anything else to their disk since erasing them. The NU program's UnErase feature can recover large files that are spread out over the disk's surface; it may also be able to recover some of the data from files that have been overwritten. In fact, you can even use the FR (Format Recover) utility to restore the entire contents of your hard disk if you format it by mistake.

EXTENDING THE CAPABILITIES OF DOS

There are some things that DOS does not do very well, and the Norton Utilities provide programs that extend the scope and capabilities of DOS. For example, the BE (Batch Enhancer) utility supplements the DOS batch-programming language with programs that give you control over the screen colors and attributes and provide true conditional branching from inside a batch file. BE also makes it easier to write batch files that create windows and boxes.

Similarly, the NCC (Norton Control Center) utility enables you to configure your system better than DOS does. It gives you more control over the PC serial communications ports, and you can use it to specify the cursor size, the video mode, and the keyboard type and delay rate. The LP (Line Print) utility's formatting options also surpass any of DOS's printing techniques. When you install the Norton Utilities, you can choose to replace the DOS FORMAT command with a quicker and safer formatting program, the SF utility.

If you work in different directories regularly, you will find that the Norton Utilities' NCD (Norton Change Directories) program makes it easier to move between them and revise them. This utility enables you to change from one directory to another without specifying the complete path for the directory.

With all the programs that the Norton Utilities package now provides, you can accomplish tasks formerly done with DOS much more quickly, without having to memorize the various forms of numerous DOS commands.

PEERING INTO THE DARK CORNERS

For the curious, the Norton Utilities' DI (Disk Information) and NU programs let you look at disk and system information that is not normally available without complex programming and a detailed knowledge of the inner workings of the computer's hardware. You can also calculate several performance indicators to determine the speed of your PC and its disk system by running the SI (System Information) utility. This program displays the amount of standard, extended, and expanded memory, as well as the number of parallel and serial ports and type of processor in your computer. You can use NU's Explore disk feature to look at your disk's data by directory, file, cluster, or sector.

THE BEGINNINGS OF THE NORTON UTILITIES

Back in 1982 when the Norton Utilities were first released, they comprised six utilities: UnErase, Hard UnErase, Disk Look, Hard Look, Disk Mod, and Hard Mod. Each one was marketed individually and could only be run on IBM PCs with a 10Mb hard-disk system.

The programs quickly caught on, especially the UnErase program. The next release, Version 2.0, came out in 1983 and contained the six original programs and many more utilities, all combined into a package. Some of these utilities provided features that DOS had not yet added. The following year saw another release, a significant one in the program's development. All the utilities were rewritten in C (originally Peter Norton wrote them in Pascal) for Version 3.0 and made compatible with all floppy-disk and hard-disk systems, including IBM-compatibles. The Disk Look, Hard Look, Disk Mod, and Hard Mod programs were revamped and grouped together in the NU program's Disk information and Explore disk features. At this point, the Norton Utilities became firmly entrenched in the DOS market.

In 1985 the Norton Utilities Version 3.1 was released. This upgrade made it possible to recover entire directories at a time, improved NU's Explore disk and Disk information features, and presented the new QU (Quick UnErase) utility.

Version 4.0, which was released in 1987, was marketed as two separate versions and became known as the Standard Edition and the Advanced Edition. The Standard Edition presented two new programs: NI (Norton Integrator), which displayed a full-screen menu for running the other Norton Utilities programs, and NCD (Norton Change Directory). In addition to these new programs, the Norton Utilities Advanced Edition included the new SD (Speed Disk) program, the FR (Format Recover) progam, and the capability to edit absolute sectors.

The next release of the Norton Utilities brings us to the present.

WHAT'S NEW IN THE NORTON UTILITIES VERSION 4.5

The current programs were released in the fall of 1988 as the Norton Utilities Standard Edition Version 4.5 and the Norton Utilities

Advanced Edition Version 4.5. If you have not yet upgraded to this latest version, I urge you do so, as it contains several new programs worth having.

THE STANDARD EDITION

The Norton Utilities Standard Edition Version 4.5 contains four new programs, as well as an installation program and additions to earlier programs. The new programs are

- BE (Batch Enhancer), which makes batch programs interactive and adds many useful screen-handling routines to the DOS batch-programming language.

- FD (File Date), which allows you to change the time and date stamp for a file or a group of files.

- NCC (Norton Control Center), which lets you set up your system's hardware, including the cursor size, the screen colors, the serial ports, and the system date and time.

- SF (Safe Format), which is a fast, easy-to-use alternative to the DOS FORMAT command.

THE ADVANCED EDITION

The Norton Utilites Advanced Edition Version 4.5 contains all the programs in the Standard Edition, along with a new program for diagnosing and fixing disk problems, the NDD (Norton Disk Doctor) utility.

The features included in the Advanced Edition Version 4.0 were also improved for Version 4.5. In particular, the SD (Speed Disk) utility was made more flexible and powerful—Version 4.5's SD utility enables you to customize its performance. The Advanced Edition's byte editors also allow you to look at and change file allocation tables, directories, or partition tables right on the screen.

REQUIREMENTS FOR RUNNING THE NORTON UTILITIES

To use the Norton Utilities on your PC, you must have at least DOS Version 2.1; however, a few utilities require DOS 3.0 or later to take advantage of all their features. When I discuss DOS in this book, I assume you are using DOS 3.X on your system and have a hard disk. You will also need at least 256K of memory available for the utilities.

HOW TO USE THIS BOOK

This book is organized into eight chapters, containing both reference and tutorial information. In each chapter I describe specific utilities and provide examples of how to use them to get the best out of your system. At the end of each chapter, you will see a short summary section that briefly restates the functions of the utilities covered in the chapter. There are also five appendices that provide additional information for using the Norton Utilities.

Chapter 1: Installing and Using the Norton Utilities   introduces the Norton Utilities, describing how to install them on your hard disk and introducing the different ways that you can run them.

Chapter 2: An Introduction to Disk and Directory Structure   provides a detailed look at disks and their internal organization and describes how to use the Norton Utilities to explore your disks.

Chapter 3: Disaster Recovery   covers rescuing files and directories that you may have deleted by mistake and shows you how to recover the contents of your hard disk after it has been accidentally reformatted with the DOS FORMAT command.

Chapter 4: Navigating Your Hard Disk   describes how you can use the LD, NCD, DS, FF, and FS utilities to organize and manage your hard disk.

Chapter 5: Finding and Printing Text   explains how to use the TS and NU utilities for text searches and how to format text files for printing with the LP utility.

Chapter 6: Evaluating and Improving System Performance   discusses how you can evaluate and improve your computer's performance with the SI and SD utilities. You'll also learn how to set up your hardware with the NCC utility and how to locate and recover from disk-related problems with the NDD utility.

Chapter 7: Safeguarding Files and Improving Directory Listings describes the DOS file attributes and how you can modify them by using NU's directory format or the FA utility. In this chapter I also explain how to use the FD, FI, and VL utilities to make it easier to identify your files, directories, and disks. You will also learn how to obliterate a file or files with the WIPEFILE or WIPEDISK utility so that they can never be recovered, not even by the Norton Utilities' UnErase feature.

Chapter 8: Programming Simple Batch Files explains batch programming in detail and describes how to extend the DOS batch-programming language with the BE utility. I also provide several batch files as examples.

Appendix A: The Complete Command Reference to the Norton Utilities provides a succinct review of each program in the Norton Utilities Standard Edition 4.5 and the Norton Utilities Advanced Edition 4.5, including the program's command syntax and available parameters. You can consult this appendix when you need just a few pointers on how a utility works.

Appendix B: Evolution gives you the background information on DOS and how the Norton Utilities fit into this context.

Appendix C: Backing Up and Restoring Files explains how to use DOS's BACKUP and RESTORE commands on your system, providing a method that helps to prevent the loss of data when even NU's UnErase feature won't work.

Appendix D: Understanding DOS's Redirection Capabilities reviews how DOS's redirection symbols, pipes, and filters work. You can use these three DOS features with the Norton Utilities programs.

Appendix E: Becoming Proficient with ASCII and Binary Files explains what the different file types are and the numbering systems you can use to refer to these files' data. You will also learn how to translate a number from one system into another system.

Although I have planned that the book be read from cover to cover, you can begin with a chapter that discusses a utility that you are currently working with; each chapter is fairly self-sufficient. If you find that you don't understand the underlying concepts of a hard-disk system, refer to Chapter 2 before delving into other chapters.

THE MARGIN NOTES

As you read through this book, you will come across notes in the margins that are prefaced with a symbol. Each symbol corresponds to the note's type.

This symbol indicates a general note about the feature being discussed. I often use it to refer you to other chapters for more information or to remind you of an important concept learned in previous chapters.

I use this symbol to denote tips or tricks that you may find useful when running the utility being discussed. These can be shortcuts that I have discovered or even just important techniques that need to be emphasized.

Pay close attention when you see this symbol in the margin; I use it to alert you to potential troublespots when running a utility and often give you methods of avoiding these problems.

INSTALLING AND USING THE NORTON UTILITIES

CHAPTER *1*

IN THIS CHAPTER I DESCRIBE HOW TO INSTALL THE
Norton Utilities onto your hard disk. An essential preliminary to this
installation process is making backup copies of the original program
disks; this protects you in case of an accident with the original disks.
You will also learn the three ways of running the Norton Utilities:
from the DOS command prompt, in full-screen mode if the utility
has one, and from inside the organizer program known as the Norton
Integrator.

THE DISTRIBUTION PACKAGE

The distribution package for the Norton Utilities consists of three
5¹/₄-inch floppy disks and two 3¹/₂-inch disks, the manual, and *The
Norton Disk Companion*, which is a short guide to hard- and floppy-disk
structure. If you have the Advanced Edition, *The Norton Troubleshooter*
manual is included as well.

Check to see if there is a READ.ME file on disk 1. The READ.ME
file contains the latest information about the package, information that
may not be in the program manual. You should examine this file before
installing the package. To do this, use the DOS TYPE command to display the contents of READ.ME on the screen, or use the DOS PRINT
command to send READ.ME to your printer.

The files which end in .EXE are the utility programs themselves.
NU.HLP is the help file for the NU (Norton Utility) main program.
The BEDEMO.BAT file is a demonstration program for the BE
(Batch Enhancer) program, which uses two other files: BEDEMO-
.DAT and MENU.DAT. The files MAKE-TUT.BIN, MAKE-
TUT.BAT, and TUT-READ.ME are all files connected with the
tutorial described in the *Norton Utilities* reference manual. The file

MARY, which has no file name extension, is a tone file that you can use with the BE program's BEEP utility to play a short tune.

THE NORTON UTILITIES IN BRIEF

Here is a short description of each of the Norton Utilities' programs. A complete listing of all options for the programs is given in Appendix A.

BE	The Batch Enhancer adds the capability of making batch files interactive, and has routines to clear the screen and manipulate screen colors and attributes. BE can also draw boxes, open windows, position the cursor at a specific screen location, and write a character at that location.
DI	Disk Information lists technical information about your disks.
DP	Data Protect saves information that other utilities can use (Standard Edition only).
DS	Directory Sort can sort directory entries by name, extension, date, time, and/or file size in ascending or descending order. In the full-screen mode you can move files anywhere you want in the directory.
DT	Disk Test checks your disks for damaged clusters. DT can mark the bad areas so they will not be used by files, moving any existing files out of these areas to undamaged areas.
FA	File Attributes displays and allows you to change any of the file's attributes, including its hidden, system, read-only, or archive attribute.
FD	File Date allows you to set or reset the timestamp on a file.
FF	File Find helps you find lost files or lost directories anywhere on a disk.

FI   File Info allows you to add, edit, and delete a message attached to a file.

FR is available only in the Advanced Edition.

FR   Format Recover allows you to recover data on a hard disk after the disk has been accidentally reformatted with the DOS FORMAT command.

The FR utility does not work with floppy disks that have been formatted with the DOS FORMAT command.

FS   File Size displays file sizes and calculates the amount of unused space in the file. FS also calculates the amount of space needed for copying a file from one disk to a differently sized disk.

LD   List Directories lists directory names in list form or graphic form on the screen.

LP   Line Print formats ASCII text files for printing. For example, LP lets you specify page length, margins, headers, and footers.

NCC   Norton Command Center gives you control over many of the computer's hardware functions, including the video mode, screen colors, and keyboard rate.

NCD   Norton Change Directory allows you to change to any directory on the disk without having to specify the whole DOS path name. Directories can be made, removed, and renamed. NCD also makes a graphic display of the whole directory structure.

NDD appears only in the Advanced Edition.

NDD   Norton Disk Doctor finds and fixes logical or physical floppy- or hard-disk problems.

NI   The Norton Integrator is a control program that allows you to run any of the Norton Utilities program from its full-screen menu. NI also displays a different help screen for each utility.

NU   The Norton Utility program is the heart of the Norton Utilities package. It allows you to display technical information about your disks, search for text strings in files, and perform a number of complex data-recovery operations.

SD is part of the Advanced Edition only.

QU	Quick UnErase is a shorter version of NU's UnErase features. It is quicker to use but is not as powerful as NU.
SD	Speed Disk examines disk files and reorganizes them to eliminate file fragmentation. You can make SD produce a report on the percentage of fragmentation in a file, a group of files, or a directory. Several levels of optimization are provided, ranging from simple directory relocation to the complete unfragmentation of all the files on your disk.
SF	Safe Format is a quick, easy-to-use alternative to the DOS FORMAT command.
SI	System Information reports on the hardware installed in your computer and calculates three performance indicators.
TM	Time Mark allows you to start and reset up to four independent stop-watch timers.
TS	Text Search allows you to search for the occurrence of specific text in a file.
UD	UnRemove Directory restores directories you have removed. If the directory's files have not already been overwritten, they will also be recoverable.
VL	Volume Label allows you to add or change a disk's volume label.
WipeDisk	WipeDisk truly erases the contents of a disk. Contents erased with WipeDisk cannot be unerased.
WipeFile	WipeFile applies the same technique when erasing a file.

MAKING FLOPPY-DISK BACKUPS

As with any software package you buy, the first thing you should do after taking it out of the box is back it up. You should do this even

Note that the Norton Utilities are distributed on write-protected disks, which means you cannot modify them.

if you plan to install the software on your hard disk. In the event that the original disks are damaged or destroyed, the backup copies ensure that the software is still available for your use.

To make a floppy-disk copy of the distribution package, place the first distribution disk in drive A and a formatted blank disk in drive B, type

DISKCOPY A: B:

at the prompt, and press the Enter key. Repeat this procedure with each of the other distribution disks in the package. Store the original disks in a safe place and work with the copies rather than the original disks.

Once you have made backup copies of the original distribution disks, you are ready to install the package on your hard disk.

INSTALLING THE NORTON UTILITIES ON YOUR HARD DISK

Do not install the Norton Utilities on a hard disk containing lost files or directories.

If you bought the Norton Utilities because you currently need to perform a recovery operation such as unremoving a directory or unerasing a file, do not install the programs on your hard disk yet. Instead, use the Norton Utilities from your floppy-disk drive to recover the file (or directory), and then once the recovery is complete, continue with the installation procedure. If you install the Norton Utilities without first recovering the file, there is a good chance that the installation program will overwrite the area of the disk occupied by the erased file, making its recovery impossible. Chapter 3 contains more information on what actually happens when you delete a file.

USING THE NORTON UTILITIES' INSTALL PROGRAM

The Norton Utilities provide an installation program that guides you through the installation procedure step by step, explaining the choices available at each stage. To use the INSTALL program, insert disk 1 into drive A and type

INSTALL

A warning screen then appears to remind you not to install the utilities on your hard disk if you want to recover an erased file. At this point, you have the choice of continuing the installation or returning to DOS.

If you continue, the program looks for any old copies of the Norton Utilities on your hard disk and if it finds them, gives you three choices: Overwrite, Backup first, or Return to DOS. Overwrite replaces the old versions of the programs with the new ones. Backup first copies the old version to a new directory called NORTON.BAK and then copies the new set of programs on top of the originals. This method preserves the old version of the utilities and isolates them in a directory that is not part of your system's PATH specification. Return to DOS stops the installation process.

As the programs are copied to the hard disk, a horizontal display at the bottom of the screen shows the progress being made by moving from the left (no files copied) to the right (all files copied). When all the files on the floppy disk have been copied, INSTALL prompts you to insert the next disk. INSTALL checks the number of each disk to verify that you insert the disks in order.

If INSTALL cannot find any old copies of the Norton Utilities on your disk, it assumes you want to install the new version in a directory on the C drive called NORTON. You are given the opportunity to change this directory name if you wish; nonetheless, it makes good sense to keep all the utilities together and not mix them up with any other files, and the name NORTON will remind you what the directory contains.

The next step in the installation process renames any files in your path called FORMAT with the name XXFORMAT, and then renames the Norton Utilities program SF (Safe Format) to FORMAT. This substitution of SF for FORMAT means that whenever you type FORMAT, SF will run instead. SF (Safe Format) has many more checks and balances built into it than does the DOS FORMAT command, and it is also quicker and easier to use. See Chapter 3 for more details on SF.

The final step in the installation process adds the NORTON directory to your PATH specification (PATH is discussed in Chapter 5) so you can start the Norton Utilities from any directory. It also adds a line to your AUTOEXEC.BAT file to run FR (Format Recover) with the /SAVE switch set. This saves all the information required for recovering the contents of your hard disk if it is ever accidentally reformated with the DOS FORMAT command (see Chapter 3). Once this is done, your computer beeps and installation is complete.

INSTALLING THE UTILITIES ON YOUR OWN

Although you can use any name for the Norton Utilities directory, this book assumes that you have installed the utilities in a directory called NORTON.

If you prefer, you can to do the installation yourself; it is a straightforward operation. First, create a directory called NORTON in your hard disk's root directory. To do this, type

MD \NORTON

from the root directory. To change to the new directory, type

CD \NORTON

You can use the DOS COPY command to transfer all the needed files to your hard disk. Place distribution disk 1 in drive A and type

COPY A:*.*

When all the files have been copied from the floppy disk to the hard disk, remove disk 1 from drive A and insert disk 2. Press F3 and Enter to repeat the copying operation for the second disk.

If you have 5¼-inch disk drives, press F3 and Enter again to copy disk 3. (All the utilities are on either two 3½-inch disks or three 5¼-inch disks.)

Do not keep the Norton Utilities 3.0 or 3.1 on your hard disk when you have Version 4.0 or later, or DOS will use the old version. If you want to keep the earlier version on the disk, be sure to put its files in a separate directory that is not on the DOS path.

If you are updating your Norton Utilities from a version earlier than 4.0, this installation procedure will not overwrite your old Norton Utilities programs. This is because Versions 3.0 and 3.1 were .COM programs while the versions from 4.0 on are .EXE programs. In this case you should delete all the old files, because when DOS processes a file name it always looks for the .COM extension before it looks for the .EXE extension. This means that the newer Norton Utilities will never be run, as DOS will always find the old version first (provided, of course, that you have not put the .COM files in a directory that is not on the DOS path).

RUNNING THE NORTON UTILITIES

The Norton Utilities can be run from the DOS command prompt and from inside NI (Norton Integrator). Several utilities can also be run in their own interactive, full-screen modes.

USING THE UTILITIES FROM THE COMMAND PROMPT

When you are learning how to use the Norton Utilities, it's a good idea to run the program only from NI (see "Using the Norton Integrator" later in this chapter).

The Norton Utilities programs can be run from the DOS command prompt, just like any other program or DOS command. For example, to print the file READ.ME, type

LP READ.ME

LP is the command form of the Line Print utility.

Most of the utilities' commands take the general form of

Appendix A contains a complete listing of the parameters for all the utilities. I use *parameters* to describe any information that is specified with a command to determine how and on what the command operates. *Switches* are special parameters that are preceded by a slash. The effect of switches may vary when used with different commands.

utility parameters

where *parameters* represents one or more of the optional parameters associated with the utility.

PAUSING A PROGRAM'S DISPLAY Since seven utilities can generate a great deal of screen output, there is a command option for pausing the output from the program when the screen is full; it's called the /P switch. You specify this switch in the program's command so the program will halt its output while it is running. The seven utilities that use the /P switch are

FA (File Attributes)

FD (File Date)

FF (File Find)

FI (File Info)

FS (File Size)

LD (List Directories)

SD (Speed Disk)

For example, to pause output from the FF (File Find) utility, type

FF /P

The FF utility will then run, pausing when its display fills the screen. Once the program has paused, you can press the space bar or almost any other key to display the next screenful. However, pressing Enter only displays an additional line of the display, and pressing Esc ends the utility and returns you to DOS.

USING THE UTILITIES IN FULL-SCREEN MODE

Nine of the utilities can replace the simple DOS prompt with screens that contain windows, menus, and a variety of helpful information. These utilities are

DS (Directory Sort)

FR (Format Recover)

NCC (Norton Control Center)

NCD (Norton Change Directory)

NDD (Norton Disk Doctor)

NI (Norton Integrator)

NU (Norton Utility)

SD (Speed Disk)

SF (Safe Format)

When you activate full-screen mode for a utility, one selection will always be automatically highlighted. The highlighted item will be the current drive or directory, the first item in a menu, or the selection that is perceived to be the most likely choice.

To enter full-screen mode with any of these utilities, simply type its command form and press Enter. You can also make some adjustments to your screen display by inserting the switches listed below after the utility's name:

/Dn where n = 0 specifies use with 100% compatibles. This is the default setting. Where n = 1 specifies use with BIOS-compatible machines.

/BW	sets the CGA display to monochrome.
/NOSNOW	removes the flickering seen with some CGA displays.

USING THE NORTON INTEGRATOR

The Norton Integrator is a program that can run all the other utilities, presenting them in an easy-to-understand menu. NI displays a great deal of information that is of considerable benefit to new users. Experienced users will also find NI helpful for infrequently used utilities. This is where you should start running the Norton Utilities from until you become familiar enough with their operation to run them from the DOS command prompt.

To start NI, simply type

   NI

at the DOS prompt. Of course, you can adjust the screen by including one of the switches you just learned about. For example, to run the Norton Integrator in monochrome on your CGA monitor, type

   NI /BW

NI then displays the opening screen shown in Figure 1.1.

Figure 1.1: The initial Norton Integrator screen

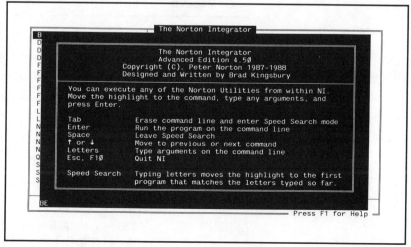 You'll learn about the commands' parameters when we examine commands individually.

The left side of the screen lists the names and command forms of the utilities. On the right side of the screen you can see a help screen. As you move the highlighting, or selection bar, down the list of programs, the help screen changes to display help for the currently highlighted utility. The command line at the bottom of the listing also changes to indicate the currently highlighted program. When you find the utility you want to run, type in any parameter you want to use and press the Enter key to run the utility. When it has finished running, you are prompted to "Press any key to continue..." After you press a key, you are returned to the NI starting screen.

The Home key moves you to the top of the list of programs, PgUp and PgDn move you up and down the list, End goes directly to the last entry in the list, and the up and down arrow keys move the selection bar up or down the list one entry at a time.

If you press the F1 key, NI's help screen is displayed (see Figure 1.2). This screen offers help on the operation of NI itself, telling you what keys you can press when you are at the initial NI screen. As you just learned, pressing Enter will run whatever program is listed on the command line, including any parameters you type in. The help screen also tells you that you can press Esc or F10 to quit NI. The remaining keys have to do with NI's Speed Search mode. Instead of moving through the list of programs, you can press the Tab key to enter Speed Search mode to find the program you want.

Figure 1.2: The Norton Integrator help screen

When you press Tab, the command line is erased, and the prompt "Speed Search" appears in the bottom left corner. Type in enough letters to make the utility name unique. As you type letters, NI moves the highlighting to the matching utility. When the correct utility is listed on the command line, press the space bar to leave Speed Search. Then type any switches you need and press Enter to run the utility.

NI keeps a list of the names of the utilities you have run in the current Norton session, as well as the parameters you used for each. Use Ctrl-E to highlight the utility you ran most recently and move backward through this list. Use Ctrl-X to start with the first utility you used and move forward through the list. At any point in the list, you can press the Enter key to rerun a utility with the same parameters that you used originally. You can also edit these entries using WordStar-like key combinations. The combinations, which are shown in Table 1.1, can be used whenever you are at the command line.

Note that the Ctrl-Y (delete line) command does not delete the name of the utility at the beginning of the line. By using this command, you can quickly run the program again with different switches. To remove the entire command line, press Tab; this also invokes the Speed Search.

Table 1.1: The Command Line's Cursor-Movement Keys

COMMAND	FUNCTION
Ctrl-D	Moves cursor right one character
Ctrl-S	Moves cursor left one character
Ctrl-F	Moves cursor right one word
Ctrl-A	Moves cursor left one word
Backspace	Deletes character to the left
Ctrl-G	Deletes character at the cursor
Ctrl-T	Deletes word to the right
Ctrl-W	Deletes word to the left
Ctrl-Y	Deletes parameters
Tab	Deletes whole line, toggles in and out of Speed Search

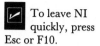 To leave NI quickly, press Esc or F10.

To leave NI and return to DOS, choose the Quit selection at the end of the list of program names, or press the Esc or F10 key. Go ahead and quit now.

HOW TO GET HELP

When you are in DOS, you can get helpful information about any of the utilities by typing the utility program's command form followed by a question mark. For example, to get help about the LP utility, type

LP ?

and the help text will be displayed on the screen. On the other hand, the BE program is different because it has two levels of help. If you type

BE ?

you will see general information about the BE program. However, if you type

BE BEEP ?

help on BE's BEEP subcommand will be displayed (see Figure 1.3).

```
C:\>BE BEEP ?
BE-Batch Enhancer, Advanced Edition 4.50, (C) Copr 1987-88, Peter Norton

     BEEP  [switches]
   or
     BEEP  [filespec]

Switches
     /Dn  Duration of the tone in n/18 seconds
     /Fn  Sound a tone of frequency n
     /Rn  Repeat the tone n times
     /Wn  Wait between tones n/18 seconds

C:\>
```

Figure 1.3: Getting help for BE's BEEP program

Thus, to get help on any subcommand, you can type BE followed by the subcommand and a question mark.

UNDERSTANDING ERROR MESSAGES

Even when you just start using the Norton Utilities, you should be able to understand what is wrong when you get an error message because the program tries to catch common typing errors and respond with a meaningful message. For example, if you ask BE BEEP to use a file called MURRAY and the file does not exist, BE BEEP responds with

Error opening MURRAY

Similarly, if you ask FA to work on a nonexistent file, it responds with

no files found

and if you ask LD to list the nonexistent directory called TEST, LD responds with the message

Directory not found
C:\TEST

telling you the path it checked.

SUMMARY

In this chapter you learned how to back up your Norton Utilities disks and two methods of installing the program on your hard disk.

The individual utilities were introduced briefly, and three ways of using them were described: from the DOS command prompt, in their interactive full-screen mode, and from inside the Norton Integrator.

In the next chapter we'll take a closer look at what goes on behind the scenes when you use your hard disk. I'll also show you how to use two of the utilities to explore your disk's structure.

AN INTRODUCTION TO DISK AND DIRECTORY STRUCTURE

CHAPTER *2* _____

BEFORE YOU CAN RECOVER FROM A DISASTER ON your system or even manage the Norton Utilities on your hard disk, you need to examine the basic concepts of disk organization. In this chapter I describe floppy disks and hard disks and how they work in DOS. Once you have become familiar with these concepts, you will explore your own system by using two utilities: DI (Disk Information) and NU (Norton Utility).

_____ *DISK STRUCTURE* _____

The better you understand how the underlying hardware works, the easier you will find it to understand what happens when you add or delete a file in DOS, and the procedures you must follow if you have to recover the deleted file.

SIDES

In early versions of DOS single-sided disks were common; that is, only one side of the disk could be used.

The most fundamental characteristic of a floppy disk is that it has two sides. Data can be written to and read from either side. The system identifies the sides with a numbering system. The first side is considered to be side 0, and the second side is side 1.

Hard disks, on the other hand, may have several recording surfaces, which are called *platters*. Platters are mounted on the same spindle inside the hard disk's sealed enclosure, and each has two sides. The numbering scheme is the same as that used for floppy disks: the first side is 0, the next 1, the first side of the second platter 2, and so on. Each side of a floppy disk and each side of a hard disk's platter can be write protected independently.

TRACKS

Each disk or platter side is divided into concentric circles known as *tracks*. The outermost track on the top of the disk is numbered track 0, side 0, and the first track on the other side of the disk is numbered track 0, side 1. Track numbering increases inwards toward the center of the disk (or platter).

The number of tracks on a disk varies with the media type. 360K floppy disks have 40 tracks per side, 1.2Mb floppy disks have 80 tracks per side, and hard disks can have from 300 to 600 tracks per platter side. On a floppy disk, the tracks cover only a small area of the disk, about three-quarters of an inch. A 360K floppy disk is recorded with 48 tracks per inch, and a 1.2Mb floppy disk is recorded with 96 tracks per inch. You will often find tracks per inch abbreviated TPI.

CYLINDERS

Tracks that are at the same concentric position on a disk (or on platters) are referred to collectively as a *cylinder*. On a floppy disk a cylinder contains two tracks (for example, track 0, side 0 and track 0, side 1); on a hard disk with four platters, a cylinder comprises eight tracks. Figure 2.1 shows cylinders on such a hard disk.

SECTORS AND ABSOLUTE SECTORS

When DOS reads or writes data, it must read or write at least one complete sector.

Each of the tracks on a disk are in turn divided into the same number of *sectors,* which are areas of equal size. In all DOS versions a sector consists of 512 bytes, and each sector is separated from the next by an inter-sector gap. The number of sectors contained in each track on the disk (as well as the total number of sectors) varies according to the media type. Most 360K and 720K floppy disks have 9 sectors per track, a 1.2Mb floppy disk has 15, a 1.4Mb floppy has 18, and most hard disks have 17. Figure 2.2 shows the relationship between tracks and sectors.

In the absolute-sector numbering scheme, the first sector on a disk is identified as side 0, cylinder 0, sector 1.

DOS identifies all the sectors on a disk by numbering them sequentially. On a 360K floppy, for example, the sectors are numbered 0–719, and a specific sector might be identified as, say, sector 317. Another way to reference a given sector is to identify it according to its disk side and cylinder and then specify its position in that

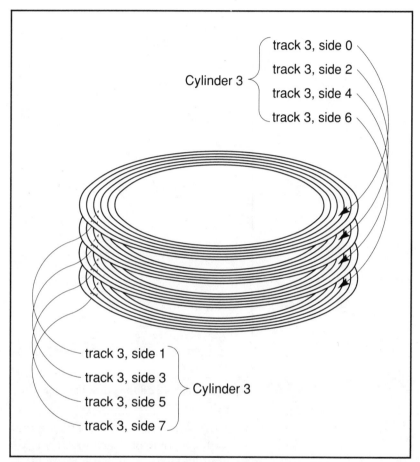

Figure 2.1: Cylinders on a hard disk with four platters

cylinder. In this case, you might give a sector's location as side 0, cylinder 25, sector 7. When you use the latter method, you are referring to *absolute sectors*.

CLUSTERS

Although DOS is capable of writing and reading a single sector, it allocates disk space for files in *clusters*, which consist of one or more sectors. So, no matter how small a file is, it will always occupy at least one cluster on the disk. A 1-byte file will occupy one cluster, and a 511-byte file on a 1.2Mb disk will also occupy one cluster. Figure 2.3 shows an example of this with a file of 1025 bytes and a cluster size of

The number of sectors per cluster varies depending on the disk media and the DOS version. 360K and 720K floppy disks have 2 sectors per cluster, while the 1.2Mb and 1.4Mb floppy disks have clusters of a single 512-byte sector. Hard disks have clusters of 4, 8, or 16 sectors.

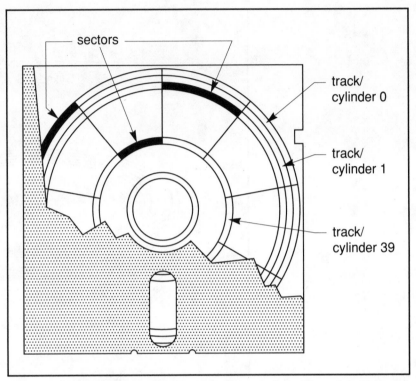

Figure 2.2: *A 360K floppy disk has 40 tracks, numbered from 0 to 39, and 9 sectors in each track.*

1024 bytes, or two sectors. The file data occupies all of one cluster and only one byte of a second cluster, yet the area of the second cluster not filled with data is not available for another file. This unused area is called *slack*. The next file must start at the next available cluster. If the first file increases in length, it will occupy more of the second cluster. If the cluster is filled up and more space is needed, the file will continue in the next available cluster—in this case, the fourth cluster.

DOS identifies clusters by numbering them sequentially, with the first cluster labeled cluster 2. Cluster numbering begins in the data area of the disk, so the first cluster on a disk (cluster 2) is actually the first cluster in the data area. This is less confusing when you understand that, unlike tracks and sectors, clusters are not physically demarcated on the disk. DOS merely ''decides'' to view groups of sectors as clusters for its own convenience.

Clusters are called *logical* units. Tracks and sectors are *physical* units.

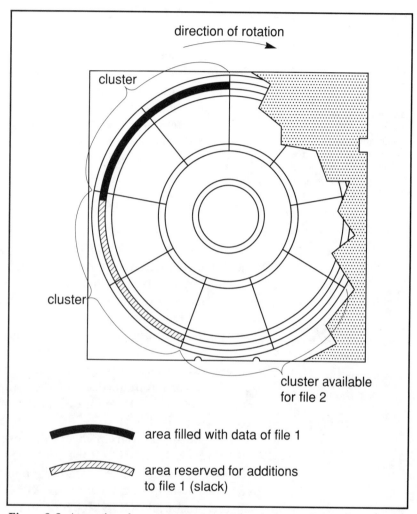

direction of rotation

cluster

cluster

cluster available
for file 2

area filled with data of file 1

area reserved for additions
to file 1 (slack)

Figure 2.3: Assuming there are two sectors per cluster, a file that needs 1025
bytes of disk space is 1 byte bigger than one cluster and will occupy
two complete clusters.

Remember that the absolute-sector method of referencing sectors
locates them according to their physical position on the disk. Because
clusters have no physical manifestation, there is no comparable, or
''absolute,'' method of referencing them.

EXAMINING THE SYSTEM AREA

When you format a disk, DOS reserves the outermost track on side 0 for its own use. This area is called the system area and is subdivided into three parts: the boot record, the *file allocation table*, or FAT, and the root directory. On a hard disk the boot record is part of a larger area called the *partition table*. The remaining space on the disk after the system area is called the data area. This is the part of the disk where application programs and data are located. The data area is far larger than the system area.

> You can reference sectors in the system area with the DOS numbering system or the absolute-sector method. You cannot reference clusters in the system area because cluster numbering begins in the data area.

THE BOOT RECORD

The boot record, which is on all formatted disks, contains the BIOS parameter block (BPB). This block holds information about the disk's physical characteristics, which is needed by device drivers. The information contained in the BPB is shown in Table 2.1.

The boot record also contains the boot program used to start the computer after a system reset or after power is applied. When you turn on the computer, it runs a set of diagnostic routines to ensure the hardware is in good order before proceeding. If you have a hard disk or have loaded a floppy disk, the ROM bootstrap program next loads the boot record from the disk into the computer's memory and turns control over to it. (When a disk is not present, most PCs run the ROM-based BASIC.)

> Note that the disk space occupied by the boot record is one sector, which includes the BPB, boot program, and slack.

The bootstrap program checks the disk for the DOS system files (IO.SYS or IBMBIO.COM and MSDOS.SYS or IBMDOS-.COM). If they are there, it loads them into the computer and passes complete system control over to DOS's COMMAND.COM. During this process, the CONFIG.SYS and AUTOEXEC.BAT files are loaded, as are any installable device drivers that a mouse or a RAM disk may need (for example, the device driver VDISK.SYS). Once everything has been loaded and you see the DOS prompt, your computer is ready for use.

However, when the computer can't find DOS's system files, it displays the error message

> If you have a hard disk but accidentally place or leave a nonsystem floppy disk in drive A and attempt to boot, your computer won't find your DOS files because it will try to use the floppy disk and will ignore the hard disk's presence. Just remove the floppy and reboot.

```
Non-System disk or disk error
Replace and strike any key when ready
```

on the screen and waits for you to either remove the nonsystem disk from the floppy-disk drive so it can use the hard disk, or place a system disk in your floppy-disk drive.

Table 2.1: Information Contained in the BIOS Parameter Block (in the boot record)

INFORMATION STORED	NUMBER OF BYTES USED	ADDITIONAL INFORMATION
Version of DOS used to format the disk	8	
Number of bytes per sector	2	
Number of sectors per cluster, per track, and per disk (or hard-disk partition)	1	
Number of reserved sectors used by the system area	2	
Number of FAT copies and sectors used	1	
Number of root directory entries	2	112 entries on 360K floppy or 1024 entries on hard disk
Number of sectors on disk	2	720 sectors for 360K floppy, thousands for hard disk
Media descriptor	1	Indicates the type of disk
Number of sectors per FAT	2	Sectors per FAT vary depending on disk's capacity (FAT references every cluster)

Table 2.1: Information Contained in the BIOS Parameter Block (in the boot record) (continued)

INFORMATION STORED	NUMBER OF BYTES USED	ADDITIONAL INFORMATION
Number of sectors per track	2	360K floppy has 9 sectors per track, 1.2Mb floppy has 15, hard disk usually has 17
Number of heads	2	Floppy-disk drive has 2, hard disk has 4
Number of hidden sectors	2	Hidden sectors are the system area

THE PARTITION TABLE

Floppy disks do not have partition tables and cannot be partitioned.

The DOS command FDISK creates the partition table. You can use it to repartition a disk and select the active partition.

The partition table, present on all hard disks, allows you to divide a hard disk into areas (called *partitions*) that appear to DOS as separate disks and to reserve disk space for other operating systems (which you can then install and use to create their own partitions). A DOS disk can contain as many as four partitions, though only one of these may be active at a time. The partition table begins with a code called the *master boot record*. This code contains a record of which partition was the active partition—the one used to boot the system. The master boot record also contains the locations of the boot records for the operating system of the active partition (and any other operating system installed on the disk). When the machine is restarted, it uses this information to boot the active partition's operating system.

THE FILE ALLOCATION TABLE

On a 360K floppy the area occupied by both copies of the FAT (plus slack) is four sectors.

The next part of a disk's system area is occupied by the file allocation table (FAT), which is also created by the FORMAT command. The FAT is part of the system that DOS uses to keep track of where files are stored on a disk. The FAT is so important that DOS actually creates two copies of it. If the first copy becomes corrupted, DOS uses the second copy. Think of the FAT as a two-column table. In one column is a sequential list of numbers that, from DOS's point of view, are the "addresses" of each of the clusters in the disk's data area. In the other column is a number that gives specific information about that cluster. If the cluster is being used to store file data, the second column contains the "address" of the next cluster in that file. (Remember that the data in a file is not necessarily stored in consecutive clusters.) Otherwise, the second column contains a special number that indicates one of the following:

- the cluster is available for storing data
- the cluster is bad and will not be used for storing data
- the cluster is reserved and will not be used for storing data
- the cluster is the last cluster in a file

Remember that cluster numbering begins with 2.

Figure 2.4 illustrates how FAT entries are chained together. File A starts in cluster 2 and then continues in cluster 8. The entry for cluster 8 points to cluster 11. Cluster 11 in turn points to cluster 12, where the file ends. Thus, File A is split up into four clusters, three of which are not in sequence. File B is less fragmented. It occupies clusters 3, 4, 5, 6, 7, 9, and 10. The entry for cluster 7 points to cluster 9, where the file continues. Cluster 9 points to 10, which contains the end-of-file value.

THE ROOT DIRECTORY

On a 360K floppy the root directory takes up seven sectors of disk space.

IBMBIO.COM and IBMDOS-.COM are *hidden* files, which means their names do not appear in a directory listing and you can't use them in a command at the DOS prompt.

Directly following the FAT sectors is the root directory, which is the third part of the system area found on the formatted disk. The root directory's size cannot be changed, but it is proportional to the media type. For example, a 360K floppy has space for 112 entries in the root, while a hard disk has space for 512 or 1024 entries.

If the disk is a system disk, the first two files in the root directory are always the files containing the MS-DOS BIOS and the DOS kernel. The disk's bootstrap program loads these files into memory when it starts up DOS.

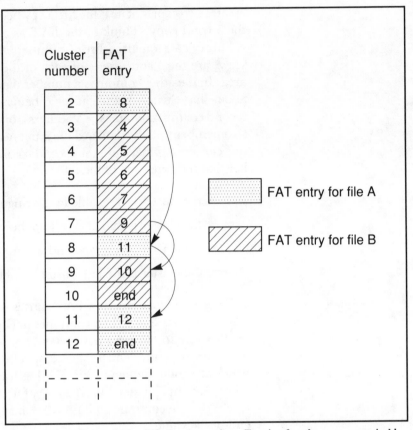

Figure 2.4: FAT entries are chained together. Entries for clusters occupied by file data contain the number of the next cluster used by the file. A special entry indicates the end of the file.

Each directory entry is 32 bytes long. The entry may contain information about a file or a subdirectory. The format of a file entry is as follows:

Base name	8 bytes
Extension	3 bytes
Attribute	1 byte, each bit represents an attribute
	bit 0, file is read-only
	bit 1, file is hidden
	bit 2, file is a system file

	bit 3, entry is a volume label
	bit 4, entry is a subdirectory
	bit 5, archive bit
	bit 6, 7, unused
Reserved	10 bytes, reserved for future use
Time of creation	2 bytes
Date of creation	2 bytes
Starting FAT entry	2 bytes
File size	4 bytes

The file name is an 11-byte entry, divided into an 8-byte base name and a 3-byte extension, which are separated by a period. The period is not stored as a byte but you must type it between the eighth and the ninth characters to use a file extension.

■ You can use letters, numbers, and any character except . '' / \ [ ] ¦ < > + : , = ; in your files' base names and extensions.

The attribute byte can have one or more of the attribute bits set at the same time. For example, a system file can also be hidden. An attribute is said to be set if the appropriate attribute bit has a value of 1. If the attribute byte has no bits set, or a value of 0, the file is a normal data or program file and may be written to or erased. This probably applies to the majority of your files.

■ See Chapter 7 for information on viewing and changing file attributes.

- Read-only files can be used, but you can't make any changes to their contents.

- Hidden files do not appear in directory listings made by DIR. You can't duplicate them with COPY or delete them. However, you can copy them by using the DISKCOPY command; this makes a sector-by-sector duplicate of the original disk.

- System files are read-only files.

- The volume label is a short piece of text used to identify the disk. You can specify up to 11 characters for it when you label your disk. The label's directory entry resembles that of an empty file.

- Subdirectory names have the same format as file names.

- The archive bit is used with BACKUP. If a new file is written to disk or an existing file is modified, this bit is set (changed to 1). After the BACKUP program has copied the file, it resets the bit to 0. This way, BACKUP knows which files need to be copied.

If the first byte of a directory entry has a value of 0, the entry is unused and indicates the end of the active directory entries. If the first byte of a file name is a period (that is, the . and .. files), the file is reserved by DOS.

EXAMINING THE DATA AREA

The rest of the DOS partition (or unpartitioned hard disk or floppy disk) is the data area and can store files and subdirectories. This is the largest part of a disk and is where all your programs—spreadsheets, word processors, program language compilers, data files—are found.

Subdirectories differ from the root directory in that they do not have fixed locations on the disk and can be created and deleted.

Figures 2.5 and 2.6 illustrate disk structure in different ways and draw together the concepts presented so far in this chapter. Both figures assume a 360K floppy.

EXPLORING YOUR DISK WITH DI

DI (Disk Information) provides you with a wealth of technical information about your disks that is not normally available without complex programming. To run DI from the DOS command line to display information about drive A, type

DI A:

Figure 2.7 shows the result of this command.

DI gets its information either from the boot record on the disk or from DOS itself, and always identifies the origin of the data. In Figure 2.7 MS-DOS 3.3 indicates the operating system that was used to format the disk.

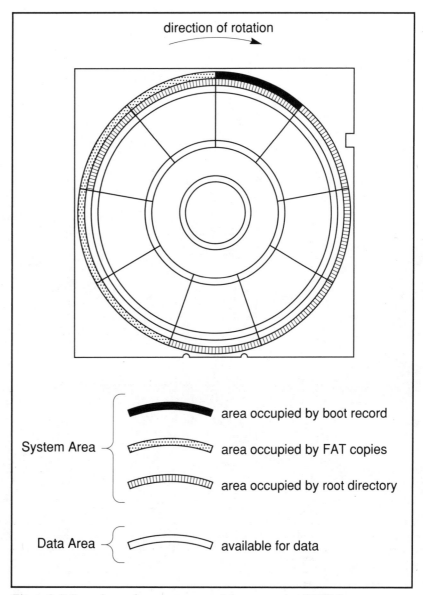

Figure 2.5: Locations of system area and data area on a 360K floppy.

To make DI report on drive C, type

DI C:

Figure 2.8 shows the resulting data.

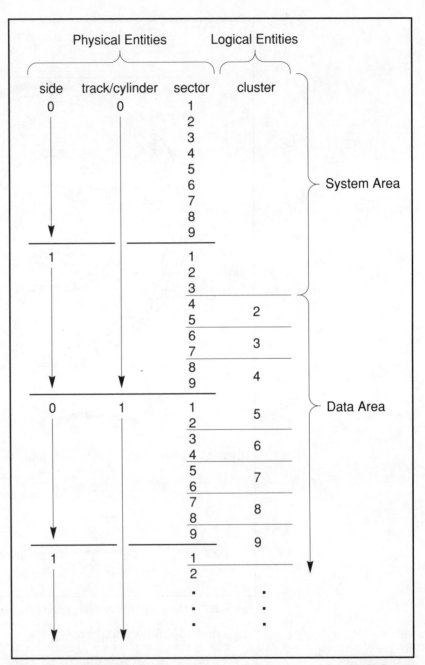

Figure 2.6: Relationships between elements of disk structure on a 360K floppy

```
C:\>DI A:
DI-Disk Information, Advanced Edition 4.50, (C) Copr 1987-88, Peter Norton

  Information from DOS          Drive A:        Information from the boot record
  --------------------------------------------------------------------------------
                              system id        'MSDOS3.3'
                       media descriptor (hex)       FD
          0                 drive number
        512                bytes per sector          512
          2              sectors per cluster           2
          2                number of FATs              2
        112            root directory entries        112
          2               sectors per FAT              2
        354             number of clusters
                         number of sectors          720
          1                 offset to FAT              1
          5             offset to directory
         12                offset to data
                         sectors per track            9
                             sides                     2
                         hidden sectors               0

C:\>
```

Figure 2.7: A typical DI display for drive A

```
C:\>DI
DI-Disk Information, Advanced Edition 4.50, (C) Copr 1987-88, Peter Norton

  Information from DOS          Drive C:        Information from the boot record
  --------------------------------------------------------------------------------
                              system id        'MSDOS3.3'
                       media descriptor (hex)       F8
          2                 drive number
        512                bytes per sector          512
          4              sectors per cluster           4
          2                number of FATs              2
        512            root directory entries        512
         64               sectors per FAT             64
     16,250             number of clusters
                         number of sectors       65,161
          1                 offset to FAT              1
        129            offset to directory
        161               offset to data
                         sectors per track           17
                             sides                     9
                         hidden sectors              17

C:\>
```

Figure 2.8: Running DI for drive C

The differences in the information shown for the floppy-disk drive and the hard-disk drive have to do with storage capacity; in other words, they involve the number of sectors and clusters, as you would expect.

You can make a useful one-page summary of this technical information by printing the output of DI. To do this for drive C, type

DI C: > PRN

The information will then be printed instead of appearing on the screen. If you want to store this information in a file, type

DI C: > DISK.INF

DOS will then create the DISK.INF file in the current directory and write the output from DI into it. You can then print the file or display it on the screen at some later time when it is more convenient.

Most of the technical information displayed by DI is also available as an option in NU (Norton Utility), but NU has many other advanced features for displaying this information.

LOOKING AT DISKS WITH NU

NU, the Norton Utilities' main program, has four primary uses:

In Chapter 5, I discuss text searches. In Chapter 3, I discuss file recoveries.

- to view or edit file and directory data
- search for text
- to recover erased files
- to look at disk information

NU has its own full-screen menu system, providing both graphic and textual displays of information. To start NU, type

NU

The initial NU starting screen is shown in Figure 2.9.

If you want help with NU's Main menu selections, press the F1 key, and the help screen shown in Figure 2.10 will appear. When you are done with the help screen, press any key to return to the Main menu. To leave NU and return to DOS, press the Esc key at the Main menu screen. If you press Esc at one of the Main menu's sub-menus, you move up one level in the menu structure. Pressing F10 at any menu or display screen will return you to DOS immediately. If you try to exit NU after you have made editing changes but before you have saved them, NU will issue a warning and require confirmation from you before returning to DOS.

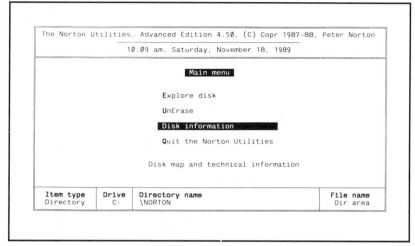

```
The Norton Utilities, Advanced Edition 4.50, (C) Copr 1987-88, Peter Norton

            10:09 am, Saturday, November 18, 1989

                        Main menu

                     Explore disk

                     UnErase

                     Disk information

                     Quit the Norton Utilities

                 Disk map and technical information

 Item type    Drive   Directory name                    File name
 Directory     C:      \NORTON                            Dir area
```

Figure 2.9: The NU startup screen

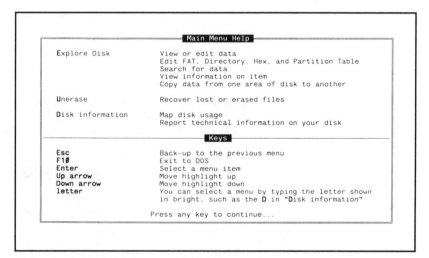

```
                        Main Menu Help

 Explore Disk            View or edit data
                         Edit FAT, Directory, Hex, and Partition Table
                         Search for data
                         View information on item
                         Copy data from one area of disk to another

 Unerase                 Recover lost or erased files

 Disk information        Map disk usage
                         Report technical information on your disk

                           Keys
 Esc                     Back-up to the previous menu
 F10                     Exit to DOS
 Enter                   Select a menu item
 Up arrow                Move highlight up
 Down arrow              Move highlight down
 letter                  You can select a menu by typing the letter shown
                         in bright, such as the D in "Disk information"

                    Press any key to continue...
```

Figure 2.10: NU's Main menu Help screen

Until you have selected an item from one of the submenus' display screens, the left box will give the item type as directory and the right box will give Dir area or Root dir as the file name. Once you have selected an item, information about it will be listed until you select another item, even if you return to the Main menu.

Each menu screen in NU contains a single line of help, usually at the bottom of the main window. As you cycle through the different menu selections, this short line of text changes to remind you of what the currently highlighted menu selection does. For example, in Figure 2.9 the selection bar is on the third entry in the menu, Disk information. The help line indicates that this selection generates a disk map and displays technical information about the disk.

On the bottom of many NU screens, you can see a row of four boxes containing details about the currently selected item. The leftmost box contains a description of the item type (file, directory, cluster, and so on), the next box shows the current drive, the largest box displays the name of the current directory, sector, or cluster range, and the box on the right displays the name of the directory or file.

CHOOSING DISK INFORMATION

The Main menu contains four selections: Explore disk, UnErase, Disk information, and Quit the Norton Utilities. Choose Disk information by moving the selection bar from Explore disk to Disk information with the down arrow key and then press Enter. Alternatively, you can type the letter D (shown on the screen as a bold character) for Disk information.

The next screen, shown in Figure 2.11, contains the Disk information submenu. Type M for Map disk usage or press Enter since the selection is already highlighted to choose it. A graphic display of the hard disk's usage then appears (see Figure 2.12).

Each of the small squares represents disk space occupied by your files. Each square is proportional to several clusters. For example, in Figure 2.12 each square represents six clusters. The display's shaded

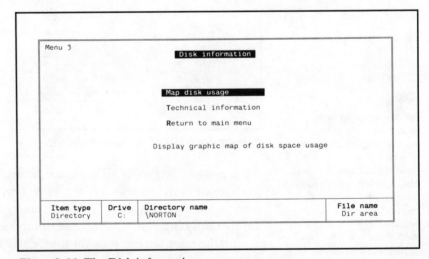

Figure 2.11: The Disk information screen

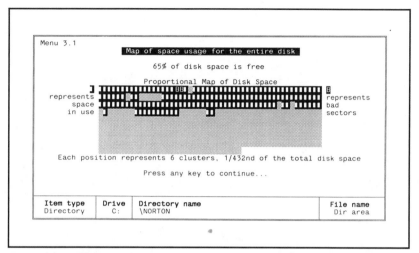

Figure 2.12: The map of space usage for the entire disk

area is the unused space on the disk. In this case, the available space is 65 percent of the whole disk.

Free space is sometimes surrounded by clusters in use. These gaps result when you delete files and the disk space is deallocated from the FAT. The space then becomes available for other files and will eventually be used again.

The blinking B represents an area of bad sectors. These sectors were found damaged when the disk was formatted, or by either DT (Disk Test) or NDD (Norton Disk Doctor). A special entry in the FAT indicates the area is bad, reserving it from use.

From this display press any key to return to the Disk information screen (Figure 2.11). From there, choose Technical information. The Technical information screen, shown in Figure 2.13, is then displayed.

Again, I made this example with drive C, the hard disk. The display shows that the disk's capacity is 21 million characters, or 21 megabytes. Of this capacity 65 percent is still available.

The lower portion of the display contains information similar to that shown by DI, although the information shown here is much less detailed. There are 2,590 clusters on the disk, and each cluster consists of sixteen 512-byte sectors, which makes each cluster 8,192 bytes in size. There are 17 sectors in each track, 4 sides to the disk, and 611 cylinders. The root directory can contain 1,024 files.

Press any key to leave this display and return to the Disk information menu. Then press R or Esc to return to the Main menu.

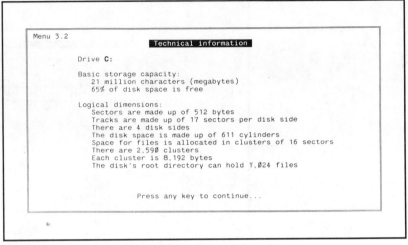

```
Menu 3.2
                            Technical information
          Drive C:

          Basic storage capacity:
              21 million characters (megabytes)
              65% of disk space is free

          Logical dimensions:
              Sectors are made up of 512 bytes
              Tracks are made up of 17 sectors per disk side
              There are 4 disk sides
              The disk space is made up of 611 cylinders
              Space for files is allocated in clusters of 16 sectors
              There are 2,590 clusters
              Each cluster is 8,192 bytes
              The disk's root directory can hold 1,024 files



                       Press any key to continue...
```

Figure 2.13: The Technical information screen

USING EXPLORE DISK

This feature has several danger spots, so it is important that you understand what you are doing with it and any resulting implications.

Explore disk is a very powerful feature in NU. It allows you to browse through any area of a disk and look at (and edit) data in that area in either ASCII form or hex notation. You actually edit this data at the byte level, which can be dangerous—make sure you read the warnings on the appropriate help screen, especially before attempting to edit a directory, FAT, or partition table.

The partition table and FAT editors and disk access via the absolute-sector numbering scheme are only available in the Advanced Edition.

To follow my discussion of Explore disk, be sure to stay in the NORTON directory.

The Explore disk menu is shown in Figure 2.14. There are several selections in this menu.

Because Search item/disk for data is such a complex feature, I dedicated most of Chapter 5 to it and do not discuss it in this chapter.

- Choose item allows you to select a cluster, a sector, a file, a directory, the FAT, or the partition table (Advanced Edition only) to work on.

- Information on item displays data on the item requested.

- Edit/display item lets you look at and edit the data.

- Search item/disk for data enables you to find specified text.

- Write item to disk saves the information you have just edited to a location on the disk.

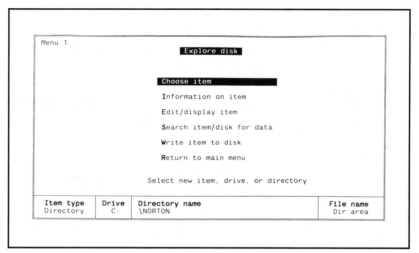

Figure 2.14: The Explore disk menu

> • Return to Main menu is a selection you are already familiar with.

CHOOSE ITEM From NU's Main menu choose E for Explore disk. Now you need to choose an area of the disk to explore, so type C for Choose item. In the Choose item menu you can select another drive, change to another directory, select a particular file, cluster, sector, or absolute sector (Advanced Edition only). The Choose item menu is shown in Figure 2.15. We'll examine each of these selections in turn. Remember, however, that choosing one of these selections simply makes its item current; you can then work with the current item by choosing the appropriate selection on the Explore disk menu.

Change Drive The Change drive selection asks you to choose between drives A, B, and C.

Change Directory The change Directory selection (which you select by typing D rather than C, as typing C chooses Change drive) brings up the display shown in Figure 2.16. This graphic display is much like that used in the NCD (Norton Change Directory) program. Use the arrow keys to move the highlighting to a directory and then press the Enter key to select it.

Figure 2.15: The Choose item menu

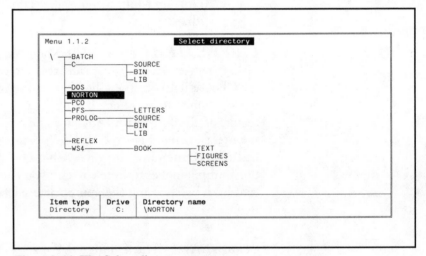

Figure 2.16: The Select directory screen

File   To select a file or subdirectory from the Choose item menu, press F for File. This brings up the display shown in Figure 2.17. Subdirectory names are capitalized and listed first (no subdirectories are listed in Figure 2.17), followed by the lowercased file names. As always, you can use the arrow keys and Enter to make your selection. However, you can also press the Tab key to enter Speed Search

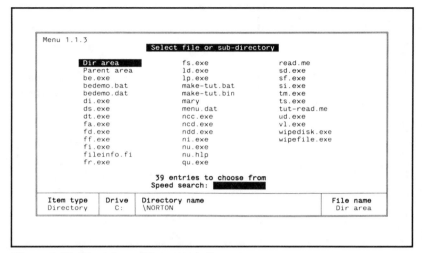

```
Menu 1.1.3
                         Select file or sub-directory
           Dir area                fs.exe                read.me
           Parent area             ld.exe                sd.exe
           be.exe                  lp.exe                sf.exe
           bedemo.bat              make-tut.bat          si.exe
           bedemo.dat              make-tut.bin          tm.exe
           di.exe                  mary                  ts.exe
           ds.exe                  menu.dat              tut-read.me
           dt.exe                  ncc.exe               ud.exe
           fa.exe                  ncd.exe               vl.exe
           fd.exe                  ndd.exe               wipedisk.exe
           ff.exe                  ni.exe                wipefile.exe
           fi.exe                  nu.exe
           fileinfo.fi             nu.hlp
           fr.exe                  qu.exe

                         39 entries to choose from
                         Speed search:
 ─────────────────┬───────┬──────────────────────────────────┬────────────
  Item type       │ Drive │ Directory name                   │  File name
  Directory       │  C:   │ \NORTON                          │  Dir area
```

Figure 2.17: Choosing a file or a subdirectory

mode. In Speed Search mode you start typing the name you want, and NU immediately moves the selection bar to the first file name that matches the letters you have typed so far. When NU reaches the file you want, press Enter to complete your selection. The boot record, the root directory, and the FAT can be specified as though they were files, even though they are not.

Cluster   You request a cluster or range of clusters by typing L at the Choose item menu. You then specify the starting and ending cluster, as prompted by the display screen. Use the Tab key to move between the data-entry boxes. You can specify a single cluster by entering its number in the Starting Cluster box and pressing the Enter key twice. This specifies a range that is one cluster long.

Sector   The Choose item menu's Sector choice is also requested by giving starting and ending numbers (see Figure 2.18). You are also shown the range of sectors on the current disk and how they are being used. In Figure 2.18 sector 0 is the boot area, sectors 1 through 16 are reserved for the FAT, sectors 17 through 80 are used by the root directory, and the remaining sectors on the disk, sectors 81 through 41,520, are the data area where files are stored.

Figure 2.18: The Select sector screen

Absolute Sector If you have the Norton Utilities Advanced Edition, you can also access absolute sectors directly. This bypasses the DOS numbering scheme to use the BIOS numbering scheme, which actually adresses physical sectors by disk side, cylinder, and sector number within the cylinder.

For example, say you made the NORTON directory current. In this case, you did not need to know the cluster or sector number— you selected the directory as you would a file.

INFORMATION ON ITEM Press Esc twice to return to the Explore disk menu, whose next selection is Information on item. If you choose this selection, NU displays the screen shown in Figure 2.19.

In this display the amount of disk space occupied by the directory or by a file is shown graphically in the Proportional Map of Disk Space. The display is interactive; by using the arrow keys, you can scroll through the whole NORTON directory, entry by entry, and the information on this screen will change to reflect the new entry. Each time, the file's name, attributes, date and time of its last modification, starting cluster number, and size, including the total number of clusters, are given.

If you previously chose a cluster (through the Choose item menu), the sectors that make up the cluster will be described here, and the file

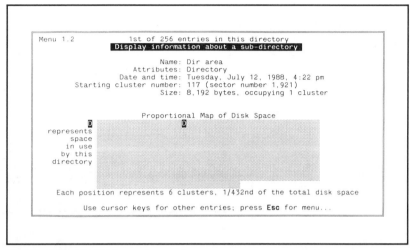

```
Menu 1.2              1st of 256 entries in this directory
                 Display information about a sub-directory

                         Name: Dir area
                   Attributes: Directory
                 Date and time: Tuesday, July 12, 1988, 4:22 pm
       Starting cluster number: 117 (sector number 1,921)
                         Size: 8,192 bytes, occupying 1 cluster


                  Proportional Map of Disk Space
                     D                     D
     represents
        space
       in use
      by this
     directory



     Each position represents 6 clusters, 1/432nd of the total disk space

           Use cursor keys for other entries; press Esc for menu...
```

Figure 2.19: The Information on item screen

name to which the cluster is allocated will be given.

If you selected sectors, the cluster number that the sector is in is given, along with a display showing the disk's sector use.

If you specified an absolute sector (Advanced Edition only), the DOS sector and cluster numbers are given.

After viewing the displayed information, press the Esc key to return to the Explore disk menu.

EDIT/DISPLAY ITEM   Type E to select Edit/display item, and you will see the NORTON directory, as shown in Figure 2.20. Since only the first portion of the NORTON directory is displayed, you mostly see the utilities themselves. Use PgDn to look at the rest of this listing. The last part shows several unused directory entries.

Using the Byte Editors   You can use the byte editors to change data displayed after you have chosen Edit/display item. The function keys used by the byte editors are labeled on the last line of the screen. If you have the Standard Edition, you can use

- F1 to display a help screen

- F2 to show the data on the screen in hex notation

- F3 to show the data as text

Before editing an item, use the Explore menu's Write to disk selection to copy it to another disk and work on the copy. This way, you can save your changes and test them without doing irreversible damage. Once your changes are correct, use Write to disk again to copy the revised item back to its original location.

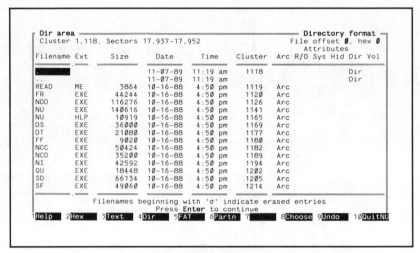

```
┌─ Dir area ──────────────────────────────── Directory format ─┐
│  Cluster 1,118, Sectors 17,937-17,952       File offset 0, hex 0  │
│                                                    Attributes      │
│  Filename Ext     Size     Date     Time    Cluster  Arc R/O Sys Hid Dir Vol │
│                                                                   │
│  █                         11-07-89  11:19 am  1118            Dir │
│  . .                       11-07-89  11:19 am                 Dir │
│  READ    ME     3864      10-16-88  4:50 pm   1119   Arc         │
│  FR      EXE    44244     10-16-88  4:50 pm   1120   Arc         │
│  NDD     EXE    116276    10-16-88  4:50 pm   1126   Arc         │
│  NU      EXE    140616    10-16-88  4:50 pm   1141   Arc         │
│  NU      HLP    10919     10-16-88  4:50 pm   1165   Arc         │
│  DS      EXE    36000     10-16-88  4:50 pm   1169   Arc         │
│  DT      EXE    21080     10-16-88  4:50 pm   1177   Arc         │
│  FF      EXE    9020      10-16-88  4:50 pm   1180   Arc         │
│  NCC     EXE    50424     10-16-88  4:50 pm   1182   Arc         │
│  NCD     EXE    35200     10-16-88  4:50 pm   1189   Arc         │
│  NI      EXE    42592     10-16-88  4:50 pm   1194   Arc         │
│  QU      EXE    18448     10-16-88  4:50 pm   1202   Arc         │
│  SD      EXE    66134     10-16-88  4:50 pm   1205   Arc         │
│  SF      EXE    49060     10-16-88  4:50 pm   1214   Arc         │
│  .   .                                                           │
│        Filenames beginning with 'σ' indicate erased entries     │
│                  Press Enter to continue                        │
│ 1Help  2Hex  3Text  4Dir  5FAT  6Partn  7    8Choose 9Undo 10QuitNU │
└───────────────────────────────────────────────────────────────┘
```

Figure 2.20: Displaying the NORTON directory in directory format

- F4 to present the data in a special directory format (you'll get an error message if you use this key for data that isn't a directory)

- F8 to open a window in which you can choose a new item without leaving Edit/display item

- F9 to undo the last changed character if you are in the text portion of the display; if you are in the hex portion of the screen, this replaces the entire byte

- F10 to return directly to DOS

To see the information shown in Figure 2.20 in hex notation, press F2; to see it as text, press F3. You can edit the data in the directory format or the hex notation display by moving through the data with the cursor keys.

In the directory format the PgUp, PgDn, End, and Home keys move the cursor through the display as you would expect. You can also press Tab to move between columns, and the space bar becomes a toggle key that turns the file attributes on or off or switches the time descriptor from am to pm.

Hex bytes that do not correspond to printable ASCII characters are represented in the text window as dots. If you want to edit text, switch to the hex format and edit in the right-hand text window. You press Tab to move from window to window. Data you enter is highlighted, and you always enter it in overstrike mode, never in insert mode. You can see the modifications you make at the hex window when you change to one of the other display types. For example, press F4 to put the data back into the directory format.

If the selected item is a file or a range of clusters or sectors, you can press PgUp and PgDn within the range you originally requested, but you cannot use these keys to move out of the specified range. However, if you chose a single cluster or sector, you can press PgUp or PgDn to view the next or previous cluster or sector.

If you have the Advanced Edition, you can use F5 to invoke the FAT editor. You can only enter the FAT editor after selecting the FAT through the Choose item menu, either by choosing its name from the file listing or by specifying the appropriate clusters or sectors. In the FAT editor display you use the Tab key to move from entry to entry. Typing B sets the FAT entry for the selected cluster to a value that shows the cluster is bad and should not be used by a file. Typing E sets the FAT entry to the end-of-file value.

If you have the Advanced Edition, you can also edit the partition table, but I strongly advise you not to do so unless you know exactly what you are doing. You can make a disk completely unbootable if you make a mistake here. The preferable way to change the partition table is to use the DOS command specifically designed to do the job—FDISK.

You cannot edit the partition table unless you first use Choose item to specify that you want to work on that area of the disk. The easiest way of doing this is to accept all the default values in the Select physical sector screen under Absolute sector. Accept the values of side 0, cylinder 0, sector 1, and request that sector 1 be loaded. Then you go back to Edit/display item and choose F6 from the resulting display.

In the display that then appears, the four lines represent the four possible partitions. If DOS-12 appears at the beginning of a line, it indicates a DOS partition with a 12-bit FAT, and DOS-16 indicates a DOS partition with a 16-bit FAT. A question mark indicates a non-DOS partition or the absence of a partition. In this editor you use the space bar to cycle through the system and boot values. You can also edit the starting and ending location of each partition, as well as the length of the partition in sectors.

Do not edit the partition table unless you know exactly what you're doing.

Ending an Editing Session   When you have finished revising your selected item, press Esc or Enter to leave the display screen. NU will then prompt you to save your changes, return to the editing screen, or discard your changes. For example, if you choose Discard the changes after editing a file, the file will keep its original version; your changes will be lost. If you change your mind about ending the editing session, choose Review the changed data to continue editing or double-check your changes. When you choose Write the changed data, NU saves your file and you are returned to the Explore disk menu. If you want, you can exit NU at this point; your changes will be in effect. (You don't need to use the Explore disk menu's Write to disk selection after you have ended an editing session.)

WRITE ITEM TO DISK   The Explore disk menu's Write item to disk selection provides an effective safety net for editing items. Before you begin editing a selected item, you should copy it to another location with Write Item to disk. When you choose this selection, the Write item to disk menu appears (Figure 2.21), allowing you to write the selected item back to disk as a file, which is the most common and safest way of copying an item. You can also choose to save it as clusters, sectors, or absolute sectors.

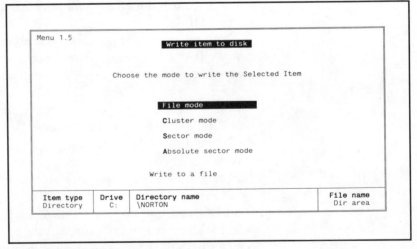

Figure 2.21: The Write item to disk menu

If you select File mode, you specify a file name, and NU then writes the data back to disk as a DOS file. If the file already exists, NU will overwrite the old file. Since you are always asked to specify the disk to which the file should be written, you can easily copy the item to another disk. If you copy it to the same disk, you can rename it to avoid overwriting the original item.

In cluster, sector, or absolute-sector mode, you are prompted for the starting cluster or sector number. The data is written into the appropriate number of contiguous clusters or sectors, whether or not they are in use. For example, if you save a cluster in sector mode and the disk in question has four sector clusters, the data will be written into the starting sector and the next three contiguous sectors. Be very sure that this is what you want to do before proceeding. Note that if you save a single sector to a cluster, the sector is written into the first sector of the cluster, and the remaining sectors in the cluster will keep their original data.

Once you have made a copy of the item, go ahead and edit it. When you have completed your changes to your satisfaction, use Write item to disk again to copy the revised item to the original item's location. If, however, you are unsure about any changes you made, simply leave the original version alone. You can then delete the revised item, if necessary, without doing any damage to the original version.

SUMMARY

In this chapter I have concentrated on the details of disk organization that provide the basis for the following chapters' discussions of hard-disk management and disaster recovery.

You are now familiar with

- DI (Disk Information), which displays detailed technical information about your disks.

- NU (Norton Utility), which allows you to look at disk information in a slightly different way.

In the next chapter you will learn how to restore files that have been erased and how to recover from an accidental formatting of your hard disk.

CHAPTER *3* _____

IN THIS CHAPTER I DISCUSS SOME OF THE MISHAPS that can befall your data and the means by which you can recover from them. Both floppy and hard disks can be mechanically damaged by careless handling, files can be deleted accidentally, and disks can be reformatted inadvertently. The Norton Utilities programs provide several elegant solutions to these problems, but there are preventive steps that you should become familiar with; following them helps reduce the impact of these problems.

TAKING CARE OF YOUR DISKS

Disks, both hard and floppy, can deteriorate through extended use, and floppy disks especially can be easily damaged through mistreatment and careless handling.

SAFEGUARDING FLOPPY DISKS

Here are some suggestions for handling floppy disks:

- When you are not using a floppy disk, keep it in its jacket in a disk storage tray or in its box.

- Do not leave floppy disks anywhere where they will get hot, such as on a window sill, on top of your monitor, or in a car parked in the sun. The disks will warp, becoming unusable.

- Keep disks away from magnetic fields, such as motors, paper clip holders, and magnetic keys.

- Do not touch the recording surface of the disk. This can transfer grease to the disk's surface and destroy data.

- Label all your disks. Write on the label before attaching it to the disk. If you do write on the label after it has been stuck onto the disk, use a soft felt-tip pen—not a pencil. Add a volume label to each of your disks.

- Keep backup copies of all distribution disks, preferably in a different place from the original disks. You can often find a local company that specializes in archiving data. Such places use precisely controlled temperature and humidity to ensure long life to the media in storage. They also usually have excellent security and fire protection.

HANDLING HARD DISKS

Your hard disk is not immune from problems either. Here are some suggestions relating to its care:

- When you are using the hard disk, do not move the disk unit if the drive is external, or the computer cabinet if the drive is internal.

- Use a head-parking program to stabilize the heads on the hard disk before turning off your computer or moving the system.

- To protect your system against power outages or "brown-outs," use a voltage regulator or surge suppresser.

- Do not obstruct the air flow to the back of the computer, as the air flow cools your system.

- Perform timely backups.

RECOVERING FROM FORMATTING PROBLEMS

One of the most appalling prospects for a hard-disk user is an accidentally reformatted hard disk, which means all its data and programs are lost. With FR (Format Recover), however, you can now recover data from a reformatted hard disk. Some PC manufacturers have even invented another command to use when formatting the hard disk, just to make reformatting more difficult to do by accident. The Norton Utilities provides the SF (Safe Format) program, which not only helps to protect your hard disk from being inadvertently reformatted, but can also speed up the formatting process.

USING FORMAT RECOVER

FR is part of the Advanced Edition only.

When you run DOS's FORMAT command on a hard disk, it clears the root directory and the FAT of their entries, but does not overwrite the data area on the disk. The data is still there, but as the root directory and the FAT have been cleared, you normally have no way of getting to it. The Advanced Edition's FR program provides an easy way of recovering these files. Note, however, that FR will not recover floppy disks formatted with DOS's FORMAT command because when you use FORMAT on a floppy disk, its data is overwritten.

If you install the Norton Utilities with the INSTALL program, you can have FR /SAVE added to your AUTOEXEC.BAT file automatically.

You should run FR with the /SAVE switch as a part of your daily operation. By doing so, you create a file called FRECOVER.DAT (and a copy called FRECOVER.BAK) that FR can use to recover the disk. Although these files' entries will be cleared from the root directory and FAT if the hard disk is reformatted, running the FR program from a floppy will enable you to recover their data and thereby recover your hard disk completely.

You can use the Standard Edition's DP (Data Protect) program to create FRECOVER.DAT. In this case, FRECOVER.DAT can only be used to recover directories and files, not to recover from formatting.

FRECOVER.DAT is also used to recover erased directories and files. If FRECOVER.DAT is not present, you can usually still recover directories and files, but the process may not be as smooth and you may not be able to recover all the erased data.

FR makes a FRE-COVER.DAT file of approximately 40K in size to save all the information necessary to recover 10Mb worth of files.

Once FR has created these files, you cannot delete them by accident—they are read-only files. If you do try and delete them with DOS's DEL or ERASE command, you will receive DOS's "Access denied" error message. FRECOVER.DAT is also used by the NU, QU, and UD programs when you run them to recover files and directories. If you want to have FR make only the FRECOVER-.DAT file (to save space, for example), run it with the /NOBAK switch. To do this, type

FR /SAVE/NOBAK

at the DOS prompt.

If you want to recover a hard disk using a FRECOVER-.DAT file made by an earlier version of the Norton Utilities, use the earlier version of FR. Version 4.5's FRE-COVER.DAT file is not compatible with any of the previous versions' FR programs.

Complete recovery can only be achieved if FRECOVER-.DAT is absolutely accurate and up-to-date.

Always run FR on a reformatted hard disk before writing anything to the disk—otherwise you may overwrite FRECOVER-.DAT, making recovery impossible.

If you run FR on a hard disk when FRECOVER.DAT is not up-to-date, the recovery will be less than complete. If you have added or removed files and these changes were not stored in FRECOVER-.DAT, FR will not know about them. For example, if you deleted files, FR will assign data to those files even though they no longer exist. Furthermore, data in files created since FRECOVER.DAT was updated will not be recovered. Once FR has done all it can to recover data with an outdated FRECOVER.DAT file, run NDD (Norton Disk Doctor) to sort out the few remaining file fragments. If your hard disk has been reformatted with DOS's FORMAT command, insert a floppy disk that contains FR into drive A. (You have to run FR from a floppy disk because your hard-disk copy of FR can't be accessed.) Do this immediately—before loading any backup copies to the reformatted hard disk. If you try to load programs first, you may overwrite the FRECOVER.DAT file, in which case a complete recovery will be impossible.

To run FR in full-screen mode, type

FR C:

The program then displays the screen shown in Figure 3.1.

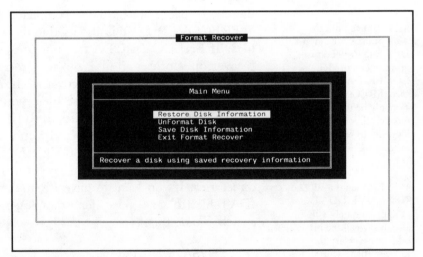

Figure 3.1: The Format Recover screen

The four menu choices are Restore Disk Information, UnFormat Disk, Save Disk Information, and Exit Format Recover. You can also press F10 or Esc to exit FR and return to DOS.

When one of the menu choices is highlighted, a brief description of its capabilities is shown in the lower box on the screen. Here's an elaboration of the descriptions:

- You can use Restore Disk Information to recover data on the hard disk if FR has previously saved data to the FRE-COVER.DAT file.

- You can use UnFormat Disk if your hard disk's data has not been saved to the FRECOVER.DAT file.

- You can use Save Disk Information to create or update the FRECOVER.DAT file. (This is equivalent to specifying FR /SAVE at the command line.)

- You can also save the FRECOVER.DAT file to a floppy disk with the Save Disk Information menu choice.

The combination of an up-to-date FRE-COVER.DAT file and a complete set of current backup disks greatly increases the chances of a complete recovery of all the files on your refor-matted hard disk. Be prepared.

RECOVERING DATA WITH FRECOVER.DAT   If you have an up-to-date copy of FRECOVER.DAT, use Restore Disk Information to rebuild your hard-disk structure. When Restore Disk Information has finished, you should run the NDD utility to see if any sectors remain unallocated to a file. For example, NDD would probably report errors if you hadn't updated the FRECOVER.DAT file recently by using FR /SAVE. NDD can fix these errors as well as find them.

USING FR IN A BATCH FILE   Invoking FR with a batch file is an excellent way to safeguard your hard disk against accidental refor-matting. By including the line FR /SAVE in your AUTOEXEC-.BAT file, FR will automatically update the FRECOVER.DAT file each time you boot your system. If you install the Norton Utilities on your hard disk with the INSTALL program, you can choose to have FR /SAVE added to your AUTOEXEC.BAT automatically. Better still, you can place FR in a batch file that you run just before you turn off your computer. Running FR after you have finished using the computer will make sure that FRECOVER.DAT reflects your most recent disk structure.

If you are prompted for a DOS disk during the recovery process, copy COMMAND.COM to your root directory to make the hard disk a bootable disk.

NCD is described in Chapter 4.

FR's UnFormat Disk choice cannot recover files in the root directory, although it can recover files in all other directories.

RECOVERING DATA WITHOUT THE FRECOVER.DAT FILE   If you have not saved details of your hard disk to FRE-COVER.DAT, you should use the UnFormat Disk option from the menu to recover as much data as possible. FR may prompt you to insert a floppy disk containing your current version of DOS into drive A.

When UnFormat Disk is finished, subdirectories will be called DIR0000, DIR0001, DIR0002, and so on. Use NCD (Norton Change Directory) to rename the directories more appropriately.

As with the Restore Disk Information menu choice, you should run NDD to find any remaining file allocation errors when Unformat Disk has finished. Next, check that all your files and subdirectories are on the hard disk.

Finally, copy any files that you need for normal operation to the root directory. Check that AUTOEXEC.BAT, CONFIG.SYS, and COMMAND.COM are all present. If they are not there, copy them to the root directory from your backup floppies.

USE SF TO AVOID FORMATTING PROBLEMS

The SF (Safe Format) utility provides a faster, easier-to-use alternative to DOS's FORMAT command. It adds many useful safety features, including the ability to store information about the disk's original contents so that the original data on the disk can be recovered even after the formatting process is complete. If you use Norton's INSTALL program to load the Norton Utilities onto your hard disk, you can substitute SF for DOS's FORMAT command. The installation program renames the FORMAT command to XXFORMAT, so when you type FORMAT, SF runs instead.

RUNNING SF IN FULL-SCREEN MODE

SF always gives you a chance to change your mind before it starts carrying out your instructions.

The Safe Format menu screen appears when you type SF with nothing after it and press Enter (see Figure 3.2). A window opens immediately in the center of the screen, prompting you to specify which drive to format and listing the available drive letters on your system. Use the cursor keys to highlight the drive you want to format

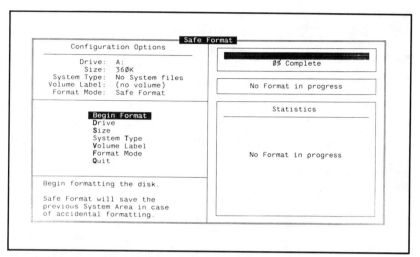

Figure 3.2: The Safe Format screen

and press the Enter key. You can also simply type the drive letter to choose it. SF does not start working straight away; you have to choose one of the menu items. By making this a two-step procedure, SF provides a safety net of sorts—you have time to change your mind.

Once you have chosen the drive letter, the window closes and you can see the menu on the left side of the screen. The menu choices are Begin Format, Drive, Size, System Type, Volume Label, Format Mode, and Quit. The left side also contains a configuration display for the current drive and a message area below the menu. SF uses the right side of the screen to give disk statistics, showing you how much progress is being made with its % Complete display and providing a brief description of the current operation.

Begin Format   This menu choice starts the formatting process. If the disk contains data, SF asks if you wish to continue with the formatting. This welcome safety feature allows you to remove an important disk you have inserted by accident.

Drive   This choice lets you change the current drive setting to another drive. Use the arrow keys to choose the drive letter you want and press the Enter key to confirm your choice.

You cannot use this menu choice to change the size of the hard-disk partition.

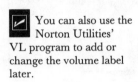 If you try to change the size of a hard disk, an error message appears to tell you that it is not possible.

Size   This selection specifies how to format the disk for the amount of data you want to put on the disk. When you select it, SF offers a range of sizes that the current drive can support. Your choices here are likely to be limited to the common sizes (360K, 1.2Mb, and so on). Use the arrow keys to highlight your choice and press the Enter key.

System Type   This choice enables you to install the DOS system files on the formatted disk. You can also use it to reserve space for these files without adding them to the disk.

You can also use the Norton Utilities' VL program to add or change the volume label later.

Volume Label   This choice lets you create or change the disk's 11-character volume label.

Format Mode   This choice brings up another window, where you select the format mode you want to use (see Figure 3.3). Here are descriptions of the modes you can choose from:

- Safe Format formats a disk without erasing its existing data. This means that Quick UnErase and Undelete Directory can both recover data on a disk with this format.

- Quick Format is extremely fast because it only creates a new system area on the disk and does not overwrite the data area.

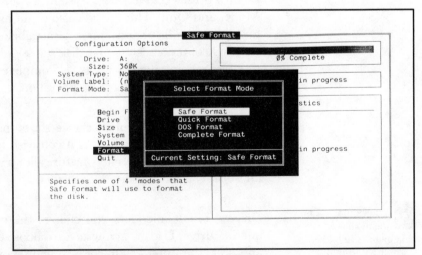

Figure 3.3: The Select Format Mode window

- DOS Format invokes the regular DOS formatting procedure. Everything on the floppy disk is overwritten.

- Complete Format is only available for floppy disks, not hard disks. It functions like Safe Format, except it also reformats any bad sectors found on the disk to make the disk more reliable.

- Quit returns you to DOS.

As a disk is formatted, the % Complete display shows the progress being made and the amount of work that remains. The area below it displays which head is in use and which cylinder is being formatted. The Statistics display presents the following information: the size of the disk, the estimated time it will take to format the disk and the actual elapsed time, the number of total sectors and bad sectors, and finally, the total disk space, system space, bad sector space, and usable disk space in bytes.

When formatting is complete, you can format another disk or use the Quit selection to return to DOS.

RUNNING SF DIRECTLY FROM DOS

SF can also be run from the DOS command prompt with one or more of the many SF switches. To put the system files on a disk, use the /S switch. To leave space for the system files without copying them, use the /B switch. /Q specifies the Quick Format, and /D specifies the DOS format. /C is for use with floppy disks only, and specifies the Complete Format.

RECOVERING ERASED FILES

It is easy, especially if you use wildcards in file names, to specify more than you meant to specify in a DEL operation; you end up deleting more files than you wanted to, maybe even the entire contents of the directory. For example, both EDLIN and WordStar create .BAK files when files are modified and saved. Most people delete these files to save space, relying on their backup disks for copies of the original files. Suppose in this case you misstype

DEL *.BAK

as:

    DEL *.BAT

Instead of deleting your .BAK files, you have just deleted all your batch files.

Careful disk organization can help prevent some of these accidental erasures. To protect your batch files, for example, you should keep them in a directory separate from your EDLIN or WordStar files. No matter how good your organization is, however, sooner or later you will erase a file by accident or want to recover a file that you erased intentionally. This is where the Norton Utilities come into play; the product is probably the most famous for its ability to restore deleted files.

WHAT REALLY HAPPENS WHEN YOU DELETE A FILE?

Before going on to describe how the utilities do their job, I need to explain precisely what happens when you delete a file. When you use DEL or ERASE on a file, the file's entries are cleared from the FAT. DOS also changes the first character of the file name in its directory to a Greek sigma character (ASCII E5 hex or 229 decimal) to indicate to the rest of the DOS system that the file has been erased. The file's entry, including its starting cluster number and its length, remains in the directory, hidden from your view by DOS's inclusion of the sigma character in the file name. The data itself is still in its original place on the disk. DOS does not do anything to the data until it is instructed to write another file over its clusters. Thus, the first cluster of a file can be found and recovered quite easily as long as it has not been overwritten.

To illustrate this, make a very small text file on a blank formatted floppy disk by typing

    COPY CON A:MYFILE.TXT
    This is a short example of text.

Press F6 to terminate your text input and then press Enter to close the file. Use the NU program to look at the directory entry for this file by typing

NU A:

Then press E for Explore disk, C for Choose item, and F for File. Next select Root dir from the Select file or sub-directory screen. You will be immediately returned to the Explore disk menu and should then type E for Edit/display item. The result is shown in Figure 3.4.

The first line of the display shows that the file MYFILE.TXT is 32 bytes long. The file's creation time and date are also shown, as well as that its archive bit is set. This tells DOS that the file should be backed up the next time the BACKUP command is run.

Leave NU and return to DOS by pressing F10. Delete MYFILE-.TXT by typing

DEL MYFILE.TXT

Now rerun the NU program and display the root directory again. Notice that the the file name's first character has been changed to a sigma character (see Figure 3.5).

If you try to make a DIR listing of this disk, however, you will only see an empty listing.

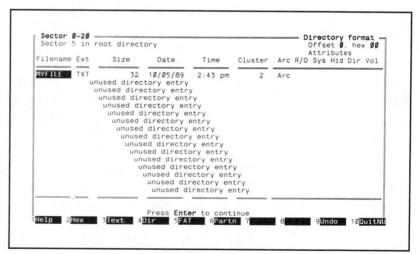

Figure 3.4: Displaying the root directory in directory format

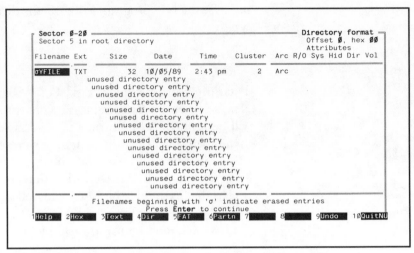

```
┌ Sector 0-20 ══════════════════════════════ Directory format ┐
│   Sector 5 in root directory                       Offset 0, hex 00 │
│                                                        Attributes   │
│ Filename Ext    Size     Date      Time   Cluster  Arc R/O Sys Hid Dir Vol │
│ ───────────────────────────────────────────────────────────────── │
│ σYFILE   TXT      32  10/05/89    2:43 pm     2     Arc            │
│             unused directory entry                                  │
│             unused directory entry                                  │
│             unused directory entry                                  │
│              unused directory entry                                 │
│              unused directory entry                                 │
│              unused directory entry                                 │
│               unused directory entry                                │
│               unused directory entry                                │
│               unused directory entry                                │
│                unused directory entry                               │
│                unused directory entry                               │
│                unused directory entry                               │
│                 unused directory entry                              │
│                 unused directory entry                              │
│ ──────────────────────────────────────────────────────────────── │
│          Filenames beginning with 'σ' indicate erased entries       │
│                   Press Enter to continue                           │
│ 1Help   2Hex   3Text   4Dir   5FAT   6Partn  7       8       9Undo  10QuitNU │
```

Figure 3.5: Displaying the file entry for the deleted file

WHAT HAPPENS WHEN YOU ADD A NEW FILE?

> To learn how to reduce fragmentation, see Chapter 6's discussion of the Speed Disk utility.

When you add a new file to your disk, DOS looks for the next available piece (cluster) of free disk space. If the file is small enough to fit into this space, DOS slots it in. If the file is larger, DOS splits it up into several pieces, recording it into clusters that are not numbered consecutively. In other words, the file becomes fragmented.

Thus, saving a new file on the disk destroys the deleted file's data. If the new file is larger than the old one, the old file is completely obliterated. If the new file is smaller than the old one, some unknown amount of the old file will remain on the disk until it is finally overwritten during another write-to-disk operation.

> Do not save anything after you delete a file or files inadvertently, or you may be unable to recover the file(s).

The most important point to remember about file recovery is you must not save anything on the disk until you have completed the recovery operation. Do not even copy the Norton Utilities to the hard disk; instead, you should run them from a floppy disk, installing them on the hard disk only when the recovery is completely finished. By following this rule, you will not overwrite the erased file's data, and you will increase the chances of a complete recovery.

USING QU TO UNERASE FILES

Using QU (Quick UnErase) is the easiest way to recover erased files. If the file is just a short file or is on a floppy disk, there is an

QU will not recover files that have been partially overwritten. If QU cannot recover a file, use the UnErase item under NU (which is explained in the next section).

excellent chance that QU will be able to restore it on the first attempt. If the file is badly fragmented, or part of it has been overwritten by another file, the chances of a complete recovery are substantially less. Always try QU on the file first. If QU cannot recover the file completely, you can erase it again and then use the NU program's UnErase item to recover the file.

You can run QU in automatic mode, in which it tries to recover all the deleted files on the disk without stopping to ask you for confirmation, or in interactive mode, in which it asks for confirmation before trying to recover each file. To demonstrate QU, let's continue with the file MYFILE.TXT that we earlier created and deleted on drive A. To run QU in automatic mode on drive A, type

> **QU A: /A**

QU replies that it has found one erased file that it can unerase and tells you that erased files lose the first character of their name (see Figure 3.6).

QU lists the names of all the deleted files it can find on the disk, with a question mark as the first character of each file. This is to remind you that QU does not know what this letter should be. QU then supplies the first letter of the alphabet that, if used as the first character of this file name, would make the file name unique among

```
A:\>QU /A
QU-Quick UnErase, Advanced Edition 4.50, (C) Copr 1987-88, Peter Norton

Directory of A:\
    Erased file specification: *.*
    Number of erased files: 1
    Number that can be Quick-UnErased: 1

    Erased files lose the first character of their names.
    Quick-UnErase will automatically replace them.

    ?yfile.txt        16 bytes      4:31 pm  Sat Nov 18 89
'ayfile.txt' Quick-UnErased

A:\>REN AYFILE.TXT MYFILE.TXT

A:\>
```

Figure 3.6: Running Quick UnErase in automatic mode with the /A switch

the file names on the disk and saves the recovered file to that name. As this is the only file on this floppy disk, QU uses the letter A and calls the recovered file AYFILE.TXT. It is now a simple job to use DOS's RENAME command to change the name back to the correct one. The proper syntax for the command in this case is

REN AYFILE.TXT MYFILE.TXT

as you can see in Figure 3.6.

You can use QU to restore a group of files if you include wildcard characters in the file name. For example, if you have accidentally deleted several Lotus 1-2-3 spreadsheet files, which all have the .WK1 extension, you can use QU to restore them automatically by typing

QU *.WK1 /A

QU will restore each of the files in turn, using the first letter of the alphabet that results in a unique file name for each one. These names may look a little strange at first since most of them will probably begin with the letter A or B. As before, you simply use the RENAME command to give them more appropriate names.

For this example delete MYFILE.TXT from the floppy in drive A once again. To run QU in interactive mode, type

QU

at the DOS prompt.

QU follows essentially the same procedure in this mode as in automatic mode, except that it asks you to provide the letter to use as the first character of the file name. If you can remember the original name, you can give QU the correct letter and won't have to use DOS's RENAME command (see Figure 3.7).

USING NU TO UNERASE FILES

Now that you are familiar with QU, you are ready to examine NU's UnErase feature.

Change to the NORTON directory on your hard disk. Use DOS's TYPE command to look at the contents of the READ.ME file. You should see the text shown in Figure 3.8.

```
A:\>QU
QU-Quick UnErase, Advanced Edition 4.5Ø, (C) Copr 1987-88, Peter Norton

Directory of A:\
     Erased file specification: *.*
     Number of erased files: 1
     Number that can be Quick-UnErased: 1

     Erased files lose the first character of their names.
     After selecting each file to Quick-UnErase, you will be
     asked to supply the missing character.

     ?yfile.txt            16 bytes      4:31 pm  Sat Nov 18 89
'myfile.txt' Quick-UnErased

A:\>
```

Figure 3.7: Running QU in interactive mode lets you specify the first letter of the file name.

```
        Late Additions to Version 4.5 of the Norton Utilities
                        Advanced Edition

We've added a few new commands to the Batch Enhancer,
program, have included new switches in Speed Disk, and
have made minor adjustments to the Norton Disk Doctor.


                      BATCH ENHANCER (BE)

  There are two additional subcommands available with the
Batch Enhancer program beyond those listed in the manual:
CLS and DELAY.

        CLS

    Purpose:  To clear the screen and reposition the cursor
              at the home position.

    Format:  BE CLS


        DELAY
-- More --
```

Figure 3.8: The contents of the Norton Utilities' READ.ME file

Now erase the file READ.ME by typing

DEL READ.ME

To use NU to restore READ.ME, start NU by typing

NU

From NU's Main menu, which then appears, select UnErase. This brings up the Recover erased file menu screen (see Figure 3.9).

The first menu choice allows you to change to a different drive or directory. You must be in the correct drive and directory to recover any files. In this case, you should be in the NORTON directory. Choosing this first selection takes you to the Change drive or directory submenu. To change the drive, type C for Change drive. Then select the drive you want by typing its drive letter or by moving the highlighting to the correct letter and pressing Enter. If you want to change to another directory instead, type D and you will see a graphic display of the directory structure on your disk. Use the cursor-control keys to move the highlighting to the directory you want to work with and press the Enter key. You are then returned to the Recover erased file menu. The menu entry to get to the unerase

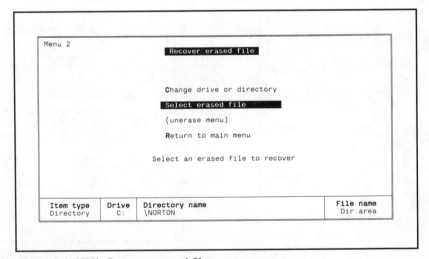

Figure 3.9: NU's Recover erased file menu screen

menu is shown in parentheses, which indicates that the selection is not available yet—you must select the erased file from this menu first. You choose the file to work on by typing S for Select erased file or by highlighting this menu choice and pressing Enter. The Select erased file or sub-directory screen then appears (see Figure 3.10).

NU looks for all the erased files it can find in the directory you have chosen and lists their names at the top of the screen. Like QU, NU does not know the first letter of the file name and uses a question mark to take its place. In this example there is one erased file called ?EAD.ME.

Use the cursor-control keys to move the highlighting to the file you want to restore, or use the Speed search box at the bottom of the screen to enter the name of the file. If you use Speed search, you do not have to type the question mark character. As soon as you have typed enough characters to make the file name unique, NU moves the highlighting to the file, and you can press the Enter key to choose it. If the file you want to restore is not shown on this list, check that you have specified the correct drive and directory. If you are in the right directory, the directory entry for the file may have been over-written. In this case, you would have to make a new directory entry. (This technique is discussed in the next section.)

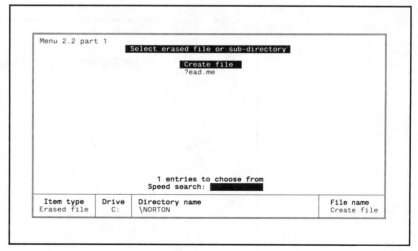

Figure 3.10: The Select erased file or sub-directory screen

When you choose a file, NU displays all the information it can find about the file, as shown in Figure 3.11. NU confirms that the file name is ?EAD.ME. As you can see in Figure 3.11, the file's archive bit is set, and the file was created Sunday October 16th, 1988, at 4:50 p.m. The file starts at cluster 8,158 and contains 3,864 bytes, occupying two clusters. NU also tells you that a successful unerase is possible (as opposed to unlikely) and shows that the first cluster of the file is not being used by another file.

To correct the file name, type R. Press the Enter key, and you are returned to the Recover erased file menu. Note that the parentheses have been removed from around the UnErase menu selection. This shows that it is now available. Press U for UnErase menu, and you will see the screen shown in Figure 3.12. (You are not done yet because you must select the actual clusters or sectors that you want to include in the file you just specified.)

You first use this screen to specify the clusters or sectors that you want to include in the file that you are recovering. The screen looks different from the others in NU, because it is really two menus on the same screen. You use the right-hand menu to find lost clusters, and you use the left-hand menu to save, display, or rearrange the clusters once they have been found. Press the Tab key to move from one side of the screen to the other. The number of clusters needed for the file

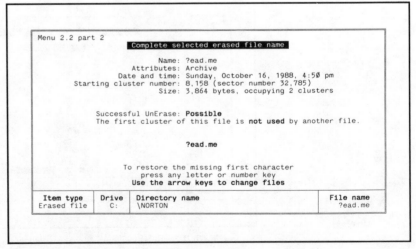

Figure 3.11: The Complete selected erased file name screen

and the number of clusters found so far are given at the top of the screen. Not all the clusters in the original file may be recoverable, of course. The Clusters added to the file line at the bottom of the screen tells you which clusters have been found so far.

Press F1 to get information about the screen shown in Figure 3.12.

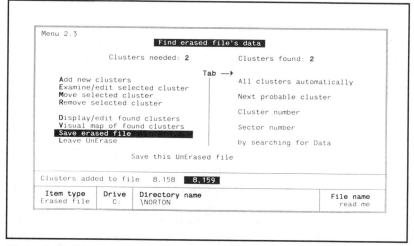

Figure 3.12: The Find erased file's data screen

FINDING CLUSTERS OR SECTORS TO BE RECOVERED

To find the file's clusters, you can choose from the following list:

- All clusters automatically provides the most straightforward method of recovering the file's data. It is the same as running QU.

- Next probable cluster lets NU choose the next likely cluster to include. (Clusters are chosen one at a time.)

- Cluster number requires that you know which cluster to add. You can specify a single cluster or a range of clusters. Enter a starting cluster number and an ending cluster number. If the range contains clusters already in use in a file, NU finds the first free cluster within the range. (This is called *zooming.*)

- Sector number presupposes you know which sector you want to work with. You specify starting and ending sector numbers. Choosing sectors always adds the contents of entire clusters.

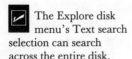 The Explore disk menu's Text search selection can search across the entire disk.

- Searching for data lets you specify and then look for specific text. This selection only searches across the erased data space of the disk.

The simplest way of finding the data for the file is to select All clusters automatically from the right-hand menu. Choose it now. The program will find all the clusters that the READ.ME data occupies and list them on the Clusters added to file line. The highlighting will then move to Save erased file in the left-hand menu. Before completing the recovery process by actually saving the file, you can look at the information contained in the found clusters in several different ways or unselect clusters by using menu selections from the left-hand menu.

VIEWING OR UNSELECTING FOUND CLUSTERS If you do want to work with the clusters, read through these brief descriptions to determine which selection you want:

- Examine/edit selected cluster allows you to look at and edit a single cluster. By choosing this item, you can look at the contents of the cluster and make sure it is one that you want to add to your file.

- Move selected cluster lets you change the order of the clusters.

- Remove selected cluster permits you to delete the highlighted cluster. Use this selection if you have mistakenly added the wrong cluster.

If you just want to change which cluster is selected on the Clusters added to file line, use the arrow keys. For example, pressing the left arrow key in this case would select cluster 8,158.

- Display/edit found clusters allows you to move through the clusters listed on the Clusters added to file line. Use this selection if you want to work with any of the found clusters.

- Visual map of found clusters creates a map of the disk in question, displaying the relative location and size of the data recovered so far.

- Save erased file completes the recovery. You use this selection after you have finished selecting the clusters.

- Leave UnErase ends the recovery process and returns you to the Recover erased file menu.

To display a map of cluster 8,158, press the left arrow key to select the cluster and choose Visual map of found clusters. The resulting screen is shown in Figure 3.13.

You can now look at the actual contents of cluster 8,158 by using the Display/edit found clusters selection from the left-hand menu. When you choose this menu item, the cluster will be displayed in text format (see Figure 3.14). Compare this figure with Figure 3.8 to confirm that

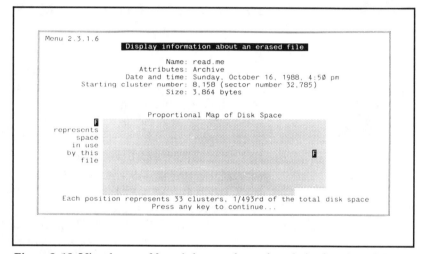

Figure 3.13: Visual map of found clusters shows the relative location of cluster 8,158.

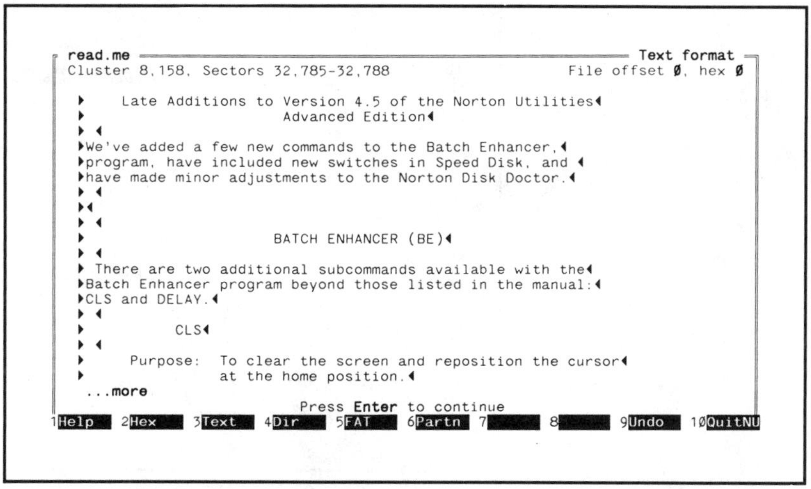

Figure 3.14: Displaying cluster 8,158

what you see is indeed the start of the READ.ME text file.

Now that you have made sure that you have selected the correct file to unerase, use Save erased file to complete the recovery process. This menu selection stores the data to READ.ME's directory entry and also restores the FAT data so that DOS can find the file again. As the information is updated, the screen shown in Figure 3.15 is displayed.

RECOVERING PARTIAL FILES

Often, recovering files is not as straightforward as recovering the READ.ME file was. DOS may have overwritten all or part of the erased file with another file before you realize that you want to recover the erased file. Whether recovery is possible depends on many factors, including the length of the new and erased files, and the existence or nonexistence of the erased file's directory entry.

However, the single most important aspect of this kind of file recovery is how much you know about the contents of the erased file. If you know nothing about the file, it may be impossible to determine whether you have recovered it completely.

To serve as an example of a more complex file-recovery operation, copy the file MAKE-TUT.BAT from your NORTON directory to a 360K floppy disk that has been recently formatted with DOS's FORMAT command.

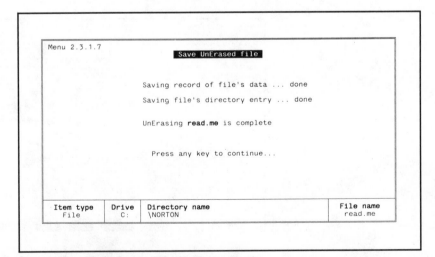

Figure 3.15: The Save UnErased file screen

The MAKE-TUT.BAT file is 2980 bytes long, which means that on this 360K floppy disk it occupies the first three clusters, 2, 3, and 4 (that is, sectors 12–17). Now delete the file with DOS's DEL command. Type

   DEL A:MAKE-TUT.BAT

Next, use DOS's COPY command to make a short text file and save it to the floppy disk. First type

   COPY CON A:MYFILE.TXT
   this is more stuff

Then press F6 to terminate your text input and press Enter to close the file. This new file will overwrite some of the space previously occupied by the MAKE-TUT.BAT file.

   The first step in the recovery process is to try QU to see if anything can be recovered quickly. Type

   QU A:

QU reports that there are no erased files on the disk. This suggests that the directory entry for MAKE-TUT.BAT has been overwritten and lost. The file name, file size, and starting cluster number are therefore no longer available. More complex methods of file recovery are needed, so load NU by typing

   NU A:

From the Main menu, type U for UnErase and S for Select erased file. As you might have expected, no files are listed in the Select erased file or sub-directory screen. Choose the Create file selection, which is designed for exactly these circumstances. When you want to recover a file that no longer has a directory entry, using Create file will create the necessary directory entry. Choosing this selection displays the Complete selected erased file name screen, which prompts you to enter a file name (see Figure 3.16).

   Enter a file name, press Enter, and select UnErase menu. The Find erased file's data screen displays most of its selections in paren-

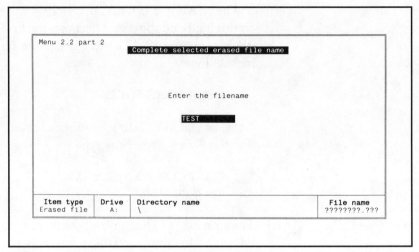

Figure 3.16: Specifying a file name for the erased file

theses, which means they are not yet available. For example, the selection for automatic recovery, All clusters automatically, is not available because NU does not know the starting cluster number or length of the file. (This information was erased when the original directory entry was overwritten.) This time choose Cluster number from the right-hand menu. (The other available choices in this menu work in a similar manner to the following example.)

As MYFILE.TXT is the first file on the disk and is only a short file, there is a good chance that it only occupies the first cluster on the disk, cluster 2. Therefore, enter cluster 3 as the starting and ending cluster number (of MAKE-TUT.BAT). The screen for choosing clusters by number is shown in Figure 3.17.

If one of the clusters you specify in a range is already being used by a file, NU prevents you from accessing *any* of the clusters in your selected range and asks if you want to zoom to the next available clusters.

Press Enter to see the Review cluster(s) menu shown in Figure 3.18. Choose the Add cluster(s) to file menu item to add clusters 3 and 4 to the file TEST. Choosing this item returns you to the Find erased file's data screen.

If you want to double-check that you chose the correct clusters, repeat the cluster selection process for the next free cluster on the

The exact cluster numbers used in this example may vary with DOS versions.

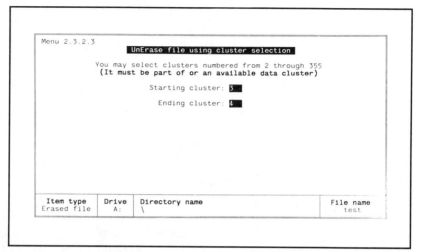

Figure 3.17: The UnErase file using cluster selection screen

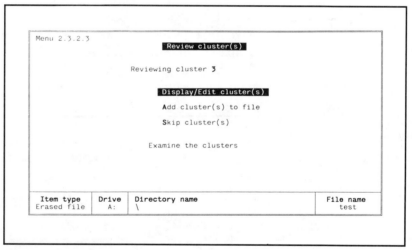

Figure 3.18: The Review cluster(s) screen

disk, cluster 5. Remember, to do this, you follow these steps:

1. Choose Cluster number from the Find erased file's data screen and specify cluster 5 as the starting and ending cluster.

2. At the Review cluster(s) screen that then appears, choose Display/edit cluster(s). You will see that the entire cluster

consists of F6 hex characters, which shows that this area has been newly formatted—nothing has been written here since the disk was formatted.

This confirms that the information in cluster 4 is the end of the MAKE-TUT.BAT file. Press Enter to leave the display and press Esc to return to the Find erased file's data screen.

From the Find erased file's data screen's left-hand menu, choose Save erased file. This will save the recovered clusters (clusters 3 and 4) using the file name TEST. However, because NU originally allotted zero clusters to this file and the file requires two clusters, NU suggests that the length of the file should be adjusted (see Figure 3.19).

You can also choose to keep the current file size (0), or return to the Find erased file's data screen to collect more data. In this case, use the Adjust file size selection and then press F10 to return to DOS. You have now recovered the MAKE-TUT.BAT file as best you could.

Recovery of the entire MAKE-TUT.BAT file was impossible since its first part had been overwritten by MYFILE.TXT. You will have to recreate that part of the file. Nonetheless, this has been a simple example of a partial recovery because the MAKE-TUT.BAT file was not fragmented; it was recorded into contiguous clusters. The more fragmented an erased file is, the less likely it can be recovered

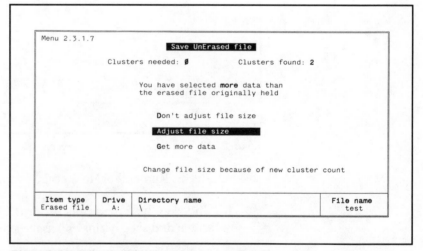

Figure 3.19: Adjusting the size of the recovered file

completely, as it gets increasingly difficult to find and identify its pieces. If the file has some characteristic text that you recall, you can try to find the data by using the by searching for Data selection from the Find erased file's data menu.

RECOVERING AN ERASED DIRECTORY

To recover files, you must sometimes recover a directory first so that you can gain access to them. Note that if a directory contains *any* files, it cannot be deleted.

USING UD TO UNREMOVE DIRECTORIES

You can also use NU to restore directories. The procedure is the same as for restoring deleted files.

The UD (UnRemove Directory) program was made expressly for this purpose. UD restores a directory, allowing access to its erased files. Once the directory has been recovered, all its files can be restored. If FR (Format Recover) has been run on your disk using the /SAVE switch, UD can use the FRECOVER.DAT file to help recover the directory. (If this file is not present, UD can often complete the recovery anyway.)

DOS treats the removal of a directory in the same way that it treats the removal of a file. The first character is set to the same special character, and the removed directory's entry remains in its parent directory (unseen, of course), just like a removed file's entry.

Let's look at an example to review this procedure briefly. Suppose you erased all your spreadsheet files that were in drive C's 123 directory, erased the directory itself, and then realized that this was not the directory you had intended to delete. The QU program will not be able to find the spreadsheet files to restore them, as their names, starting cluster numbers, and file lengths are all stored in the 123 directory that has also been deleted. You must recover the directory before attempting to recover the files. To run UD on the 123 directory, go to the directory that was the parent of the 123 directory (the root in this example) and type

UD 123

You will see the display shown in Figure 3.20.

UD first looks for the FRECOVER.DAT file, and since it is present, uses that file's information to help recover the 123 directory automatically.

Once you have recovered the directory, you can proceed to recover the files that were in the 123 directory. The files were all small files, each a single cluster, so try QU on them first. Move to the 123 directory and type

    QU L*.WK1

> If you specify QU L as the command, QU will attempt to recover all erased files and will make L the initial character for each file's name. If this isn't appropriate for a particular file, you can simply rename it later.

Specifying a file name with the QU command tells QU which files to recover. By giving an initial letter (in this case, L for Lotus), you instruct QU to replace the missing character in the file names. The rest of this file specification, *.WK1, narrows QU's search to only those erased files that have the .WK1 extension.

QU finds three files and tells you it can unerase the first two. It can't recover the last file because the file's data space is being used by another file. Figure 3.21 demonstrates this file-recovery sequence.

```
C:\>UD 123
UD-UnRemove Directory, Advanced Edition 4.50, (C) Copr 1987-88, Peter Norton

Directory of C:\
     Removed directory specification: 123.*
     Number of removed directories: 1
     Number that can be UnRemoved: 1

     ?23          <DIR>          4:48 pm   Sat Nov 18 89
Enter the first character of the filename: 1

     ?otus.wk1          43 bytes    4:49 pm   Sat Nov 18 89
     ?23.bat           120 bytes    4:49 pm   Sat Nov 18 89
     ?otus2.wk1        190 bytes    4:50 pm   Sat Nov 18 89
     ?otus3.wk1        118 bytes    4:52 pm   Sat Nov 18 89

Files included in C:\123

'123' UnRemoved

C:\>
```

Figure 3.20: UD uses information from FRECOVER.DAT to restore the 123 directory.

```
C:\>CD 123

C:\123>QU L*.WK1
QU-Quick UnErase, Advanced Edition 4.50, (C) Copr 1987-88, Peter Norton

Directory of C:\123
     Erased file specification: L*.WK1
     Number of erased files: 3
     Number that can be Quick-UnErased: 2

     ?otus3.wk1           118 bytes      4:52 pm  Sat Nov 18 89
   'lotus3.wk1' Quick-UnErased

     ?otus2.wk1           190 bytes      4:50 pm  Sat Nov 18 89
   'lotus2.wk1' Quick-UnErased

     ?otus.wk1             43 bytes      4:49 pm  Sat Nov 18 89
   It is not possible to Quick-UnErase this file
   Its data space is being used by another file
   Press any key to continue...

C:\123>
```

Figure 3.21: Specifying the file name's first character

USING THE OTHER NU MODES

If you start NU by typing NU and a file name at the DOS prompt, NU starts up its Explore disk program and opens an editor on the file.

If the file you specify on the command line is an erased file (type a question mark as the first character of the file name to indicate that the file is an erased file), NU starts up its UnErase program. The file you specified is the file selected for unerasing.

NU also has a *maintenance mode.* When NU starts running, the program reads the directory structure of the whole disk. If your disk is so badly damaged that NU cannot read it, the program will not start up. However, if you type

NU /M

You can only work with absolute sectors in the Advanced Edition.

to specify maintenance mode, NU will bypass the attempt to read the directory structure and start. In this mode you can work with clusters, sectors, and absolute sectors. You cannot work with files or use the UnErase selections. (Remember, unavailable selections are enclosed in parentheses.)

SUMMARY

In this chapter I discussed the importance of taking care of floppy and hard disks, giving you tips on how to do so. You also learned how to use the following utilities:

- FR (Format Recover), which allows you to recover the contents of your hard disk if you accidentally reformatted it with DOS's FORMAT command.

- SF (Safe Format), which can format a disk safely and quickly. The original data on the disk is not overwritten, which makes file recovery a little more certain.

- QU (Quick UnErase), which can make simple recoveries of erased files.

- NU (Norton Utility), which can restore files partially when the files' data has been damaged or overwritten.

As you now know, file recovery is by no means certain. Many aspects of the process influence the success of any recovery attempt, most of which you examined in this chapter. Although the file-recovery process can be more difficult than was shown in this chapter's examples (for instance, recovering program files can be messy), you should have enough knowledge of the Norton Utilities' recovery programs to attempt difficult recoveries on your own. Chances are the file can't be recovered if you can't rescue it with the Norton Utilities.

CHAPTER *4* _____

ONE OF THE TOUGHEST PROBLEMS IN THE MANAGE-
ment of your hard disk is deciding how to organize your files into
directories. You want to implement a system that enables you and
others to find files easily.

The Norton Utilities contain several programs that can help you
organize and work with your files. Before I present them in this chapter, however, I describe how the file system in DOS works.

THE DOS DIRECTORY STRUCTURE

The most useful feature of DOS's file system is its ability to organize directories hierarchically. What this means is that directories can
contain subdirectories as well as files; in fact you can consider a subdirectory to be another type of file.

As so many others before me have advised, think of this hierarchical file system as a filing cabinet. The hard disk is the filing cabinet,
the information (file) you need is in there, and the root directory
is the index to the drawers of the filing cabinet, telling you which
drawer to look in for the file you want.

All disks start with the root directory, so called because it is like the
roots of a tree, with all the other directories branching off it.

THE ROOT DIRECTORY

Don't clutter up
your root directory
with files; place them in
subdirectories, reserving
the root for directories.

The concepts of the root and ordered hierarchical directories originated in UNIX, which is another operating system. You should be
careful to install few files in the root directory, AUTOEXEC.BAT,
CONFIG.SYS, and COMMAND.COM being the three main
exceptions to this rule. The remaining entries in the root should be

subdirectories; for example, one might contain your word processor, another your spreadsheet, another the DOS files, another your batch files, another the Norton Utilities, and so on. In this way you will be able to find your way around the disk easily and quickly, and DOS will run more efficiently.

ORGANIZING YOUR HARD DISK

The key to maneuvering through your hard disk is organization. You should start to group like things together in their own subdirectories, rather than putting all files in the root directory. Placing all your files in the same directory defeats the purpose of DOS's hierarchical file system—to enable you to find the file you want quickly.

Keep each software package you install on your system (the program files, the device drivers, the help files, and so on) all in the same directory. For example, if you are a Lotus 1-2-3 user, create a directory called 123 in the root directory and install Lotus 1-2-3 into it. If necessary, you can create additional subdirectories below the 1-2-3 directory. Suppose you want to separate your quarterly budget files from all your other files. You could place them in a subdirectory of 123 called BUDGETS. Note, however, that you would only want to separate an easily identifiable group of files and that this group should contain more than just a few files. Otherwise, you will quickly forget where your files are. By the same token you don't want to create too many subdirectories or levels of subdirectories.

I recommend that you limit yourself to three levels (root, subdirectories, and subdirectories of those subdirectories); with any more you will find it time-consuming to move through your directory structure.

When you want to use a file or directory, you tell DOS where it is in the hierarchy. In other words, you give DOS the file or directory's *path*. For example, to move to your newly created BUDGETS directory from the root, you would type

    CD \123\BUDGETS

at the DOS prompt.

When you organize your directory structure, make sure you install all the DOS files except for COMMAND.COM and CONFIG.SYS in a

To learn more about PATH commands, see Judd Robbins' *Mastering DOS,* 2nd. ed. (SYBEX, 1988).

directory under the root directory. You should not install them in the root directory itself. Use the PATH command in your AUTOEXEC-.BAT file to tell DOS where to look for certain files.

LISTING DIRECTORIES

Perhaps the first step in organizing your hard disk is to take a look at the directory structure that already exists. I'll briefly discuss the DOS commands that allow you to do this and then show you how you can do the same things with less effort—not to mention some things that you simply can't do with DOS—by using the Norton Utilities.

USING THE DOS DIR COMMAND

The DOS DIR command lists the names of all the files and sub-directories in a directory. As well as the name, DIR gives the file size in bytes, the date and time of the file's creation or last modification, and the number of bytes remaining on the disk. DIR does not list hidden files. If the disk has a volume label, DIR will show the label text in the first line of the listing; otherwise DIR reports

Volume in drive *n*: has no label

To make a DIR listing of the DOS directory on drive C, type

DIR \DOS

from the root directory.

You can compare the results on your screen with Figure 4.1, which shows a typical listing from DIR.

If the listing flashes by before you have time to read any of it except the last part, you can use the Ctrl-S key combination to stop and then restart the listing. Another alternative is to cause DOS to present only one screenful at a time by entering

DIR /P

If you want to print the DIR listing, rather than display it on the screen, type

DIR > PRN

```
C:\>DIR

 Volume in drive C is DYSON
 Directory of  C:\

BATCH        <DIR>      7-22-89    9:19a
SD     INI    2494  10-17-89    3:13p
DOS          <DIR>      7-12-88    3:51p
NORTON       <DIR>     11-07-89   11:19a
PCO          <DIR>      7-12-88    3:58p
PFS          <DIR>      7-12-88    3:58p
REFLEX       <DIR>      7-12-88    3:57p
WS4          <DIR>      7-12-88    3:57p
COMMAND  COM  23210   1-24-86   12:00p
CONFIG   SYS    128   9-24-89   10:02a
FRECOVER DAT  38400  11-16-89    2:34p
TREEINFO NCD    267  11-16-89    2:45p
FRECOVER BAK  38400  11-16-89    2:34p
AUTOEXEC BAT    256  10-05-89   11:14a
      14 File(s)  11952128 bytes free

C:\>
```

Figure 4.1: A typical listing made by the DIR command

Each screenful will then be displayed until you hit any key, and then the next screenful will be displayed. To make a wide listing that gives only file and directory names, use the /W switch. Directories in this display do not have the usual <DIR> notation and may be easily confused with files (see Figure 4.2).

USING THE DOS TREE COMMAND

The DOS TREE command summarizes the directory information for all the directories on a disk and presents this data in an outline form. To make a TREE listing of your disk, type

TREE

Using the /F switch will make TREE list all the files in each directory or subdirectory. This listing will be too long to fit on the screen. You can send the listing to your printer instead of displaying it on the screen by typing

TREE > PRN

The output produced by this command will not be broken into neat pages; it will be an exact copy of what would have appeared on the screen.

```
C:\DOS>DIR /W

  Volume in drive C has no label
  Directory of  C:\DOS

                            COMMAND  COM    MODE     COM    GWBASIC  EXE
BASIC    COM    BASICA   COM    GRAPHICS COM    FORMAT   COM    FDISK    COM
SYS      COM    CHMOD    COM    SIZE     COM    ASSIGN   COM    RAMDISK  DEV
COMP     COM    ANSI     SYS    PRINT    COM    TREE     COM    DISKCOMP COM
DISKCOPY COM    AUTOEXEC BAT    CHKDSK   COM    FIND     EXE    MORE     COM
RECOVER  COM    EDLIN    COM    FC       EXE    SORT     EXE    SUBST    EXE
JOIN     EXE    SHARE    EXE    LABEL    COM    DEBUG    COM    LINK     EXE
EXE2BIN  EXE    SHIP     EXE    BACKUP   COM    RESTORE  COM
        39 File(s)  13934592 bytes free

C:\DOS>
```

Figure 4.2: A wide listing made with DIR /W

USING LD TO LIST DIRECTORIES

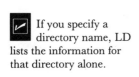 If you specify a directory name, LD lists the information for that directory alone.

The Norton Utilities' LD (List Directories) program greatly expands on the capabilities of the DOS TREE command. LD can make a textual or graphic listing of a disk's directory structure. For example, Figure 4.3 shows the textual LD display for my hard disk. Compare this to the graphic listing of the hard disk's file system shown in Figure 4.4. To make a graphic listing such as this, use the /G switch in the LD command.

To stop the display each time it fills the screen, include the /P switch in the LD command. Pressing any key will restart the display.

You can also redirect the output from LD to the printer by typing

LD /G > PRN

If your printer does not support the IBM extended character set, use the /N switch with /G to print the graphic listing. Type

LD /G/N > PRN

To get a count of the number of files in a directory and the total amount of disk space they occupy, rather than the number of bytes of disk space unused, which the DIR command gives, type

LD /T

```
C:\>LD/P
LD-List Directories, Advanced Edition 4.50, (C) Copr 1987-88, Peter Norton

  C:\ (root)
  C:\BATCH
  C:\DOS
  C:\NORTON
  C:\PCO
  C:\PFS
  C:\PFS\LETTERS
  C:\PFS\FLYERS
  C:\REFLEX
  C:\WS4
  C:\WS4\BOOK
  C:\WS4\BOOK\TEXT
  C:\WS4\BOOK\FIGURES
  C:\WS4\BOOK\SCREENS
  C:\WS4\PHOTO
  C:\WS4\SJ

16 directories

C:\>
```

Figure 4.3: LD textual output for a hard disk

```
C:\>LD /G
LD-List Directories, Advanced Edition 4.50, (C) Copr 1987-88, Peter Norton

C:\──┬──BATCH
     ├─DOS
     ├─NORTON
     ├─PCO
     ├─PFS────────┬─LETTERS
     │            └─FLYERS
     ├─REFLEX
     └─WS4────────┬─BOOK────────┬─TEXT
                  │             ├─FIGURES
                  │             └─SCREENS
                  ├─PHOTO
                  └─SJ

16 directories

C:\>
```

Figure 4.4: LD graphic output for a hard disk

Figure 4.5 shows an LD listing of the NORTON directory made with the /T switch.

To list all the directories on your disk before you back up the disk, include the line

LD > LISTFILE

```
C:\>LD NORTON /T
LD-List Directories, Advanced Edition 4.50, (C) Copr 1987-88, Peter Norton

  C:\NORTON
        37 files   909,522,678 bytes

1 directory

C:\>
```

Figure 4.5: Listing how many files there are in the NORTON directory

in your backup batch file (you can substitute a different file name for LISTFILE). If you place this line before the backup command, the file created by the redirection, LISTFILE, will also be backed up.

MAKING, CHANGING, AND REMOVING DIRECTORIES

Creating and deleting directories and moving between directories are essential tasks for hard-disk users. You can accomplish these common operations faster with the Norton Utilities than you can with DOS, and you can use the utilities' graphic display of the directory structure to view the results of your changes instantly. I'll quickly cover the DOS commands for these operations and then show you the more powerful Norton alternatives.

USING DOS COMMANDS

To make a new directory from the root for your Lotus files called 123, type

MKDIR 123

You can also abbreviate this command to

MD 123

DOS makes the new 123 directory, assigning its creation time and date. If you make a DIR listing now, you will see an entry whose format differs slightly from that of the file entries. The 123 directory had a creation time and date, but no file size. Instead, the designation <DIR> appears in the listing. This confirms that 123 is not a file but a directory. To make this new directory the default directory, type

CHDIR 123

for change directory. You can also abbreviate this command to

CD 123

The 123 directory is now the default, or current, directory. To make the root directory the default directory once more, type

CD \

When you create a directory, DOS automatically places two special entries in it. These entries (known as . and ..) are shorthand notations for the full path name of the new directory (.) and of the parent directory (..). Thus for your new 123 directory, . is equivalent to \123, and .. is equivalent to the root directory (\). Although you can change to the root directory by typing

CD \

you can also change to the root from the 123 directory by typing

CD ..

since the root is its parent directory.

So long as a directory contains only the . and .. entries, DOS considers it empty, and you can delete it. If the directory is not empty when you try to remove it, DOS responds with this message:

Invalid path, not directory,
or directory not empty

Use DOS's DEL or ERASE command to delete the files from the directory. For example, to remove all the files from a directory simultaneously, type

DEL * *

Because this is a potentially dangerous command, DOS has a safety net built into it and prompts you with

Are you sure? (Y or N)

so you have to confirm that you want to erase all the files or abort the DEL command.

If the directory also contains subdirectories, you will need to delete all their files and then remove them individually before you can erase the directory. For instance, to remove 123's BUDGETS directory, once it is empty, type

RMDIR BUDGETS

from the 123 directory. When the 123 directory is empty of all files and subdirectories, you can remove it by changing to the root and typing

RD 123

(RD is short for RMDIR).

If you stop using a directory, you really should remove it, as it will be easier to work with your hierarchical structure if it is not cluttered with old, unused entries. It will also conserve some disk space.

USING NORTON CHANGE DIRECTORY

The NCD (Norton Change Directory) utility includes all the functions of DOS's MD, CD, and RD commands. NCD also allows you to change to another directory without specifying its complete path.

USING NCD FROM THE COMMAND PROMPT   The DOS CD command requires that you specify the whole DOS path name every time you use it. With a large hard disk and a complex structure, this can be difficult to remember and can become very time-consuming.

Changing Directories   You can use NCD with a directory name to change from any directory to another directory on the disk without

When using NCD, you do not need to enter the path of a directory. You may not even need to enter the directory's complete name.

typing its path. For example, suppose you are in the root directory and want to change to the directory C:\WS4\BOOK\TEXT. Instead of typing CD with the complete path name, type

   NCD TEXT

NCD will search the disk's directory structure, find the requested directory, and change to it. In fact, you may only need to type the first few letters of the name—enough letters so that NCD can understand which directory you mean. If you have directory names that have the same initial letters (TEST and TEXT, for example), you will have to type more characters to make the entry unique.

Updating TREEINFO.NCD   When you run NCD for the first time on your disk, it reads the complete directory structure from the disk and stores the data in a small file called TREEINFO.NCD, which it keeps in the root directory. When you run NCD the next time, it reads the data from the TREEINFO.NCD file, rather than the directory structure, to find the specified directory more quickly. If you make a change to the directory structure using DOS commands, NCD will not know about it until you explicitly specify that NCD must read the disk's directory structure again. To do this, type

   NCD /R

NCD then updates the TREEINFO.NCD file with the new information. If for some reason you don't want NCD to store information to the TREEINFO.NCD file, type

   NCD /N

to stop the file being written.

Making and Removing Directories   To practice making and removing directories with NCD, let's work with a new 123 directory as an example. To make this directory, type

   NCD MD 123

from the root directory. You can also create a subdirectory in another directory using NCD MD. If you are not in the directory where you want the new subdirectory to be, you must give the new directory's full path when you create it. For example, if you are in your TEXT directory and want to create a BUDGETS subdirectory for the 123 directory, simply type

NCD MD \123\BUDGETS

If you encounter any difficulties running NCD in full-screen mode, update the TREEINFO.NCD file.

Although you normally don't have to update the TREEINFO.NCD file after making changes to your directory structure with NCD, you may find that NCD's full-screen mode doesn't work if you run it after using NCD MD from the root (trying to change directories ends NCD, sending you back to the root). To fix this problem, simply rescan your directory structure from NCD's full-screen mode or run NCD /R at the DOS prompt.

To remove the BUDGETS subdirectory using NCD, type

NCD RD BUDGETS

from the 123 directory. A directory must be empty of files and sub-directories before you can remove it. You can use the DOS command DEL or ERASE to remove the files from a directory. If you are not in the parent directory of the directory you want to remove, specify the full path of the directory. For example, if you are in the TEXT directory, you can remove the 123 directory by typing

NCD RD \123

USING NCD IN FULL-SCREEN MODE   You can run NCD in full-screen mode by entering

NCD

You must have DOS 3.0 or later to be able to rename directories in NCD.

with no parameters. You will then see a display similar to that shown in Figure 4.6.

NCD shows the directory structure in graphical form, linking sub-directories together with lines. With the full-screen version of NCD you can change, make, remove, and rename directories.

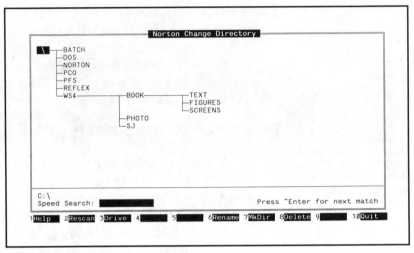

Figure 4.6: NCD's full-screen display

NCD uses function keys for its available commands. To run a command, press the appropriate function key, as indicated by the numbered labels at the bottom of the screen. The function keys and their uses are listed in Table 4.1.

When you start NCD, the highlighting is on the name of the current directory (that is, the directory you were in when you started NCD). You can move this selection bar with the up and down arrow keys. Pressing the PgUp and PgDn keys scrolls the display up and down a page at a time. The Home key returns you to the top of the display, and the End key takes you to the end of the listing.

To change to another directory, highlight it and press the Enter key. NCD will make it the new current directory, quit NCD, and return you to the DOS command prompt. Alternatively, you can use the Speed Search box at the bottom of the screen to specify the directory you want. As soon as you type enough letters to identify the directory uniquely, NCD moves the highlighting to that directory. Press Enter to confirm your choice and return to DOS. If you have several directories with similar names, Speed Search will move to the first one when you start typing. To move to the next one, hold down the Ctrl key and press the Enter key. Each time you press Ctrl-Enter, you move to the next directory name that matches the letters you typed in the Speed Search box.

If you move the selection bar, the directory that was current when you invoked NCD will appear in boldface.

Press the F1 key to get help information, and press the Esc key or the F10 key to quit NCD and return to DOS.

Table 4.1: NCD Function Keys and Their Uses

KEY	SCREEN LABEL	USE
F1	Help	Displays a help screen.
F2	Rescan	Makes NCD reread the disk's directory structure.
F3	Drive	Allows you to change to another drive by choosing another drive letter.
F4 and F5		Unused.
F6	Rename	Allows you to rename a directory.
F7	MkDir	Allows you to make a new directory.
F8	Delete	Allows you to delete a directory. As with the DOS RMDIR command, the directory must be empty before it can be deleted.
F9	Lines	If you have an EGA or a VGA, you can display more lines on the screen than the default 25 lines. The EGA can display 25, 35, or 43 lines, while the VGA can display 25, 40, or 50 lines.
F10	Quit	Leaves NCD and returns you to DOS.

Rescanning the disk is the same as running NCD /R from from the command prompt.

If the directory structure shown by NCD is not up-to-date, use the F2 key to make NCD reread the directories on the disk. NCD updates the TREEINFO.NCD file with the new data and then displays the new structure. If you make changes to the directory structure from within NCD by using the function keys (see below), TREEINFO.NCD will be updated automatically when you exit NCD.

You can use the F3 key to change drives. When you press F3, a dialog box appears on the screen. Highlight or type the drive letter you want and press the Enter key, or press the Esc key for no change. If you do not change the current drive but press Enter instead of Esc, the selection bar will return to the directory that was current when you invoked NCD.

To rename a directory, position the selection bar on it and press F6. The cursor will then appear under the first letter of that directory's name, and you can type the new name over the original. You must press Enter before you can move on.

To make a new subdirectory, move the highlighting to what will be its parent directory in the directory structure (for example, PFS) and press F7. A blank highlighted box is then added to the display for you to enter the new directory's name (see Figure 4.7). Type the new name, say LETTERS, and press Enter. To add another subdirectory under PFS called FLYERS, simply repeat the process. The resulting display is shown in Figure 4.8.

To delete a directory, highlight the victim and press F8. As with DOS's RD command, the directory must be empty before it can be deleted, and you cannot delete the root directory.

If you have an EGA or VGA monitor, you can use the F9 key to change the number of lines NCD displays on the screen. (If you do not have one of these monitors, NCD does not use F9; F9's label on the screen will be blank.) With an EGA monitor you can choose to

If you want to change the number of screen lines permanently, see the discussion of NCC in Chapter 6.

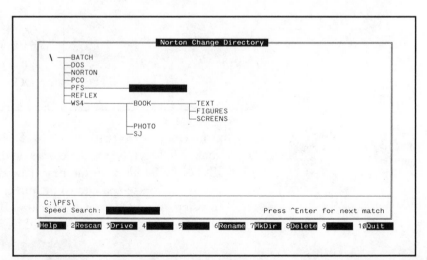

Figure 4.7: Creating a subdirectory under the PFS directory in NCD

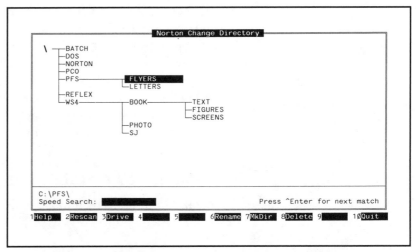

Figure 4.8: Creating another subdirectory, FLYERS, under PFS

display 25, 35, or 43 lines on the screen, and with a VGA monitor you can choose to display 25, 40, or 50 lines. The screen will revert to its normal settings when you leave NCD.

CUSTOMIZING NCD'S FULL-SCREEN DISPLAY   You can customize NCD's full-screen mode for your screen by typing

> NCD *parameters*

where *parameters* includes any of the following:

- /D0, the default setting for 100 percent compatibles
- /D1, the display setting for BIOS-compatible machines
- /BW, the monochrome setting for CGA monitors
- /NOSNOW, the setting for removing flickering from CGA monitor displays

SORTING DIRECTORIES WITH DS

Even on a well-organized hard disk, the accumulation of directories and files often forces you to look through long directory listings to find a directory or file that you want. You can improve this situation by sorting directory listings. You may also find that sorting directory entries into groups based on criteria that you choose allows you to speed your work in ways you've never thought of before.

You can sort the information listed in a directory by adding switches to the DOS DIR command, but the Norton DS (Directory Sort) utility lets you manipulate the contents of any directory in a simpler fashion and provides many more possibilities than does DOS.

USING DS IN FULL-SCREEN MODE

To invoke DS in full-screen mode, enter

DS

The resulting screen will contain a list of the contents of the current directory. Figure 4.9 shows a typical DS full-screen display.

If you type the name of a directory after DS, the contents of that directory will be listed in the resulting screen even if that directory is not the current one. For example, I can produce the screen in Figure 4.9 by entering

DS \REFLEX

The name of the directory to be sorted is shown at the top of the main box.

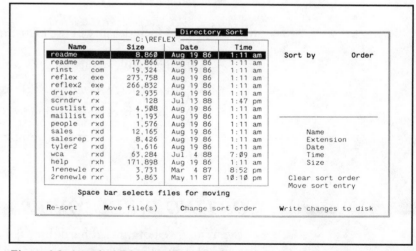

Figure 4.9: A typical Directory Sort display

regardless of what the current directory is. Note that you must specify the complete path for the directory that you wish to sort. You can sort a directory on a different drive by specifying the drive letter, as in

DS A:\[*directory name*]

You can also use the usual switches to customize your display. (See this chapter's "Customizing NCD's Full-Screen Display" section for a listing of these switches.) These switches can be used in combination with the other DS parameters. For example, entering

DS \REFLEX/BW

will list the REFLEX directory in a monochrome display (black and white).

You use the PgDn, PgUp, Home, and End keys to scroll the directory listing in the usual ways:

- PgDn brings the next page (17 lines in this case) of entries into view.

- PgUp brings the previous page into view.

- Home moves the selection bar to the first entry in the directory.

- End moves the selection bar to the last entry in the directory.

SORTING AN ENTIRE DIRECTORY   After you have invoked DS in full-screen mode, type C for Change sort order, or press Tab or the right arrow key to move the selection bar to the far right and activate the sort settings. Press Tab, the left arrow key, Enter, or Esc to move the selection bar back to the directory listing.

The sort settings, Name, Extension, Date, Time, and Size, are located in the lower-right of the screen. When they are activated, you can request them by typing the first letter of their names. For example, to sort by Name, type N and to sort by Time, type T. After you have chosen a setting, it is listed in the Sort by column, and DS initially assumes its sort direction is normal (ascending). This is indicated by the + sign in the Order column. To reverse the sort direction, change the + to a − sign by typing − . When you are ready to sort the directory, type R for Re-sort.

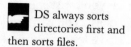
DS always sorts directories first and then sorts files.

You can choose multiple sort settings. For example, let's say you first choose Extension and then choose Size. The directory entries will first be arranged alphabetically by their extensions, and any entries with identical extensions will then be sorted by size (from the smallest to the largest, assuming there is a + in the Order column for both settings). If you want to cancel the sort settings you have chosen, type C for Clear sort order. If you want to reorder the sort settings you have chosen, you can highlight a setting that you want to move and type M for Move sort entry. Use the vertical arrow keys to move the highlighting. The selected setting will move with it, and the list of settings will be reordered immediately.

When the sort settings are active, the Move file(s) and Change sort order selections are temporarily disabled. Figure 4.10 shows a screen with the sort settings active and a directory that has been sorted by size in + order.

MANUALLY SORTING ENTRIES   DS in full-screen mode lets you reorder a directory by moving one or more entries to specific locations within the directory. This feature lets you order a directory any way you like without being limited by sort settings.

You can move both subdirectory names and file names.

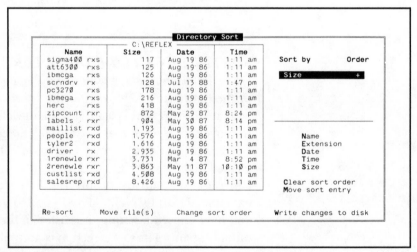

Figure 4.10: A directory sorted by size in + order

Moving One Entry at a Time To move one directory entry, follow these steps:

1. Place the highlighted selection bar on the appropriate entry and press Enter. Notice that a small arrowhead shape appears on the left of the entry.

2. Use the arrow keys to move the selection bar to the entry above which you want the selected entry to appear.

3. Press M for Move file(s). The entry you selected will now appear at the new location.

Here is a second method for moving a directory entry:

1. Highlight the appropriate entry and press M.

2. Use the arrow keys to move the highlighted entry. Notice that the directory is immediately reordered as you move the entry.

3. When the entry is where you want it, press Enter.

Moving Multiple Entries at a Time To move a group of directory entries, follow these steps:

1. Use the arrow keys to highlight an entry that you want to move and press Enter. Repeat this step until you have selected all the entries that you want to move.

2. Press M. Notice that the entries are now listed in one contiguous block and that the entire block is highlighted.

3. Use the arrow keys to move the block. The directory is reordered each time the block moves.

4. When the block is where you want it, press Enter.

SAVING THE SORTED DIRECTORY Up to this point, all the changes you have made have been made in memory only. To make the changes permanent, type W for Write changes to disk. The next time you use the DS utility or the DOS DIR command on this directory, you will see the files ordered exactly as you requested. Press Esc or F10 when you want to return to DOS.

To cancel a selection that has an arrowhead on the left, highlight the entry and press Enter.

To cancel an entry selected with this method, simply press Esc.

Both methods of canceling a selection work during this process: If the selected entry has an arrowhead on the left, highlight the entry and press Enter. When the entries have been grouped into a large highlighted block, pressing Esc will cancel the entire selection and move the entries back to their original locations. (Each entry that was in the block will now have an arrowhead next to it.)

RUNNING DS FROM THE COMMAND PROMPT

To run DS from the DOS prompt to sort the entries in the current directory alphabetically, type

DS N

To sort them into reverse alphabetical order, type

DS N –

The other sort keys (E for file extension, T for time, D for date, and S for size) work in the same sense—the specified letter alone invokes the ascending sort, and a minus sign after it reverses the direction of the sort. You can even group sort letters (with or without minus signs) together on the command line to produce more complex sorts.

To sort a directory other than the current one, type its name, giving its full path, after the sort keys. If you make a spelling error when typing a directory name or specify a directory that does not exist, DS presents the message

Directory not found *pathname*

where *pathname* is the entry you typed, and returns you to the DOS prompt.

To practice using these keys, first check the unsorted root directory shown in Figure 4.11. Suppose you want to sort it by file extension and name. If you type

DS E N C:

at the DOS prompt, DS will sort the root directory's entries alphabetically by extension, and then it will sort any entries with the same extension by name. As you can see in Figure 4.12, the only entries that have been sorted by name are the directories (which are all entries without extensions); the remaining entries have different extensions, so they are sorted only by their extensions. This is a particularly useful sort-key combination: not only does it separate the subdirectories from the files, making it easier to identify the directories, but it will also group your program files together and your data files together, provided you (and the programs) use file extensions consistently.

```
Volume in drive C has no label
Directory of  C:\

REFLEX          <DIR>      7-12-88    3:57p
DOS             <DIR>      7-12-88    3:51p
AUTOEXEC BAT       256     7-19-89   10:44a
NORTON          <DIR>      7-12-88    4:22p
PCO             <DIR>      7-12-88    3:58p
CONFIG   SYS       128     7-12-88    4:09p
PFS             <DIR>      7-12-88    3:58p
PROLOG          <DIR>      7-12-88    3:58p
WS4             <DIR>      7-12-88    3:57p
COMMAND  COM     23210     1-24-86   12:00p
C               <DIR>      7-12-88    3:58p
TREEINFO NCD       315     7-19-89   10:58a
        12 File(s)  15065088 bytes free

C:\>
```

Figure 4.11: An unsorted root directory

```
C:\>dir

Volume in drive C has no label
Directory of  C:\

C               <DIR>      7-12-88    3:58p
DOS             <DIR>      7-12-88    3:51p
NORTON          <DIR>      7-12-88    4:22p
PCO             <DIR>      7-12-88    3:58p
PFS             <DIR>      7-12-88    3:58p
PROLOG          <DIR>      7-12-88    3:58p
REFLEX          <DIR>      7-12-88    3:57p
WS4             <DIR>      7-12-88    3:57p
AUTOEXEC BAT       256     7-19-89   10:44a
COMMAND  COM     23210     1-24-86   12:00p
TREEINFO NCD       315     7-19-89   10:58a
CONFIG   SYS       128     7-12-88    4:09p
        12 File(s)  15056896 bytes free

C:\>
```

Figure 4.12: The same root directory sorted by file extension and name

Including the /S switch in the DS command extends the sort to the entries in the current directory's subdirectories. For example, type

DS N /S

to sort entries in the current directory and its subdirectories alphabetically by name.

RUNNING DS AUTOMATICALLY

By including DS in a batch file, you can sort your files and sub-directories automatically. You can use different sort-key combinations for different directories. The advantage of using a batch file to invoke DS is that you can run the batch file at the end of every work session, and all the specified directories will be resorted quickly—any changes you made will be incorporated.

If you want to sort all the files and subdirectories on your hard disk alphabetically, include the following line in your batch file:

DS N \ /S

Every time you run the batch file DS will sort by name, starting with the root directory and working through all subdirectories.

LOCATING FILES AND SUBDIRECTORIES WITH FF

Sometimes you know the name of a subdirectory or file that you want to work with, but you can't remember its location. Sometimes you can't even remember the complete name of the item. The DOS DIR command is of little use in this situation. However, you can use FF (File Find) to locate files or directories.

FF always searches an entire drive regardless of what the current directory is.

If you do not specify otherwise, FF searches throughout the current drive. To find all copies of AUTOEXEC on a hard disk (assuming that the current drive is C), type

FF AUTOEXEC

The results of running this command on my hard disk are shown in Figure 4.13.

To tell FF to search a drive other than the current one, specify the drive before typing the file or directory that you want to search for. For example, entering

FF A: AUTOEXEC

```
C:\>FF AUTOEXEC.*
FF-File Find, Advanced Edition 4.50, (C) Copr 1987-88, Peter Norton

C:\
        autoexec.bat        256 bytes  11:14 am  Thu Oct  5 89

C:\DOS
        autoexec.bat          3 bytes  12:00 pm  Fri Jan 24 86

C:\WS4
        autoexec.bat        256 bytes   9:52 am  Tue Oct  3 89

3 files found

C:\>
```

Figure 4.13: Using FF to find all copies of AUTOEXEC on the hard disk

would cause drive A to be searched regardless of what the current drive is. Using the /A switch, as in

FF AUTOEXEC /A

tells FF to search all drives.

When FF finds a match, it first lists the directory that contains the matching name and then gives the match's entry information (file or directory name, extension, size, time, and date of creation or modification). You can even use FF to find hidden files, including IBM-BIO.COM and IBMDOS.COM.

If you don't specify a file name, FF finds all the files in all the directories on the drive. Figure 4.14 shows an example from the root directory of a hard disk. In this case, I used the /P switch to force the display to pause when the screen was full. You can also press the space bar to pause the screen output.

Compare the information shown in Figure 4.14 with that in Figure 4.15. By adding the /W switch to my previous command, I instructed FF to give a wide listing showing only file names and extensions.

If you would prefer to examine FF's information on paper than by screenfuls, send FF's output to the printer by typing

FF > PRN

```
C:\>FF /P
FF-File Find, Advanced Edition 4.50, (C) Copr 1987-88, Peter Norton

C:\
        ibmbio.com        7,836 bytes   12:00 pm   Fri Jan 24 86
        ibmdos.com       27,760 bytes   12:00 pm   Fri Jan 24 86
        BATCH               <DIR>         9:19 am   Sat Jul 22 89
        sd.ini            2,494 bytes    3:13 pm   Tue Oct 17 89
        DOS                 <DIR>         3:51 pm   Tue Jul 12 88
        NORTON              <DIR>        11:19 am   Tue Nov  7 89
        PCO                 <DIR>         3:58 pm   Tue Jul 12 88
        PFS                 <DIR>         3:58 pm   Tue Jul 12 88
        frecover.idx         29 bytes    2:34 pm   Thu Nov 16 89
        REFLEX              <DIR>         3:57 pm   Tue Jul 12 88
        WS4                 <DIR>         3:57 pm   Tue Jul 12 88
        command.com      23,210 bytes   12:00 pm   Fri Jan 24 86
        config.sys          128 bytes   10:02 am   Sun Sep 24 89
        frecover.dat     38,400 bytes    2:34 pm   Thu Nov 16 89
        treeinfo.ncd        267 bytes    2:45 pm   Thu Nov 16 89
        frecover.bak     38,400 bytes    2:34 pm   Thu Nov 16 89
        autoexec.bat        256 bytes   11:14 am   Thu Oct  5 89

C:\BATCH
        .                   <DIR>         9:19 am   Sat Jul 22 89
Program paused; press any key to continue...
```

Figure 4.14: An initial output screen from running FF /P. (Note that the two hidden system files IBMBIO.COM and IBMDOS.COM are both visible.)

```
C:\>FF /P/W
FF-File Find, Advanced Edition 4.50, (C) Copr 1987-88, Peter Norton

C:\
    ibmbio.com      ibmdos.com      BATCH           sd.ini          DOS
    NORTON          PCO             PFS             frecover.idx    REFLEX
    WS4             command.com     config.sys      frecover.dat    treeinfo.ncd
    frecover.bak    autoexec.bat

C:\BATCH
    .               ..              bu.bat          menu.bat        pcobu.bat
    test.bat        menu.txt

C:\DOS
    .               ..              command.com     mode.com        gwbasic.exe
    basic.com       basica.com      graphics.com    format.com      fdisk.com
    sys.com         chmod.com       size.com        assign.com      ramdisk.dev
    comp.com        ansi.sys        print.com       tree.com        diskcomp.com
    diskcopy.com    autoexec.bat    chkdsk.com      find.exe        more.com
    recover.com     edlin.com       fc.exe          sort.exe        subst.exe
    join.exe        share.exe       label.com       debug.com       link.exe
    exe2bin.exe     ship.exe        backup.com      restore.com

C:\NORTON
Program paused; press any key to continue...
```

Figure 4.15: An initial output screen from running FF /P/W

Remember that FF without a file or directory specification finds all files on the disk and that the redirection symbol (>) sends the output to the printer.

USING FS TO EXAMINE FILE SIZE

If you need to refresh your memory about clusters, see the section entitled "Clusters" in Chapter 2.

When a file is copied between a hard disk and a floppy disk, the number of clusters it occupies will change because cluster size varies with the version of DOS used to format a disk and the size of the disk itself. (The file data will not change.) This differing cluster size can sometimes lead to unexpected results when you try to copy a file from one disk to another—there seems to be enough room on the target disk, but you find you cannot copy the file across because the disk does not have enough available clusters. To circumvent this problem entirely, use the FS (File Size) utility. FS gives information about a file's size, displaying the percentage slack for the file and determining if a file will fit onto another disk.

DOS's DIR command, on the other hand, reports the actual file size in bytes rather than the number of occupied clusters and reports the space remaining on the disk in bytes. Hence, the numbers may not add up to the expected total when you use DIR.

DETERMINING WHETHER A FILE WILL FIT ON A DISK

FS looks in the current directory for the specified file. You can tell it to look for a file in another directory by specifying the file's complete path.

FS can tell you whether a specific file will fit on a disk. For example, FS can report on whether the file COMMAND.COM on drive C will fit on the 360K floppy disk in drive A. Assuming that you are in the root directory of drive C, type

FS COMMAND.COM A:

You will get a report resembling the one shown in Figure 4.16.

In Figure 4.16 FS reports COMMAND.COM as having 25,276 bytes and occupying 26,624 bytes on the hard disk. As this hard disk has a cluster size of 4 512-byte sectors, making each cluster 2,084 bytes, COMMAND.COM occupies 13 clusters.

The 360K floppy disk has 1024-byte clusters, so 25 whole clusters are needed for COMMAND.COM to fit. As you can see in Figure 4.16, there is plenty of space on the floppy disk for the file.

FS reports the total available disk space, which in the case of this hard disk is 33,280,000 bytes, with 11,450,368 bytes (or 34 percent) unused.

```
C:FS COMMAND.COM A:
FS-File Size, Advanced Edition 4.50, (C) Copr 1987-88, Peter Norton

  C:\
     command.com      25,276 bytes

        26,624 bytes disk space occupied, 5% slack

        25,600 bytes disk space needed to copy to A:
        96,256 bytes available on A:, enough disk space

 Drive usage
   33,280,000 bytes available on drive C:
   11,450,368 bytes unused on drive C:, 34% unused

 C:
```

Figure 4.16: FS reports that there is enough disk space on the 360K floppy disk in drive A for COMMAND.COM.

FS also works with wildcards. For example, if the root directory of drive C is the current directory and you enter

FS *.BAK A:

FS will tell you whether all the files in the root directory with the extension .BAK will fit on the floppy disk in drive A.

GETTING A REPORT ON A FLOPPY DISK

Chapter 2's "Clusters" section also contains a discussion about slack.

For a floppy disk FS displays a report showing the size of each file found, the total size of the files, the total disk space occupied by the files, as well as the percentage of slack created by the file—that is, how much unused space the file wastes. FS displays this information for hidden files as well as for normal files.

To have FS report on all the files in drive A, type

FS A:

Figure 4.17 shows the results I got when I ran this command for a system disk in drive A. As you can see, there were only three files on the disk, two of which were hidden files.

```
C:FS A:
FS-File Size, Advanced Edition 4.50, (C) Copr 1987-88, Peter Norton

  A:\
    io.sys            22,398 bytes
    msdos.sys         30,128 bytes
    command.com       25,276 bytes

       77,802 total bytes in 3 files
       78,848 bytes disk space occupied, 1% slack

Drive usage
     362,496 bytes available on drive A:
     283,648 bytes unused on drive A:, 78% unused

  C:
```

Figure 4.17: Running FS for a system disk

Since this disk has a cluster size of 1024 bytes, IO.SYS occupies just over 21 clusters (in other words, 22 clusters), MSDOS.SYS occupies 30 clusters, and COMMAND.COM occupies 25 clusters, for a total of 77 clusters (78,848 bytes). The actual data in the three files fills 77,802 of those bytes, and the remaining 1046 bytes roughly equals 1 percent of slack.

FS also reports the total available space and the remaining space on the disk, both in bytes and as a percentage of the total disk capacity. In Figure 4.17 the disk has a capacity of 362,496 bytes, of which 283,648 bytes, or just over 78 percent, are unused.

GETTING A REPORT ON A HARD DISK

If your hard disk is the current drive and you want FS to report not only on the current directory but also its subdirectories, type

    FS /S

from the root directory. If the root directory is not current and you want a report on the entire disk, simply type

    FS \ /S

SUMMARIZING AND PAUSING A LONG REPORT   An FS report on an entire hard disk can obviously be very long. To see this report in summary form, type

FS \ /S/T

Figure 4.18 shows a screen after FS has been run with these switches.

If you want the display to pause when the screen is full, add the /P switch. You can also press the space bar to stop the display from scrolling. To continue scrolling, press the space bar again.

```
C:FS \/S/T/P
FS-File Size, Advanced Edition 4.50, (C) Copr 1987-88, Peter Norton

  C:\
      386,100 total bytes in 48 files
      452,608 bytes disk space occupied, 14% slack

  C:\BIN
      828,052 total bytes in 16 files
      845,824 bytes disk space occupied, 2% slack

  C:\DOS
      612,737 total bytes in 49 files
      663,552 bytes disk space occupied, 7% slack

  C:\EV
      187,406 total bytes in 4 files
      192,512 bytes disk space occupied, 2% slack

  C:\INCLUDE
      169,633 total bytes in 40 files
      210,944 bytes disk space occupied, 19% slack

  C:\INCLUDE\SYS
Program paused; press any key to continue...
```

Figure 4.18: A summary FS report on an entire hard disk

SUMMARY

In this chapter I first described the hierarchical directory structure in DOS and the DOS commands used with files and directories.

You can use many of the Norton Utilities programs to work with your directory structure. Some of the utilities extend the capabilities of the DOS commands, while others add totally new capabilities that can make your life much easier. Here's a review of the programs you examined in this chapter:

- LD (List Directories) can make a graphic or textual listing of your disk's directory structure on the screen.

- NCD (Norton Change Directory) allows you to make, change, delete, and rename directories. So it can access data quickly, NCD creates and references the TREEINFO.NCD file, which contains a copy of your disk's structure.

- DS (Directory Sort) can sort a directory's entries by name, extension, size, or creation time or date. You can also reverse the order of these sorts by using a minus sign with the sort-key letters.

- FF (Find File) gives you the locations of files or directories on a disk. Use it if you remember the file's name but not where you put it.

- FS (File Size) displays the size of a file in bytes and the percentage of slack in the file's clusters. By using FS, you can determine whether a file will fit on a different disk.

CHAPTER **5** _____

DOS PROVIDES SEVERAL GENERAL-PURPOSE PRO-grams for searching files for text and for printing from ASCII text files. These programs have their limitations, and there are several ways in which you can use the Norton Utilities to overcome these limitations.

USING THE DOS FIND COMMAND
TO LOCATE TEXT

You can use FIND to search for a string of characters in a text file. FIND identifies the lines in the file that contain the specified characters when it finds them. FIND performs a case-sensitive search, because it requires you to specify the string exactly—the upper- or lowercase letters you give must be the same in the file, or FIND will not locate the string. For example, if you want to find the word Norton in the READ.ME file provided with the Norton Utilities, you must type

    FIND "Norton" READ.ME

If you type

    FIND "norton" READ.ME

instead, the FIND will not locate a match. Notice that the search string itself must be enclosed in quotation marks.

FIND locates all occurrences of the search string in the target file, so you must make the search string as specific as possible to minimize the number of incorrect or unanticipated matches. For example, to locate all the phone numbers with the 916 area code in the

ADDRESS.TXT file, which contains names, addresses, and phone numbers, type

FIND "916/" ADDRESS.TXT

Assuming that all area codes are separated from the rest of the phone numbers by a slash, the search string "916/" pinpoints the context; it is highly unlikely that this will turn up any matches that are not phone numbers. If, however, you used "916" as the search string, FIND might locate unwanted matches in a street address or zip code.

FIND can operate on several files at a time if you specify them using the DOS wildcards or type their names on the command line, separating them by a space. With the following command FIND looks for the search string "1989 Budget" in all .DOC files in the current directory:

FIND "1989 Budget" *.DOC

FIND stops its search at the first Ctrl-Z character it encounters in a file. The Ctrl-Z character (ASCII 26) is DOS's end-of-file marker. However, many program and data files include the decimal value 26 as an instruction or a data word. When you use FIND on these files, the search is truncated at the first Ctrl-Z character that it locates, which is not necessarily the end of the file.

You can also use the following switches with FIND:

/C   displays a count of the lines that contain the string.

/N   displays the line number of the line found as well as the lines.

/V   displays the lines that do not contain the string.

USING THE TS UTILITY TO FIND TEXT

The Norton Utilities contain a program called TS (Text Search) that expands enormously on the functions of the DOS FIND filter. TS is a much more flexible and powerful program than FIND, although the basic premise is the same—to find a specific set of text characters in one or more files.

USING TS IN INTERACTIVE MODE

You can use TS in interactive mode by typing

TS

The display shown in Figure 5.1 then appears. At this point you have three choices: F, D, or E.

Press F if you want to search files. This limits TS's search to the data area that is occupied by files. This is by far the most common kind of search you will perform.

Press D to extend the search to the entire disk, including the boot record, the FAT, the root directory, and the unoccupied data area. If a match is found in this kind of search, its location is given in terms of disk sectors. A search of a 20Mb hard disk will take a long time to complete, so think carefully before starting this kind of search.

Press E to search the entire data space of the disk. This search will also report matches in terms of disk cluster or sector information, rather than by file name, and it too can take some time to complete. If you enter F, the program asks for the name of the file to search. If you do not enter a file name and press Enter, the search includes all the files in the current directory. You can also use the DOS wildcard characters to search groups of files. In the example in Figure 5.2, I entered WIPEDISK as the name of the file to search.

When you press Enter after specifying the file or files to search, you are prompted to enter the search string. As you can see in Figure 5.3, I entered the text "GOVERNMENT SPECIFICATIONS."

Searching an entire hard disk takes a while. Use this search as a last resort.

Searching a disk's data space is also time-consuming.

To specify all files in the current directory, just press Enter when prompted for a file specification.

```
C:\NORTON>TS
TS-Text Search, Advanced Edition 4.50, (C) Copr 1987-88, Peter Norton

Select search within FILES, all of DISK, or ERASED file space
Press F, D, or E ...
```

Figure 5.1: Setting up a text search with TS

```
C:\NORTON>TS
TS-Text Search, Advanced Edition 4.50, (C) Copr 1987-88, Peter Norton

Select search within FILES, all of DISK, or ERASED file space
Press F, D, or E ... F

Searching contents of files

Enter the file specification for the files to search
   File: WIPEDISK
```

Figure 5.2: Specifying a file for a TS search

```
C:\NORTON>TS
TS-Text Search, Advanced Edition 4.50, (C) Copr 1987-88, Peter Norton

Select search within FILES, all of DISK, or ERASED file space
Press F, D, or E ... F

Searching contents of files

Enter the file specification for the files to search
   File: WIPEDISK

Enter specific text to search for
Or press enter for any text
   Text: GOVERNMENT SPECIFICATIONS
```

Figure 5.3: Entering the search text

If TS fails to find text that you think it should find, try enclosing the search text in quotation marks, especially if the search text contains spaces.

In Figure 5.4 TS displays the first occurrence of the search text and asks if you want to continue the search. Note that case is unimportant in this example; g and G are treated the same. (I will show you how to make the search case sensitive shortly.) In this example the text is found at line 142. File offset 11,681 indicates that the search text begins 11,681 bytes from the beginning of the file. The line containing the search text is also displayed, with the search text shown in reverse video.

If you answer yes to the "Search for more?" prompt, TS continues. When TS does not find any more matches, it prints a short summary, as shown in Figure 5.5. It reports the location of the found string, how many files contained the string, and the number of times the string was found.

USING TS FROM THE COMMAND PROMPT

You cannot use wildcards in the search text; TS will look for the actual characters.

You can also activate TS directly from the DOS prompt. To repeat the previous search operation, type

TS WIPEDISK "GOVERNMENT SPECIFICATIONS"

```
Searching C:\NORTON\wipedisk.exe
Found at line 142, file offset 11,681
Wipe Erased data space using government specifications: %d cycle

Search for more (Y/N) ?
```

Figure 5.4: TS finds the first occurrence of the search text

```
Searching C:\NORTON\wipedisk.exe
Found at line 145, file offset 11,869
Wipe Entire disk using government specifications: %d cycles

Search for more (Y/N) ? Y

Searching C:\NORTON\wipedisk.exe

Search Complete

1 file found containing the text "GOVERNMENT SPECIFICATIONS"
4 occurrences

C:\NORTON>
```

Figure 5.5: TS's summary report

This will give the same results as those shown in Figure 5.4, finding the same occurrence of the string "GOVERNMENT SPECIFICATIONS." If you fail to specify a search string, the program will prompt you for one.

If no match is found, TS reports this as shown in Figure 5.6. In this example TS was asked to search the WIPEDISK file for the text "DOD 5220.22-M" but failed to find it.

SEARCHING THROUGH FILES IN SUBDIRECTORIES   If you want to search a number of files in the current directory and in the subdirectories of the current directory, use the /S switch. For example, if you enter

TS *.* GOVERNMENT SPECIFICATIONS /S

all the files in the current directory and its subdirectories will be searched.

SEARCHING WITHOUT PAUSING   With /A you can automate the TS search. Instead of waiting for you to answer the "Search for more?" question when a match is found, the /A switch tells TS to

```
C:\NORTON>TS WIPEDISK "DOD 5220.22-M 116b(2)"
TS-Text Search, Advanced Edition 4.50, (C) Copr 1987-88, Peter Norton

Searching contents of files

Searching C:\NORTON\wipedisk.exe

Search Complete

0 files found containing the text "DOD 5220.22-M 116b(2)"

C:\NORTON>
```

Figure 5.6: Output from TS when it does not find a match

continue the search for the next occurrence of the search string automatically. TS does not stop until it has searched the entire file, displaying each line containing the search string as it is found.

The problem with the /A switch is that it causes the screens displaying each match to be quickly erased, making them impossible to read. The result is that this switch is only useful when used with the /LOG switch, which allows you to capture the output of the search in a file or print it out directly.

LOGGING TS OUTPUT TO A FILE OR PRINTER To send the output of the TS utility to a file (called LOG.LOG, for example) enter

TS *.* NORTON UTILITY /LOG > LOG.LOG

The /LOG switch prepares output from TS into a form suitable for redirecting to a file or printer; however, it does not send the TS output to a file automatically. You must use the DOS redirection symbol (>) to send the output to a file. When you use the /LOG switch, TS presents each occurrence of the search string in each file and also counts how many times the string occurs overall. You can use the LP utility to print the LOG.LOG file. If you want to print the results of the search without creating a file, enter

TS *.* NORTON UTILITY /LOG > PRN

To capture the results of an automatic search in a file, enter

TS *.* NORTON UTILITY /A /LOG > LOG.LOG

GETTING SUMMARY RESULTS The /T switch causes TS to display only the names of the files containing text that matches the search string. It does not display the search string or the lines containing it.

To make TS find any occurrence of the text "NORTON UTILITIES" in the files in the NORTON directory, change to that directory and type

TS *.* "NORTON UTILITIES" /T

Figure 5.7 shows the results. Note that with the /T switch TS shows that the search string was found at least once in each file, but it does not show whether the search string occurs more than once in any file.

MAKING THE SEARCH CASE SENSITIVE   The /CS switch makes a TS search case sensitive; whether the letters are upper- or lowercase in the search string now becomes important. For example, "Norton" and "norton" are two completely different search strings when you use the /CS switch. This results in a more specific search and can be used to avoid unwanted matches with the search string.

USING TS IN WORDSTAR FILES   TS usually searches all bits in a byte, but the /WS switch tells it to ignore the eighth bit. Use the /WS switch if you are searching WordStar 3 or 4, or WordStar-compatible files because WordStar reserves the eighth bit for its own internal purposes. (WordStar 2000 does not use this technique.) Matches based on the the first seven bits may sometimes be misleading.

SEARCHING EBCDIC FILES   TS can search EBCDIC files downloaded from your mainframe computer when you use the /EBCDIC switch. This tells TS that the file to be searched is in the IBM mainframe computer code, EBCDIC, rather than in ASCII.

```
C:\NORTON>TS *.* "NORTON UTILITIES" /T
TS-Text Search, Advanced Edition 4.5Ø, (C) Copr 1987-88, Peter Norton

Searching contents of files

    C:\NORTON
          fr.exe
          nu.exe
          ni.exe
          fileinfo.fi
          bedemo.dat
          tut-read.me

6 files found containing the text "NORTON UTILITIES"

C:\NORTON>
```

Figure 5.7: Using the /T switch with TS to produce a summary listing

TS then translates the search string text you enter into EBCDIC coding before starting the search.

EBCDIC stands for Extended Binary Coded Decimal Interchange Code. EBCDIC is a standard for coding characters on IBM mainframes, just as ASCII is a standard on PCs and minicomputers.

If you forget what a particular switch does with TS when you go to use this utility, you can refer to Table 5.1, which summarizes the switches and their uses.

Table 5.1: TS's Switches

SWITCH	USE
/A	Automatically searches for all occurrences of search string
/CS	Makes the search case sensitive
/D	Searches the whole disk
/E	Searches the erased data area
/EBCDIC	Translates search text to EBCDIC code and searches for it
/LOG	Formats TS information for printing or storing in a file
/S	Searches subdirectories of specified directory
/T	Provides summary search information
/WS	Does not search for ASCII characters 128 to 255 (the eighth bit)
/Cn	Starts search at cluster n.

FINDING TEXT WITH THE NU (NORTON UTILITY) PROGRAM

The NU (Norton Utility) program can also be used for text searches, but its approach and results differ significantly from those of TS. If you want to search through a number of files, you will probably find it easier to use TS. If you are working in NU and need to find some text, however, NU's search capabilities might be more convenient.

Although you have worked with some of the many menu selections NU provides, you haven't seen its search feature in detail yet. In this example you will find the text "search complete" in the TS.EXE file. First make NORTON the current directory. Then start the NU program by entering

NU

The screen shown in Figure 5.8 is displayed. Type E for Explore disk. From the Explore disk menu, which then appears (Figure 5.9), select Choose item.

You will usually want to choose File as the item to work with for searches since you are looking for text within specified files and are unlikely to know the more precise locations of the data (cluster, sector, absolute sector). As this case is no exception, select File from the Choose item menu (Figure 5.10). The screen shown in Figure 5.11 is then displayed.

Use the left and down arrow keys to highlight the TS.EXE file and press Enter. Alternatively, you can use the Speed search box at the bottom of the screen to enter the file name.

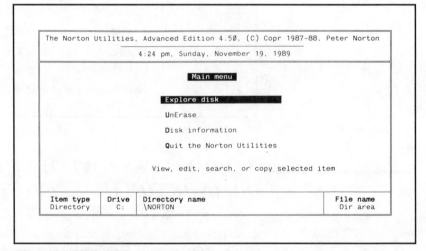

Figure 5.8: NU's Main menu screen

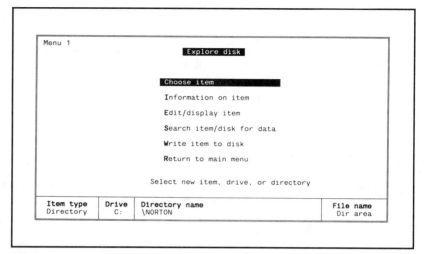

Figure 5.9: The Explore disk menu

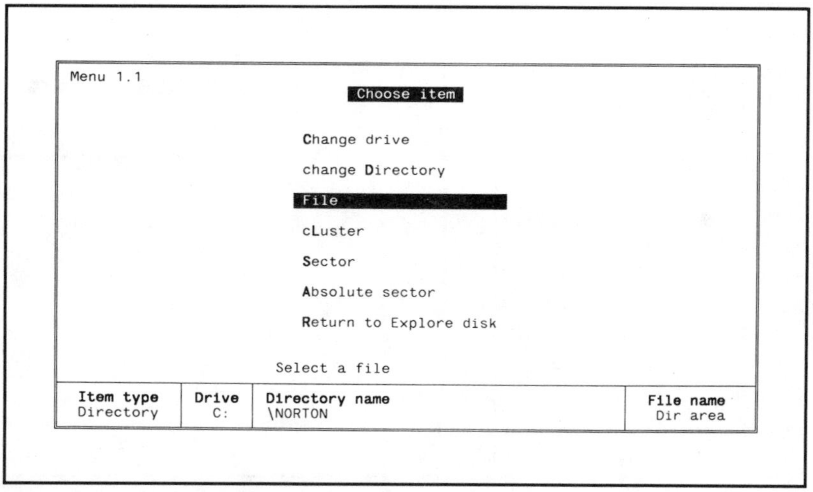

Figure 5.10: The Choose item menu

After you have selected the file, you are returned to the Explore disk menu (Figure 5.9). This time choose S for Search item/disk for data.

The Search item/disk for data menu appears next, as shown in Figure 5.12. Note that several selections in this menu are enclosed in parentheses and are not available at this point. You cannot, for

Figure 5.11: The Select file or sub-directory screen

Figure 5.12: The Search item/disk for data menu

example, choose Display found text until some text has been specified and found. Similarly, you cannot choose Continue search if the search has not yet started.

If you type F1 while this screen is displayed, the Search Help screen will overlay the menu screen (see Figure 5.13). Help in NU is not context sensitive; although you cannot get help on an individual item or selection, you can get general information about a menu screen.

Press any key to remove the help screen and go back to the Search item/disk for data screen. Now choose the first selection in the menu, Where to search, to bring up the display shown in Figure 5.14.

Since you have already selected a file to search, the menu choice Selected item: TS.EXE is highlighted. If you had chosen Where to

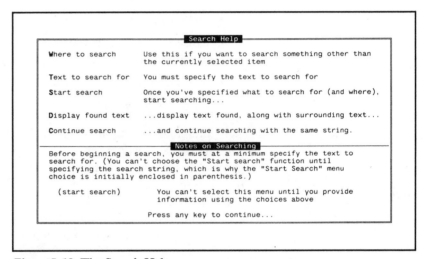

Figure 5.13: The Search Help screen

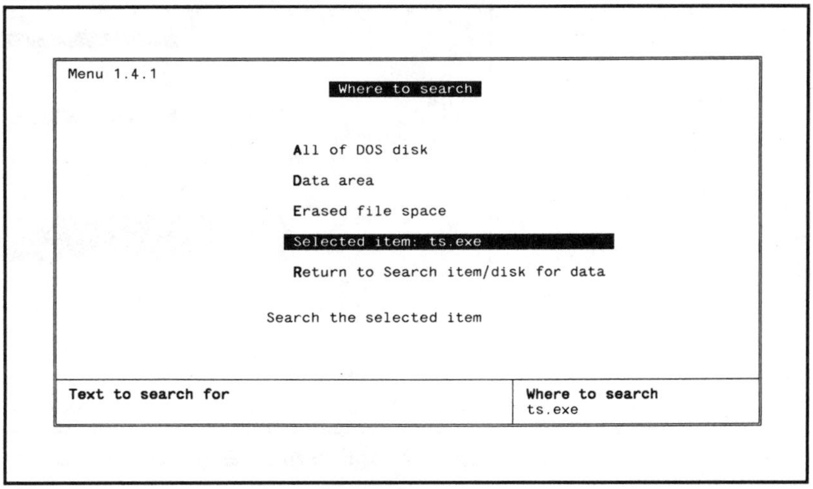

Figure 5.14: The Where to search menu

search before selecting a file, the first entry in the menu, All of DOS disk, would be highlighted. In this case, you don't need to reselect the file; however, you could choose another area of the disk to search if you changed your mind. Here are the choices the Where to search menu provides:

- All of DOS disk searches the entire DOS partition sector by sector

- Data area searches the disk's data area only

- Erased file space searches the disk area that is not currently used by files

- Return to Search item/disk for data simply returns you to the previous menu

When you make your choice, you will be immediately returned to the Search item/disk for data screen.

Now choose Text to search for. This selection displays the screen shown in Figure 5.15.

Type the characters you wish to search for, in this case, the text "search complete." Note that as you type the ASCII characters in the upper window, they are translated into hex format and displayed

NU can search for as many as 48 characters (including spaces) at a time.

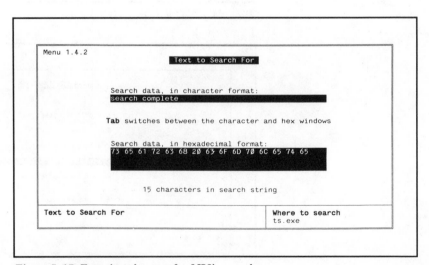

Figure 5.15: Entering the text for NU's search

in the lower window. If you want to enter the search string in hex characters, press Tab to move to the hex window and enter the characters directly in hex. NU can search for up to 48 characters at a time. As you enter characters, they are counted and the total count is displayed at the bottom of the screen. Here you have entered 15 characters (including the space). Press the Enter key to return to the Search item/disk for data menu. As you can see in Figure 5.16, the menu selection Start search is now available. Choose it to tell NU to look for ''search complete'' in the TS.EXE file.

When NU finds a match for the search string, it presents the screen shown in Figure 5.17. Press any key to return to the Search item/disk for data screen, and from its menu select Display found text. The found text can be displayed in a variety of ways, including ASCII or hex.

If you display the text in ASCII, you can switch to hex by pressing F2. To change the display back to ASCII, press F3. The Dir, FAT, and Partn function keys do not work from this display, even though they are labeled on the screen. After you have finished viewing the text, press Esc to return to the Search item/disk for data menu and choose Continue search to see if the text occurs more than once in this file.

If NU can't find any other matches with your string, it displays the screen shown in Figure 5.18; if it does locate a match, it presents the screen shown in Figure 5.17 again.

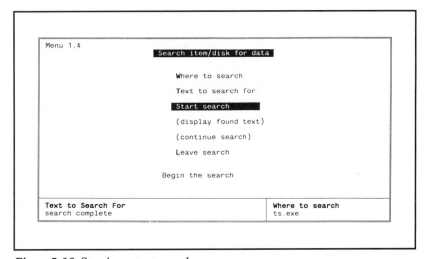

Figure 5.16: Starting a text search

Figure 5.17: NU's display when it locates the text string

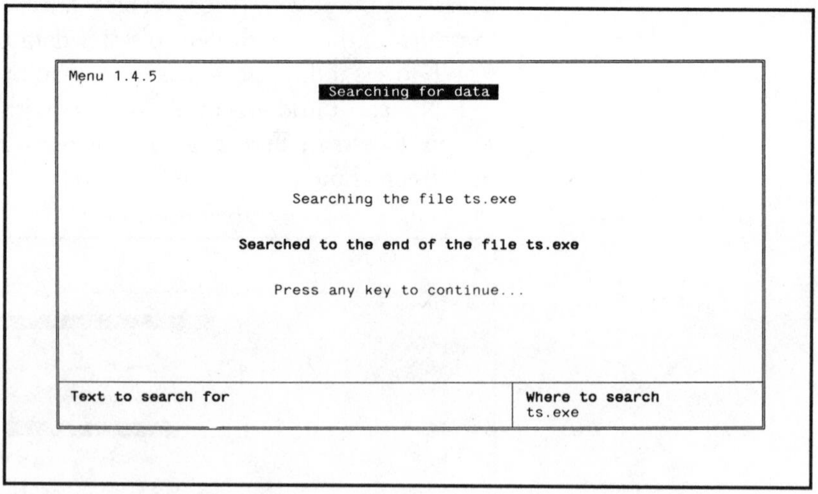

Figure 5.18: NU has not found any more occurrences of the search string.

Press any key to return to the Search item/disk for data menu and select Leave search to exit from this part of the program. This returns you to the Explore Disk menu. (Alternatively, you could have pressed F10 to return to DOS immediately.) If you want to continue working in NU, you can choose another selection from this menu or press Esc to return to NU's Main menu.

PRINTING FROM DOS

DOS provides several basic commands that allow you to print information from the screen or from an ASCII text file. However, these commands have limited usefulness, as they do not produce neatly paged output.

USING PRTSC

PrtSc copies the screen's contents to the printer. The success of this operation depends on the type of printer used and the kind of information displayed on the screen. Some printers cannot reproduce the line-drawing characters used to make boxes on the screen, and most printers cannot recreate screen colors or reverse video successfully.

USING CTRL-P

When you press Ctrl-P, DOS sends a copy of every subsequent keystroke you type to the printer. Pressing Ctrl-P again stops this output. In other words, this key combination is a *toggle*.

REDIRECTING DOS'S OUTPUT TO THE PRINTER

You used DOS's redirection symbol earlier in this chapter when you sent the output from TS to the printer. In fact, you can use the symbol with any command that produces output. For example, to make a printed listing of the directory of the disk in drive A, type

```
DIR A: >PRN
```

DOS then redirects the output from the DIR command to the printer. If the directory contains many entries, the printout will run off the page since DOS redirection commands do not paginate the printout.

USING THE DOS PRINT COMMAND TO PRINT A FILE

The DOS PRINT command sends the contents of an ASCII text file to your printer. For example, to print the Norton Utilities' READ.ME file, make the NORTON directory current and type

PRINT READ.ME

The first time you run this operation after booting the computer, DOS asks for confirmation that you want the output from PRINT sent to the default printing device, PRN, by asking

Name of list device [PRN]:

Press the Enter key to accept PRN. DOS will then reply with

Resident portion of PRINT installed

and begin printing the file. As it prints DOS adds the message

C:\NORTON\READ.ME is currently being printed.

Several files can be queued up at the same time so that they are printed one after the other. Each file is still a large slab of text, without page breaks or line numbers.

USING THE DOS COPY COMMAND TO PRINT A FILE

The DOS COPY command is often used to copy files from one disk or directory to another, or to join (concatenate) several files together. You can also use the COPY command with a device name instead of a target file name; this sends a copy of the file to the device. For example, to print the READ.ME file, type

COPY READ.ME PRN

Notice that you do not have to type the colon character at the end of the device name.

To print a file without frills and quickly resume working, use the DOS PRINT command.

The difference between using PRINT and COPY to print a file will become immediately obvious if you try to print a file using one command and then reprint it using the other command. COPY returns the system prompt after the file has been printed, but PRINT returns it almost immediately, so you can continue working. The COPY command takes the machine's whole attention, while the PRINT command works in a background mode, using only a portion of the computer's resources. This is often called *spooling*.

USING NORTON UTILITIES' LP PROGRAM TO PRINT

The LP (Line Print) utility prints text files, providing several formatting options. LP can also set up the printer for more advanced printing before it prints a file.

USING LP TO FORMAT TEXT

To use LP to print the READ.ME file, type

    LP READ.ME

You can make LP print several files, one after the other, by listing them individually in the command line. You can also use the DOS wildcards to specify files. For example, to print all the .BAK files in the current directory, you would enter

    LP *.BAK

Each file printed in this way starts on a new page and is numbered independently.

If you want to send the output from LP to a file rather than to the printer, you must specify the file name in full—you cannot use the DOS wildcard characters.

PRINTING DIRECTORIES WITH LP   If you want to print a directory that is longer than one page neatly, first use DOS's redirection symbol to capture the directory as a file. For example, entering

    DIR > LIST.DIR

would place the current directory's listing in a file named LIST-.DIR. You could then print the file by entering

LP LIST.DIR

ADDING LINE NUMBERS TO A FILE You may find it useful to have line numbers in a text file. For instance, they are often included in legal documents and early drafts of advertising copy. Suppose you want to print your ASCII text file called DRAFT.TXT and number its lines. You can use LP to do this by typing

LP DRAFT.TXT /N

Each time you reprint the file and want line numbers you need to include the /N switch in the LP command.

CHANGING THE WIDTH OF PRINTED COLUMNS Normally LP produces output that is 80 columns wide. To instruct the printer to use 132 columns (which compresses the type), type

LP MAKE.TXT /N/132

assuming MAKE.TXT is the file you want to print.

Note that LP will not reset the printer back to 80-column mode after the file has been printed. You can reset it yourself by using the /80 switch when you make the next printing.

USING LP WITH PRINT

The problem with using LP to print a number of files consecutively is that you cannot use your computer for other tasks while the files are being printed. The way to get around this problem is to use LP in combination with the DOS PRINT command.

First, use LP to combine the files you want to print into one file. For example, entering

LP *.BAK BIGFILE.TXT

would combine all the files in the current directory with the .BAK extension into one file called BIGFILE.TXT. (The original files would not be altered, of course.) You could then enter

    PRINT BIGFILE.TXT

to start the print run. The DOS prompt will quickly reappear, and you can do other tasks while waiting for the printer to finish.

BIGFILE.TXT will not print out as one continuous file. Each of the original files contained in it will start on a new page, just as if you had entered

    LP *.BAK

LP'S DEFAULT SETTINGS In most cases, if you use the default setting for LP, the formatted output will be as you might expect: 66 lines per page, a 3-line top margin, a 5-line bottom margin, and a 5-space left and right margin. LP also prints the file name, the current DOS time and date, and the page number as a header for each page. You can tell LP to omit the header altogether with the /HEADER0 switch, or expand the header to include the file creation date and time by using the /HEADER2 switch.

Table 5.2 shows the complete set of switches that you can use to format LP's output exactly as you want it. The *n* represents a number; for example, /P2 tells LP to print starting with page 2.

USING LP WITH WORDSTAR

If you want to use LP to print a file that has been saved in a Word-Star format, you must use the /WS switch. For example, to print a WordStar file named WORDSTAR.TXT, enter

    LP WORDSTAR.TXT /WS

USING LP WITH EBCDIC FILES

If you transfer files between your PC and an IBM mainframe, you may find that your files are in EBCDIC rather than ASCII. Most large IBM mainframes have their own EBCDIC-to-ASCII and

Table 5.2: LP's Switches for Formatting

SWITCH	SETS	DEFAULT
/T*n*	number of lines for top margin	3
/B*n*	number of lines for bottom margin	5
/L*n*	number of spaces for left margin	5
/R*n*	number of spaces for right margin	5
/H*n*	number of lines per page	66
/W*n*	page width (in characters)	85
/S*n*	line spacing	1
/P*n*	starting page number	1
/N	line numbering	off
/80	sets 80-column mode	on
/132	sets 132-column mode	off
/HEADER*n*	sets the header type; $n = 0$ is no header; $n = 1$ sets header to page number, file name, current time and date; $n = 2$ sets header to page number, file name, current time and date, and file creation time and date	1
/EBCDIC	file is EBCDIC rather than ASCII format	off
/WS	prints a WordStar or WordStar-compatible format	off

ASCII-to-EBCDIC converter programs. However, if the one you are working with does not, or if you forget to convert the file before downloading it to the PC, LP can do the conversion for you. Use its /EBCDIC switch to make the conversion.

USING LP TO SET UP THE PRINTER

Printers often require that you get them ready before you use them. Your printer's setup procedure could be as simple as checking that it is on-line, or it could be as elaborate as changing its ribbon color or inserting a different cartridge. You can use LP's /SET: switch to give a setup sequence to your printer before you start printing. In some cases, the sequence can carry out your entire setup procedure, while in others, it can only take care of the initial steps and then pauses the printer so you can complete the setup.

The setup sequence must be contained in a file, and the file must be specified as part of the switch. For example, if your setup sequence is in a file called PRINT.SET, you would use the following command to send it to the printer:

LP /SET:PRINT.SET

The sequence itself is similar to the sequences used by other programs, particularly Lotus 1-2-3. The setup file must be an ASCII text file, such as a DOS batch file, with no hidden characters. Use EDLIN or your word processor's nondocument mode to create it.

If you have a laser printer that supports proportional spacing, LP will ignore the proportional spacing; it can only use nonproportional spacing.

After you send the setup sequence to the printer, it stays in effect until you change or reset it. If you need to change the way your printer works for different files, use another setup file with LP's /SET: switch.

Your setup sequences can comprise decimal numbers representing the printer codes to send or alphabetical characters representing control-key combinations. You can also send individual characters to be printed.

Look in your printer's manual to find the codes you should use.

If you use a decimal number, it must have the form *nnn*, where *nnn* is the decimal number to send. All three characters are needed, so you must use leading zeros when necessary. For example, to send the code 15 to the printer, setting it in compressed mode, include the sequence

\\015

in your setup file. Similarly, to send a carriage return/line feed sequence to the printer as decimal numbers, the setup file must contain this sequence:

    \013\010

You can send the same carriage return/line feed sequence as control characters by using

    \M\J

Characters that you want printed are entered in the setup file exactly as you want them, without any coding. For example, if you want to print the message ''Printer is ready,'' followed by a carriage return/line feed, type the following sequence:

    Printer is ready \M\J

USING LP IN A BATCH FILE

If you find yourself using LP with the same set of options every time, for example, if you print a lot of numbered program listings in 132-column mode, set up a batch file to do the work for you. If you invoke the LP program with the appropriate parameters from inside the batch file, using a DOS variable for the file name, you can run the batch file for different files instead of retyping the entire LP command. For your numbered program listings, the command would be

    LP %1 /N/132

After you place it in a batch file called PRT.BAT, you can run it for a particular file by typing PRT and the name of the file you want to print. For example, to print the HELLO.C file, type

    PRT HELLO.C

This runs exactly as if you had typed

    LP HELLO.C /N/132

SUMMARY

In this chapter I discussed finding and printing text with the DOS commands and described how to use the Norton Utilities programs that augment the basic capabilities of the DOS commands. Here is a review of the utilities you worked with in this chapter:

- TS (Text Search) enables you to search for specific occurrences of text in files. TS also has an interactive mode that is easy to use.

- NU (Norton Utility) lets you search for text in files, which is particularly handy when you are using NU's UnErase feature and need to find text that will enable you to identify an erased file.

- LP (Line Print) provides formatting options for printing ASCII text files.

EVALUATING AND IMPROVING
SYSTEM PERFORMANCE

CHAPTER *6*

THERE ARE SEVERAL WAYS THAT YOU CAN EXAMINE
and quantify your computer system's performance. After describing
these, I will teach you the methods you can use to increase that
performance. I will also discuss file fragmentation and a program
that can unfragment your files. Finally, in the last section I explain
what to do when you encounter disk errors and other related hardware failures.

EVALUATING PERFORMANCE WITH SI (SYSTEM INFORMATION)

The SI utility provides a report, including three performance indices, on the computer's hardware configuration. If your job entails
installing, demonstrating, or troubleshooting hardware or software
products on unfamiliar computers, this is the program for you. SI
will save you a great deal of time and frustration. People often do not
know all the details of their computer's hardware, particularly if they
did not install it themselves. Some hardware can be used differently,
which can further confuse the issue. Running SI is a quick, efficient
way to gather this information.

To run SI from the DOS prompt, type

SI

If you want SI to compare your hard disk's operation with that of an
IBM PC/XT, include a drive letter in the command line. For
example, to compare drive C, type

SI C:

A report made by SI for a Compaq Deskpro 386 computer (including its hard disk) is shown in Figure 6.1.

Following is a line-by-line description of the SI report.

Computer Name   SI gets the name of the computer from the system's ROM (read-only memory). Depending on the make, SI may display a copyright notice instead of the computer name.

Operating System   This is the version of DOS being run on the computer.

Built-in BIOS Dated   This is the date that the ROM BIOS (read-only memory basic input/output system) was made. The BIOS is a layer of software that loads from ROM and lies between the computer's hardware and DOS. The BIOS handles the basic input and output functions in the computer.

Main Processor   This is the name of the microprocessor used in your computer. The microprocessor is the computer's engine: it turns information read from the files on the disk into instructions that

```
SI-System Information, Advanced Edition, (C) Copr 1987, 1988, Peter Norton

        Computer Name:  Compaq
      Operating System:  DOS 3.31
    Built-in BIOS dated:  Thursday, January 28, 1988
        Main Processor:  Intel 80386          Serial Ports:  1
          Co-Processor:  Intel 80287        Parallel Ports:  1
 Video Display Adapter:  Video Graphics Array (VGA)
    Current Video Mode:  Text, 80 x 25 Color
  Available Disk Drives:  3, A: - C:

DOS reports 640 K-bytes of memory:
   110 K-bytes used by DOS and resident programs
   530 K-bytes available for application programs
A search for active memory finds:
   640 K-bytes main memory    (at hex 0000-A000)
    32 K-bytes display memory  (at hex B800-C000)
ROM-BIOS Extensions are found at hex paragraphs: C000 E000

  Computing Index (CI), relative to IBM/XT: 12.5
       Disk Index (DI), relative to IBM/XT: 3.7

Performance Index (PI), relative to IBM/XT: 9.5

A:\>
```

Figure 6.1: SI's report on a Compaq Deskpro 386 computer

it can execute, and it executes them quickly. IBM used a micropro- cessor made by Intel when they released the IBM PC in November, 1981. At the time IBM chose to use the 8086/8088 family of micro- processors, so the IBM PC, IBM PC/XT, and their compatibles use the Intel 8086 or 8088 microprocessor. The more recent PC/AT machine and its compatibles use the Intel 80286. As you can see in Figure 6.1, the Compaq Deskpro 386 uses the Intel 80386 chip. Each microprocessor has proved to be several times more powerful than its predecessor. Nonetheless, you can still enhance the performance of a computer with the latest microprocessor by using a faster disk sys- tem, faster memory, and more efficient data buses.

Co-Processor   The Intel microprocessors used in PCs are designed as part of a set so that other chips can be added to them, increasing their power. One such additional chip is a math, or *floating point*, co- processor, and the PC has a socket on the main mother board for it. Each Intel chip has a matched math co-processor. For instance, the 8087 is used with the 8086, the 80287 is used with the 80286, and the 80387 is used with the 80386. These 87s take over some of the num- ber crunching from the main microprocessor, and in doing so they greatly increase the speed and accuracy of the calculations. As well as simple add/subtract/multiply/divide operations, math co-processors can do trigonometric calculations such as sine, cosine, and tangent. CAD applications and scientific or statistical programs usually benefit from the use of a co-processor, whereas word processors gen- erally do not.

The PCjr does *not* have a socket for a math co-processor.

The speed gained when using a math co-processor varies tremen- dously from application to application, but generally a math co- processor is five to fifty times faster than a regular processor. (These co-processors are not the same as the third party add-in accelerator boards that occupy a slot in the chassis and actually take over the original microprocessor's work by replacing it with a faster pro- cessor.)

Serial and Parallel Ports   These entries give the number of installed parallel and serial interface ports. DOS used to support two serial ports, but beginning with DOS 3.3 the number increased to four.

The parallel port is normally used to connect the system printer; the serial ports are used to connect a variety of serial devices, including a modem, a mouse, a serial printer, or a digitizer. As their names imply, the serial port handles data one bit after another in serial form, and the parallel port handles eight data bits at once. The data transfer rate of a parallel port is generally higher than that of a serial port. The serial port, however, is flexible and can be configured to work with a variety of devices.

Video Display Adapter   This is the name of the current video display adapter. As Figure 6.1 shows, the Compaq Deskpro uses the Video Graphics Array (VGA). Including VGA, five types of video adapter boards are available: the monochrome display adapter (MDA), the color graphics adapter (CGA), the Hercules graphics adapter, which is also known as the monochrome graphics display adapter (MGDA), and the enhanced graphics adapter (EGA). The video graphics array (VGA) was introduced with the IBM PS/2 computer in April, 1987. IBM introduced the professional graphics adapter (PGA) at the same time as it introduced the EGA. But the PGA needed a very high resolution monitor, which made it incompatible with existing standards, and it was discontinued.

Current Video Mode   This is the video mode in which your computer is currently operating. CGA video modes include 80-column-by-25-line mode or 40-column-by-25-line mode. The EGA can support up to 43 lines of text. The VGA can support up to 50 lines of text. You will normally be in text mode when running SI from the command prompt.

Available Disk Drives   This displays the number of disk drives that are available on the system. Disk drive may refer either to a real disk drive or to a RAM disk in your computer's memory.

DOS Reports 640 K-bytes of Memory   This is a short description, similar to that used by CHKDSK, of how the main memory in your computer is disbursed. Figure 6.1 shows 640K of available memory, 110K of which is used by DOS and by my TSR (terminate-and-stay-resident) programs. This leaves 530K for my application programs.

If your application memory space gets too small, consider removing some of your TSR programs to recover space.

A Search for Active Memory Finds   This section of the SI report details the amount and the location of the memory that SI found in your computer. SI actually looks for the memory—it does not just take DOS's word for it. On some computers, SI will lock up the machine if it discovers a memory parity error. This doesn't harm the computer; it just means you have to reboot the system. You can run SI without testing the memory by typing

   SI /N

The /N switch instructs SI to skip the memory test.

   SI describes main memory, display memory (used by display adapters), expanded and extended memory, and memory used by ROM BIOS extensions. The computer in Figure 6.1 contains the most conventional memory that DOS can handle—640K. If your system contains extended or expanded memory, they will be indicated on the two lines following ROM BIOS Extensions.

ROM BIOS Extensions   These are used by hardware device drivers such as those for hard-disk drives. In Figure 6.1 they are located at hex paragraphs C000H E000H.

Computing Index   This is a measure of your computer's disk-independent computing power compared to the IBM PC/XT. A basic IBM PC/XT running an 8088 at 4.77 megahertz has a computing index equal to 1. In the case of the Compaq Deskpro shown in Figure 6.1, it is 12.5. In other words, the Compaq Deskpro 386 runs the SI computing index tests 12.5 times faster than a regular IBM PC/XT.

Disk Index   This is another calculated index, intended this time to allow a comparison of the hard disk's performance. The Disk Index is only calculated if you specify a hard-disk drive after you run SI from the command line (as I did in this example).

The Compaq computer shown in Figure 6.1 has a Disk Index of 3.7, which means that the disk system is nearly four times faster than the original 10Mb hard disk on the IBM PC/XT.

If you type the drive letter for a floppy disk, SI does not calculate Disk Index and reminds you that only hard disks can be evaluated in this way.

Performance Index   If both Computing Index and Disk Index have been calculated, SI combines the results into the Performance Index, which integrates the Computing Index and Disk Index into one number. In the case of the Compaq in Figure 6.1, the Performance Index is 9.5 in comparison to the IBM PC/XT. In other words, the Compaq performs the SI tests 9.5 times faster than the IBM PC/XT.

If a hard disk is not present, the Disk Index is not calculated. Without the Disk Index, the Performance Index cannot be calculated.

You can run SI with the /A (for ANSI) switch to skip the BIOS specific features of the tests by typing

    SI /A

You can format SI's output and redirect it to your printer by typing

    SI /LOG > PRN

The SI utility alone justifies purchasing a Norton Utilities package—it saves time and frustration when you are working on an unfamiliar computer.

In the next section of this chapter, I describe how you can control some of the hardware devices installed in your computer without detailed knowledge of complex programming or DOS.

CONTROLLING HARDWARE WITH NCC (NORTON COMMAND CENTER)

NCC brings many of the computer's hardware configuration settings under simple menu control without requiring extensive knowledge of programming or of the DOS MODE command.

To run NCC from the DOS prompt, type

NCC

NCC displays its Norton Command Center startup screen (Figure 6.2). There are eight menu choices in the Select Item list on the left side of Figure 6.2, but all of them may not work on your computer. To use Palette Colors, you need an EGA or VGA display card. To use Keyboard Rate, you need a PC/AT or clone with the 80286 processor, or an 80386-based PC. All other menu choices in the Norton Control Center window will run on most PCs and clones.

To make a choice from the Select Item list, use the cursor-control keys to move the highlighting up or down the list and press Enter. You can also type the first letter of the menu choice. The right side of the screen is the area where you will work with your choice from the Select Item menu.

CURSOR SIZE

The rate of the cursor blink is built into the computer hardware and cannot be changed.

Cursor Size allows you to set the cursor size on your computer. Adjusting cursor size is useful if you have a lap-top computer whose cursor can be difficult to see.

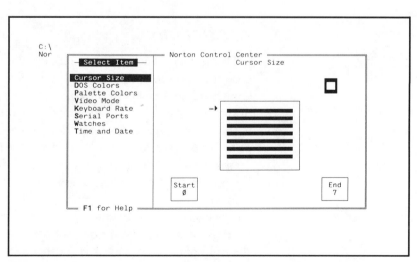

Figure 6.2: The Norton Control Center startup screen

You can configure the cursor several ways depending on your video display adapter:

- A CGA cursor can be configured to seven sizes in a single block
- An EGA cursor can be configured to thirteen sizes in two separate blocks
- A VGA cursor can have up to fourteen sizes

The Start box on the lower-left of the screen shows the starting position of the cursor, and the End box on the lower-right shows the ending position. The center box shows an enlargement of the cursor, and the cursor itself is shown in the box on the upper-right side of the screen. To reconfigure the cursor, use the arrow keys to add or remove lines from the cursor character. The changes you make will register in the box in the center of the screen and in the box in the upper-right. When you have completed your changes, press Enter. This saves your changes and returns you to the main Select Item list. Your cursor is now in effect until you turn your computer off at the end of the session. To return to the Select Item list without making changes to the cursor, press Esc.

DOS COLORS

DOS Colors allows you to change the color of the screen's foreground, background, and border. By foreground color, the Norton Control Center refers to the color used for text characters and boxes drawn on the screen with the line drawing set. The background color is the color behind the text characters—usually the main screen color. The screen border color refers to the color of the border around your screen if there is one. As the EGA video display has no borders, the border color setting has no effect.

In the middle of the Norton DOS Colors screen there are three color charts—one showing the current foreground, one showing the current background, and one showing the current border color. To the right of the color charts is another window, the text box, that lets you see exactly how your color selections will look on your screen. The text in the box is set to the foreground color selection, the background behind these characters is set to the background color selection, and the border of the box is set to the border color selection. Some of the color combinations that are theoretically possible as far as the hardware is concerned are impossible to read or very difficult to work with at best. The display boxes will help you make the most effective color combinations choices for your display. Some monochrome screens can display shades of their one color, which is usually gray, green, or amber, that correspond to color settings.

To move from one color chart to another, use the up and down arrow keys or the Tab key. You'll know you have selected a chart when the chart title is highlighted. Use the right and left arrow keys to change the color selection inside each chart. As you press the arrow keys, the colors in the text box will change to give you an idea of what a particular color combination looks like. Press Enter when your changes are complete, or press Esc to exit without making any changes.

On an EGA video display, you can choose the foreground and background colors from the selections listed in Table 6.1. You wouldn't want to make a selection from the second set of eight colors for the background as they make the text on the screen blink. All sixteen border colors can be used with a VGA video display.

PALETTE COLORS

Palette Colors is only available on computers with EGA (Enhanced Graphics Adapter) or VGA (Video Graphics Array) boards installed. It is not available with monochrome or CGA (Color Graphics Adapter) equipped computers. If you try to run Palette Colors without the proper hardware, nothing bad will happen. You will see a message informing you that this particular option is not available on your hardware.

If you have an EGA or VGA, your computer is capable of displaying 16 colors derived from a total selection (or palette) of 64 colors. Palette Colors lets you choose which 16 colors you want to display on the screen. With 64 colors to choose from, you can set some very exotic color combinations for your daily use.

The names and numbers of the 16 base colors are shown in the working window. Use the Tab key or the up arrow and down arrow keys to move from color to color. Press the plus (+) or minus (−) key

Table 6.1: DOS Color Settings Available for EGA Monitors

FOREGROUND COLORS	BACKGROUND COLORS
Black	Black
Blue	Blue
Green	Green
Cyan	Cyan
Red	Red
Magenta	Magenta
Brown	Brown
Light Gray	Light Gray
Dark Gray	
Light Blue	
Light Green	
Light Cyan	
Light Red	
Light Magenta	
Yellow	
Bright White	

to get a darker or lighter shade of color. Color changes are displayed on the screen as you make them.

Press the right arrow key to open a window that displays a color menu. In this window an arrow points to the current color setting and shows the next four colors on either side of the current color. Press the left or right arrow key to move through the colors and make your selection. Again, as you select different colors, these colors are immediately shown on the screen. Press Enter to accept the changes and return to the Select Item menu. Press Esc to exit without making any changes.

VIDEO MODE

Video Mode allows you to choose the video mode for your computer—the number of characters that fit across the screen and the number of lines that fit down the screen. The work area to the right of the Video Mode screen shows the possible selections for your system, and a checkmark shows the setting that is currently being used. Figure 6.3 shows the settings for a CGA video display.

How many columns and screen lines you can have depends on your video display:

- The CGA can support 80 columns by 25 screen lines.

- The EGA can support 80 by 25, 80 by 35, or 80 columns by 43 lines.

- The VGA can support 80 by 25, 80 by 40, or 80 columns by 50 lines.

Press Enter to accept your new choice or press Esc to return to the Norton Control Center window.

KEYBOARD RATE

Be careful about setting the keyboard rate parameters at too short an interval—it may cause you to make typing errors.

Keyboard Rate only works on computers equipped with 80286 or 80386 microprocessors. This selection specifies in keystrokes per second the rate at which "keystrokes" repeat if you simply hold down one key. At the bottom of the work area is a small window in which to type some text and evaluate your changes. It is surprising what a

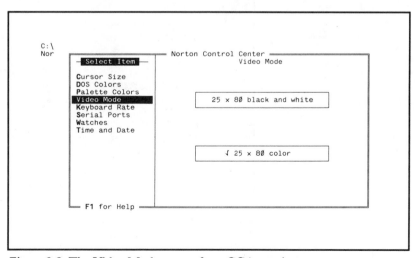

Figure 6.3: The Video Mode screen for a CGA monitor

difference a subtle change in these parameters can make to your typing. If you set these parameters at too short an interval, you will type more characters than you intend to and will see a lot of "Bad command or file name" messages as a result.

The keyboard rate can be set anywhere from 2 characters per second, the slowest rate, to the fastest rate, 30 characters per second. The time it takes for one character to automatically repeat itself can be set at a quarter of a second, a half a second, three quarters of a second, or one second.

SERIAL PORTS

Serial Ports allows you to configure the serial ports attached to your computer. The ports and their current settings are shown in the work area on the right side of the Serial Ports screen (Figure 6.4). A checkmark appears next to the current setting for each of the serial port parameters, and a short summary of these settings is shown at the bottom of the screen.

You can set the baud rate, the parity type, the number of data bits in a data word, and the number of stop bits at the end of the data word for each serial port.

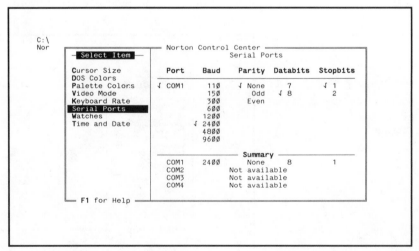

Figure 6.4: The Serial Ports screen

Mismatched baud rates are a common cause of communication errors.

Baud Rate   Baud rate is loosely used to mean the speed, measured in bits per second, at which data bits are transmitted through the serial port to another device. The baud rate can be selected on the computer end of the link or be selected separately on the peripheral device itself, usually by a hardware switch. Both the computer and the peripheral switch settings must be set to the same value for communications to work. For example, if data is sent at 2400 baud, it must also be received at 2400 baud. The most common communications errors are caused by mismatched baud rates.

Baud rates on computer serial boards can be set to 110, 150, 300, 1200, 2400, 4800, 9600, in all versions of DOS, and 19,200 in DOS 3.3 or later. An acoustic coupler might run at 150 or 300 baud; a modern modem at 300, 1200, 2400, or 9600; a printer at 4800 or 9600; and a direct computer-to-computer link at 9600 or 19,200 baud.

Parity   In communications, *parity* can be set to odd or even, meaning that the sum of each group of data bits (defined below) plus one extra bit should always be odd or should always be even. The receiving computer checks to see if the total is correctly odd or even. If the total is not correct, the receiving computer knows that a transmission error has occurred, and it can ask for the affected data to be sent again and alert you that an error has occurred.

The extra bit is called a *parity bit.* If the sum of the data bits is an even number, say, four, and parity has been set to odd, then the parity bit will be set to one so that the total is odd. If parity was set to even in this case, the value of the parity bit would be zero.

If parity is set to none, there is no parity bit and parity checking is not performed.

Data Bits   The actual information that you send through a serial port (for example, the file you are transmitting to another computer) is encoded in seven or eight *data bits* (collectively called a *data word*). A seven-bit data word is sufficient if you are sending nothing but standard ASCII characters. You must use an eight-bit data word if you want to send anything else (for example, a file containing any of the mathematical, Greek, foreign-language, or other special characters in the extended ASCII set).

Stop Bits   Stop bits are used to indicate the end of each group of bits, or *frame.* They follow the parity bit at the end of the dataword, telling the receiving device that there are no more data bits in this frame.

Consult your communications software's documentation for the proper serial port settings to use. If any of the settings is wrong—if you set the wrong baud rate, parity setting, and so on—you will see scrambled communications as the data bits are misinterpreted. Use the left and right arrow keys to move from parameter to parameter, and the up and down arrow keys to change the settings of the parameters. Press Enter to confirm your selections or Esc to exit without saving your changes.

WATCHES

Watches allow you to start, stop, or reset one of four stopwatch timers using full-screen entry techniques. The Watches screen is shown in Figure 6.5.

Press the up or down arrow key to select the timer to use, and the right or left arrow key to select the Start/Pause or Reset Clock function. Press Enter to start the timer, or Esc to return to Select Item.

TIME AND DATE

Time and Date allows you to set or reset the system time and date. The top box in the work area of the screen (Figure 6.6) controls the date, and the bottom box controls the time.

Press the up arrow, down arrow, or Tab key to select the Time box or the Date box. Once you have chosen one function, the title at the top of the appropriate box is highlighted. You can use the left arrow or right arrow key to select hours, minutes, seconds, or meridian in the Time box, and month, day, or year in the Date box. When you're ready, press Enter to confirm your entries or Esc to return to the Norton Control Center window.

On some PC/AT and most PC/XT computers, the DOS TIME and DATE commands do not actually change the setting on the clock connected to the internal battery. You must use a special program to change that clock's setting. This program is usually on the disk that contains the hardware diagnostic programs. NCC will usually change the internal clock, however. If it can't change it, you will have to use the program on the diagnostic program disk.

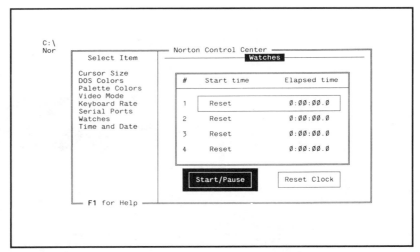

Figure 6.5: The Norton Control Center Watches screen

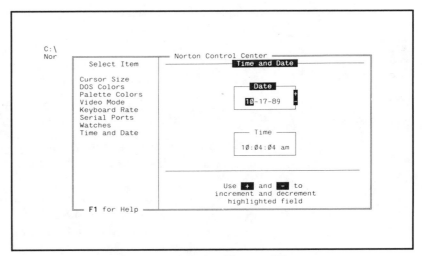

Figure 6.6: The Norton Control Center Time and Date screen

LOADING NCC CHANGES FROM THE COMMAND LINE

To save the settings you have made in NCC, press F2. NCC prompts you for a file name, as Figure 6.7 shows. Enter a file name,

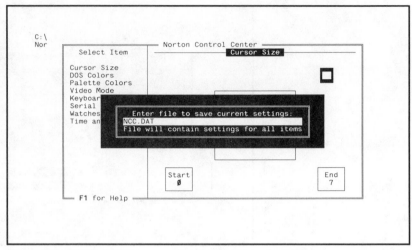

Figure 6.7: NCC allows you to save your settings in a file.

and just before you leave NCC you will be reminded to save the settings in the file.

Once you have saved the NCC settings in a file, you can load one or all of them back into your computer by using NCC from the command prompt. To load all the NCC settings from the NCC.DAT file, type

Stopwatch timer settings can only be set or reset inside NCC by way of the Watches option in the Select Item list.

NCC NCC.DAT /SETALL

To load just one setting from the file, add the appropriate switch to the command-line sequence. File-loading switches are shown in Table 6.2.

To set the Video Mode or Keyboard Rate, you can also use a group of quick switches from the command line. For example, to set the Video Mode to color and 80 columns by 25 lines, enter

NCC /CO80

Table 6.3 summarizes the other NCC quick switches.

The stop-watch timer settings cannot be set or reset except with the Watches option in NCC's Select Items menu list.

The next part of this chapter deals with several kinds of disk problems and gives guidelines on the best ways to fix them—if indeed they

Table 6.2: NCC's File-Loading Switches

SWITCH	DESCRIPTION
/COM*n*	Sets the serial port parameters for port *n*.
/CURSOR	Sets the cursor size.
/DISPLAY	Sets the video mode.
/DOSCOLOR	Sets the DOS foreground, background, and border colors.
/KEYRATE	Sets the keyboard repeat delay and repeat frequency.
/PALETTE	Sets the 16 colors chosen from the palette.
/SETALL	Sets all the options saved in the file.

Table 6.3: NCC's Quick Switches for Setting the Video Mode and Keyboard Rate

SWITCH	DESCRIPTION
/BW80	Sets the display mode to monochrome, 25 lines by 80 columns.
/CO80	Sets the display mode to color, 25 lines by 80 columns.
/25	Sets the display mode to 25 lines (same as /CO80).
/35	Sets the display mode to 35 lines by 80 columns on an EGA only.
/40	Sets the display mode to 40 lines by 80 columns on a VGA only.
/43	Sets the display mode to 43 lines by 80 columns on an EGA only.
/50	Sets the display mode to 50 lines by 80 columns on a VGA only.
/FASTKEY	Sets the keyboard rate to the fastest rate.

can be fixed. SD (Speed Disk), DT (Disk Test), and NDD (Norton Disk Doctor) are the utilities you use to evaluate and correct disk problems.

DIAGNOSING AND ELIMINATING FILE FRAGMENTATION

Files are written to the disk in groups of sectors called clusters. When you write a short file to disk, it occupies the first available cluster. When you write another short file to the same disk, this file occupies the next available cluster. Then, if you modify the first file by increasing its size above that of a cluster and save it under the same file name, DOS will not be able to push the second file up the disk to make room for the larger first file. Instead, DOS *fragments* this file by splitting it in two pieces, one occupying the first and one occupying the third cluster. This is the way DOS was designed to work.

The potential problem with fragmentation is that the disk heads have to move to different locations on the disk to read or write a fragmented file. This takes more time than reading the same file from a series of contiguous clusters. By reducing or eliminating fragmentation, you can increase the performance of your disk.

Another benefit of unfragmenting a disk is that DOS is less likely to fragment files that you subsequently add to the disk. If you should delete and then try to unerase any of these added files, your chances of success would be higher because it is easier to unerase unfragmented files. On the other hand, unfragmenting, or *optimizing,* your disk will probably make it impossible to recover any files that were deleted before the optimization. The reason for this is that SD "moves" data by rewriting it at new locations and will probably write over any erased files in the process.

To remove the effects of file fragmentation, all the files on the disk must be rearranged so that they consist of contiguous clusters. You can do this yourself by copying all the files and directories to backup disks, reformatting the hard disk, and reloading all the files back onto the hard disk, but that would be a tremendous amount of tedious work. It is much easier to use a program designed for dealing with file fragmentation—the Norton SD (Speed Disk) utility.

If there are erased files that you want to recover, do so before you unfragment a disk with SD.

REPORTING FILE
FRAGMENTATION WITH SD (SPEED DISK)

You should have SD prepare a report on the degree to which a file, directory, or disk is fragmented before you decide whether to carry out the file reorganization process. Daily and weekly file fragmentation reports will tell you how fragmentation on your disk is changing over time and how often you should run SD on your individual system. SD can also change the order in which files or directories are recorded on the disk.

To make an SD report on the fragmentation status of an individual file, type

You can enter /R instead of /REPORT.

SD FRECOVER.DAT /REPORT

for a report on FRECOVER.DAT. The result of an SD report is shown in Figure 6.8. Here, the file is 60 percent unfragmented. In other words, 60 percent of the internal cluster boundaries are contiguous. Remember, when you select the /REPORT switch, you get a report only; reorganization is not carried out.

To have SD report on a whole directory, you must specify the directory (including its path), even if you want SD to report on the

```
C:\>SD FRECOVER.DAT /REPORT
SD-Speed Disk, Advanced Edition 4.50, (C) Copr 1987-88, Peter Norton

  Reading disk information...
C:\
frecover.dat  60%

C:\>
```

Figure 6.8: SD's fragmentation report on the FRECOVER.DAT file in the root directory

current directory. SD will operate on the specified directory regardless of what the current directory is.

To get a report on the root directory, enter

SD \ /REPORT

The report for my disk is shown in Figure 6.9. A ''percent unfragmented'' figure is given for each file in the directory. A value of 100 percent means that the file is not fragmented at all and all its clusters are contiguous. A value lower than 100 percent means that there is some degree of fragmentation in the file.

SD's report can be condensed into a short summary if you use the /T switch to generate totals only. To see the fragmentation total for the root directory only, type

SD \ /T/REPORT

The results of a summary report are shown in Figure 6.10.

To make a file fragmentation report for all the files on a hard disk, type

SD \ /REPORT/S

```
C:\>SD \/REPORT
SD-Speed Disk, Advanced Edition 4.50, (C) Copr 1987-88, Peter Norton

   Reading disk information...

C:\
sd.ini       100%   command.com 100%   config.sys   100%   frecover.bak  60%
treeinfo.ncd 100%   frecover.dat 60%   autoexec.bat 100%

Directory Total: 73% unfragmented


C:\>
```

Figure 6.9: SD reports on all the files in the root directory.

```
C:\>SD \/T/REPORT
SD-Speed Disk, Advanced Edition 4.5Ø, (C) Copr 1987-88, Peter Norton

  Reading disk information...

C:\
Directory Total: 73% unfragmented


C:\>
```

Figure 6.10: SD's report for the root directory showing a total fragmentation percent value only

SD starts in the root directory, and the /S switch tells SD to include all files in all subdirectories. The report gives fragmentation values for each file, a total percentage for each directory, and a final total percentage for the whole disk. If you have many files on your hard disk, this report will be a long one, and you can redirect the output to your printer or to a file for later analysis. To redirect output to the printer, type

SD \ /REPORT/S > PRN

To redirect the output to a file called FRAGMENT.LST, type

SD \ /REPORT/S > FRAGMENT.LST

PRECAUTIONS TO TAKE BEFORE RUNNING SD ON YOUR HARD DISK

Be sure to make a complete hard-disk backup before you use SD to reorganize your files.

Before you have SD actually reorganize the files on your disk, you must take a few precautions.

- Make a complete hard-disk backup for use in the event that there is some kind of incompatibility between your system and the SD utility. Problems sometimes occur because of the enormous number of potential combinations of disks and disk controllers.

- Do not turn your computer off while SD is running. The only safe way you can interrupt SD is by pressing Esc. SD will not stop working immediately but will continue to run until it reaches a convenient, safe point in which to do so.

- Make sure that any memory-resident software that might access the disk while SD is running is turned off and disabled. For example, some programs save your work to the hard disk automatically at set time intervals. This software must be turned off.

Do not turn your computer off while SD is running.

If you are using the DOS FASTOPEN utility, or any other disk-buffering program, you will probably have to reboot your computer after running SD. This is because SD changes directory and file locations on the disk when it optimizes the disk, and FASTOPEN may not find the files where it expects to find them. If you see the message "File not found" after running SD, reboot your computer and try again.

DT and NDD are covered later in this chapter.

You should run the DOS CHKDSK command and the DT (Disk Test) utility before running SD to find and perhaps fix any hardware-related problem for your files or disk. If you have the Advanced Edition, you could run NDD (Norton Disk Doctor) to detect and correct disk problems. Either approach will give SD a clean system to work with.

UNFRAGMENTING YOUR HARD DISK WITH SD

Though SD can report on specific files and directories, you cannot unfragment only selected files or directories.

To start SD at the DOS prompt, type

    SD

After selecting the drive to optimize, pressing Shift-F9 will display various technical statistics of relevance to SD.

The program will start with the display shown in Figure 6.11.

Select the drive letter of the disk you want to optimize by using the arrow keys. Press Enter when you have made your selection. After SD reads and analyzes the chosen drive's data, it draws a display of its space usage. A display for the hard disk used in the previous figure is shown in Figure 6.12.

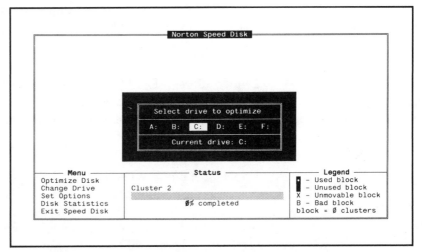

Figure 6.11: SD's startup screen

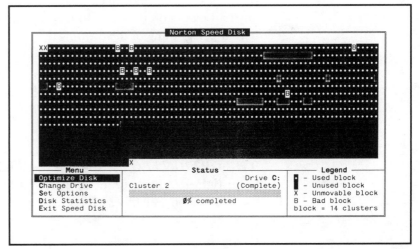

Figure 6.12: An SD disk map for drive C of an 80Mb hard disk

The Legend box, found in the lower right-hand corner of the screen, defines the graphic characters used to make the disk-usage map. Following is a discussion of the characters found in the Legend box.

Used Block   The Used block character designates the area of the disk currently occupied by files. It represents all the directories and files in the data area of the disk.

Unused Block   The Unused block character designates the area of the disk occupied by clusters not allocated to files. SD can recover this space and make it available as part of the unused disk space at the end of the files' area on the disk.

Unmovable Block   The Unmovable block character, an uppercase X, marks the position of any files or directories that SD cannot move. The X characters in the upper left-hand corner of the display represent the DOS hidden system files. To avoid interfering with copy-protection schemes, SD does not move hidden files.

Bad Block   The Bad block character, an uppercase B, represents any bad blocks on the disk. In this case there are several bad blocks near the beginning of the disk.

Clusters   Depending on the size of the disk that you are working with, each Legend character on the screen represents a specific amount of disk space. In Figure 6.12 each character represents 14 clusters.

THE OPTIONS BOX   You use the Options box, located in the lower right-hand side of the screen, to interact with SD. It lists five menu selections, all of which are discussed below.

Don't start optimizing until you're sure that all options are set correctly.

Optimize Disk   Optimize Disk begins the process of unfragmenting the drive. Don't choose it until you're sure that all the other options are set correctly.

Change Drive   Change Drive allows you to change to another drive if you wish. It opens a window very like the drive selection screen shown in Figure 6.11. Use the right and left arrow keys to select the drive letter, or just type the drive letter and press Enter.

Set Options   Set Options allows you to select the file sorting parameters for SD. If you choose this selection, a window opens showing seven more menu selections, as in Figure 6.13. Following is a summary of the SD Sort Options:

- Optimization method

    Complete Optimization: This option initiates the most complete optimization offered by SD. It will give the greatest performance increase, but it is also the slowest of all the sort methods because of the amount of work it does. When you select Complete Optimization, all directories are moved to the front of the disk, all (non-hidden) files are unfragmented, and all unused space is collected into one large block at the end of the files on the disk.

    File Unfragment: This selection unfragments as many files as it can, but leaves some files still fragmented, and may leave the unused space between files untouched.

    Quick Compress: This selection rearranges the files, making sure that all unused space between files on the disk is filled. Unused space is then collected and stored in a large area at the end of the disk.

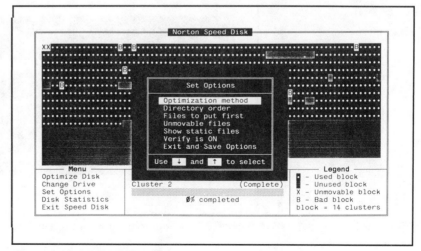

Figure 6.13: SD's Set Options menu

Only Optimize Directories: This selection only moves directories. No files are unfragmented, and unused space remains between files. Due to the relatively small amount of work this option does, it executes very quickly.

- Directory order: This allows you to manipulate the order in which SD arranges the directories. You do this by working with a graphic display of the disk's directory like the one shown in Figure 6.14. Notice the menu line in the lower right-hand corner.

Delete: To delete a directory, highlight its name, select Delete, and press Enter.

Move: To move a directory, highlight the name, and use the up and down arrow keys to place the directory where you want it. Press Enter to confirm the position of the directory.

Finished: When you are satisfied with the placement of directories, select Finished and press Enter to return to the Sort Options menu.

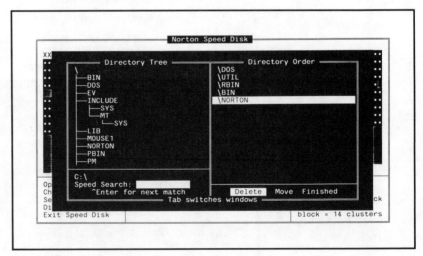

Figure 6.14: SD's graphic directory order screen

Putting program files near the outer edge of the disk will help prevent fragmentation.

- Files to be put first: This allows you to choose which files to put at the "front" (the outer edge) of the disk. Use this option to position your program files, which do not change in size, close to the FAT. Position your data files, which do change size when you modify them, after your program files. This arrangement prevents file fragmentation by preventing space from opening up near the front, or outer edge, of the disk.

  You can use wildcards to help relocate files. For example, to relocate all .EXE files, you would type

  *.EXE

  into the highlighted box.

- Unmovable files: Use this selection to enter the names of files that you do not want to be moved during optimization.

- Show static files: This selection presents a list of special files that will not be moved. (See "SD and Copy-Protection Schemes," later in this chapter.)

- Verify: This selection toggles the Verify setting on or off. If Verify is on, all data being moved during optimization will be read to check that it was written accurately. Choosing Verify makes optimization take longer.

- Exit and Save Options: This selection saves the options you have chosen to a small file (called SD.INI) in the root directory and returns you to the SD startup screen. When you next run SD on your disk, the options are loaded from the SD.INI file and used as the default SD startup settings.

Disk Statistics   Disk Statistics provides information concerning the drive you selected for unfragmentation. Figure 6.15 shows a display for an 80Mb hard disk.

Exit Speed Disk   This selection returns you to DOS.

THE STATUS BOX   The Status box in the center of the screen tells you what percentage of the disk has been unfragmented as

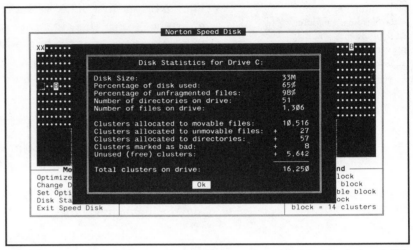

Figure 6.15: SD's display showing the disk statistics for drive C of a hard disk

optimization proceeds. The number of the cluster being operated on is also shown.

RUNNING SD   When you are sure that all the options have been set correctly, choose Optimize Disk to start the process. SD unfragments the selected item or items, collecting all the free space together and placing it at the end of the used blocks. The disk usage map shows you this process as SD works. As data is read from the disk, the *r* character moves across the screen. When the data is rewritten back to the disk, *W* is used to indicate writing. If you turn the Verify option on, *V* indicates the progress of the verification process.

You can press Esc if you want to interrupt SD, but SD will not stop instantly—it will take a few moments to complete the current operation and tidy up before stopping.

SD AND COPY-PROTECTION SCHEMES

Some copy-protection methods that rely on hidden files insist that the hidden files stay in exactly the same place on the disk. If your copy-protection method uses hidden files and you move them to another location on the disk, your application program will often refuse to work—it thinks you are using an illegal copy. SD recognizes

Optimization can take a long time, especially if you are unfragmenting an entire disk. Monitor the Status box to get an idea of how long it will take to complete the job. Press Esc to stop optimization.

To make sure SD doesn't interfere with an application's copy-protection scheme, remove the application before running SD and then reinstall it after running SD.

this problem and it does not move hidden files in case moving them interferes with the copy-protection system. In fact, SD goes further than this: it will not move any .EXE file that does not have a standard file header. All such files are left alone. Also, SD will not move the hidden files—IBMBIO.COM and IBMDOS.COM—that DOS places at the beginning of all bootable disks. Remember, though, that the only way to be absolutely sure that SD will not interfere with a copy-protection scheme is to completely remove the software package before running SD, and then reinstall it after SD is finished.

UNDERSTANDING AND FIXING DISK ERRORS

What if there are files on the disk that you cannot read? You can use several Norton facilities to diagnose and fix unreadable files.

CHECKING YOUR DISKS WITH DT (DISK TEST)

Disk errors can appear in a variety of forms, and you can use DT (Disk Test) to help isolate, and in some cases cure, problems associated with read errors. Because DT actually reads or attempts to read the data from each cluster on the disk, it differs from the DOS CHKDSK command, which tests only for logical errors in the data contained in the FAT and the directories.

When a disk-read error occurs, DOS can respond with a variety of messages. The typical DOS prompt following such a device error is likely to be "Abort, Retry, Ignore, Fail?", although the actual selections in this sequence depend on which version of DOS you are using and the nature of the error. In any case, this prompt is DOS's way of giving you the choice of how to deal with the error. If you choose Abort, DOS stops executing the program that initially performed the read. Retry tells DOS to try the operation once again. Choosing Fail causes DOS to return control to the original application with an error code indicating failure. Choosing Ignore causes DOS to return control to the application without such a code, giving the illusion that the operation has been performed. Sometimes Fail will be disallowed and promoted to Abort, and sometimes Ignore will be disallowed and promoted to Abort or to Fail.

RUNNING THE DISK-READ TEST

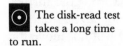 The disk-read test takes a long time to run.

You can use DT to check the entire disk for physical damage by typing

DT /D

The /D switch selects the disk-read test. This test reads every part of the disk, including the system area and the data area. Because it is so thorough and checks the entire disk, the disk-read test can take a long time to run. While the test is being made, the number of the cluster currently being tested is shown on the screen (Figure 6.16). DT first checks the system area of the disk. Any errors encountered are displayed on the screen, but if no errors are found, DT displays the message, "No errors reading system area." In Figure 6.16 DT found two bad clusters, one at number 109 and one at number 110. Because these clusters were already marked as bad by the low-level hard-disk formatting program or by a previous DT run, they do not indicate a deteriorating hard disk. When the DT program is running, press Ctrl-C if you want to interrupt it at anytime.

Many bad-sector errors can be corrected with programs such as SpinRite, from Gibson Research Corp., and Disk Technician, from Prime Solutions, Inc.

If the number of errors that DT uncovers increases, you should replace or repair the hard disk as soon as possible. When DT reports

```
C:\>DT /D
DT-Disk Test, Advanced Edition 4.50, (C) Copr 1987-88, Peter Norton

During the scan of the disk, you may press
BREAK (Control-C) to interrupt Disk Test

Test reading the entire disk C:, system area and data area
   The system area consists of boot, FAT, and directory
      No errors reading system area

   The data area consists of clusters numbered 2 - 2,591
      109th cluster read error: already marked as bad; no danger
      110th cluster read error: already marked as bad; no danger


C:\>
```

Figure 6.16: DT's display when run with the /D disk-read test switch

problems on a floppy disk, try cleaning the disk heads. Then reformat the disk and run DT on it again to see if the errors have been removed.

RUNNING THE FILE-READ TEST

To select the file-read mode of DT, type

DT /F

The file-read test checks all current files and directories for errors. This switch does not check the erased file space, the unused file space, or the system area, which is why it does not usually take as long as the disk-read test. While DT performs the file-read test, the names of each directory and all the files in each directory are displayed as they are checked. The names of any files that contain unreadable clusters are displayed on the screen with an error message. When DT has checked all the files in the directory, that directory name remains on the screen and DT moves on to the next directory on the disk. The DT file-read display is shown in Figure 6.17. Here, all the files in all the directories on the hard disk were checked, and no errors were found.

```
C:\>DT /F
DT-Disk Test, Advanced Edition 4.50, (C) Copr 1987-88, Peter Norton

During the scan of the disk, you may press
BREAK (Control-C) to interrupt Disk Test

Test reading files
   Directory C:\
   Directory C:\BATCH
   Directory C:\DOS
   Directory C:\NORTON
   Directory C:\PCO
   Directory C:\PFS
   Directory C:\PFS\LETTERS
   Directory C:\REFLEX
   Directory C:\WS4
   Directory C:\WS4\BOOK
   Directory C:\WS4\BOOK\TEXT
   Directory C:\WS4\BOOK\FIGURES
   Directory C:\WS4\BOOK\SCREENS
   Directory C:\WS4\PHOTO
   Directory C:\WS4\SJ
      No errors reading files

C:\>
```

Figure 6.17: DT's display when run with the /F file-read test switch

You can make the file-read test examine a specific file if you want to. If you suspect there is a problem in one particular file, include its file name on the command line. DT assumes you want to use the file-read test so you do not have to include the /F switch. To test the file COMMAND.COM, you would type

DT COMMAND.COM

You can also include DOS wildcard characters in a file name. For example, to check all the Lotus 1-2-3 spreadsheet files in the 123 directory, type

DT *.WK1

To check all Reflex database files in all the directories of the hard disk, type

DT *.RXD /S

As with many other utilities, the /S switch includes all subdirectories in the search for the specified file name.

You can invoke both the disk-read and the file-read modes at the same time by typing

DT /B

DT runs the disk-read test first, then the file-read test.

If you run DT and it reports that a file is already using a bad cluster, use DT to move the file to a location of the disk you know to be good. For example, to move a file called WHO.DAT that contains bad clusters, type

DT WHO.DAT /M

The /M switch tells DT two things: to move the bad clusters to a safe location, and to mark the clusters that contain read errors as bad clusters. You can also include the DOS wildcard characters instead of giving a complete file name in the command line.

DT tries to read the file containing the bad cluster and transfer its contents to a new area on the disk. If the transfer is successful, DT displays the message

File WHO.DAT: error reading file. Moved to safe area.

There is no guarantee that DT will be able to read the contents of the cluster giving the read error, but it will do the best it can. Sometimes the copied clusters contain data errors that prevent a program from running. Reading these clusters will not cause the disk controller to generate read errors.

To test all the files on a disk, copy any questionable clusters to a new location, and mark the original clusters as bad, type

DT /F/M

The /F switch selects the file-read test, and the /M switch moves any questionable clusters and marks them as bad.

If you want to see DT's error message output but do not have time to study it, use the /LOG switch. This arranges the output from DT in a format suitable for saving in a file or sending to the printer. To send output to the printer, type

DT /D/LOG > PRN

To send the output to a file called DISKTEST.DOC, type

DT /D/LOG > DISKTEST.DOC

You can print this file later on, whenever it is convenient, by using LP (Line Print). For example, to print the DISKTEST.DOC file, type

LP DISKTEST.DOC

LP uses the default settings for margins and page length if you do not specify new settings when you invoke LP.

Finally, you can use DT in manual mode to mark a particular cluster as bad or good. The /C switch selects manual mode. To mark a cluster as bad, type

DT /Cnnn

where *nnn* is the number of the cluster to mark as bad. To mark a cluster as good, type

DT /Cnnn –

where *nnn* – is the number of the bad cluster.

UNDERSTANDING DT'S ERROR MESSAGES   If DT finds errors, it uses one of three messages to notify you of the error. The message

109th cluster read error: already marked as bad; no danger

means that DT found an error while reading cluster number 109, and that the cluster is already marked as bad. It was probably marked that way by the low-level hard-disk formatting program. Because the cluster is already marked as bad, there is no danger that the cluster will be used by DOS for a file in the future. A cluster already marked as bad is not usually an indication of a deteriorating disk, as almost all hard disks have a small number of clusters containing sectors that are marked as bad by the low-level formatting program.

The message

109th cluster read error: not currently in use—DANGER TO COME

indicates that DT found a read error in cluster 109 that was not marked as bad by the low-level formatting program. This cluster is currently available to DOS for use with a file, although using the cluster would be dangerous. When DT has finished its scan of the disk, you are asked if you want to mark this cluster as a bad cluster. Do so—the bad cluster will be locked out of the list of clusters available to DOS. You can use DT in manual mode to locate and mark bad clusters well before they are ever assigned to a file.

The third message

109th cluster read error: in use by file; DANGER NOW

means that DT found a read error in a cluster currently in use by a file (hence the ''DANGER NOW'' warning), and some or all of the data in this cluster cannot be read successfully. The disk-read option of DT does not tell you the name of the file to which the cluster belongs. To find the file, DT automatically runs the file-read test when the disk-read test is finished.

How dangerous the error is depends where the bad cluster is on your disk. If the error is in the system area of the disk, in the boot record, in the FAT, or in the root directory, you may lose all the data on the disk. In the case of a hard disk, this is a great deal of data. (Here is another reason to make sure your floppy disk or tape backups are always up-to-date.) If the bad cluster contains the boot record, the hard disk may refuse to boot. The remedy to this situation is to make a complete hard-disk backup if you do not already have one, reformat the disk with the DOS FORMAT command or with SF, and reload the contents of the hard disk.

The remedy for fixing a floppy is to back it up and reformat it; if that does not work, throw the disk away. Never use a dubious disk as a backup disk for archive storage. Make your backups onto error-free disks only. This is because, when you need to reload your system from your backup disks, you will not be able to tolerate any errors.

A bad cluster in the data portion of the disk that is not being used by a file is a potential danger. Use DT to mark the cluster as bad. This prevents DOS from using the cluster with a file at some time in the future.

FIXING DISKS IN NDD'S (NORTON DISK DOCTOR'S) FULL-SCREEN MODE

NDD is provided with the Advanced Edition only.

DOS provides the CHKDSK command for finding and fixing FAT errors and the RECOVER command for dealing with files that contain bad sectors. However, DOS does not have programs to find or fix physical errors on a floppy or hard disk. The diagnostics program disk that was probably supplied with your system may be able to locate errors, but it usually can't fix them. Fortunately, NDD (Norton Disk Doctor) finds and fixes any logical or high-level physical errors on your floppy or hard disk. I do not go into great depth on the cause and nature of disk errors in this chapter. Suffice it to say, you should run NDD after DOS reports a disk error.

You can run NDD either from the DOS prompt or in its full-screen mode. To run NDD interactively, type

NDD

with no parameters or switches. The opening NDD screen is shown in Figure 6.18.

There are three menu selections in NDD: Diagnose Disk, Common Solutions, and Exit Disk Doctor.

FINDING DISK PROBLEMS WITH DIAGNOSE DISK

Diagnose Disk is the most important part of the Norton Disk Doctor. After choosing this selection, you are asked to select a disk drive from the list of active drives (Figure 6.19).

Use the arrow keys to make your selection and press the space bar to confirm it. This makes a small checkmark appear opposite the drive letter. Press Enter to make NDD start its analysis. If it finds a problem, NDD describes the problem and asks whether you want to fix it. Next, you are given the option of running a complete sector-by-sector test of the entire disk. This test can take some time to run, so skip it if you wish. If you do run the test, a map of the disk space is

To check only one disk drive in NDD, simply highlight it and press Enter.

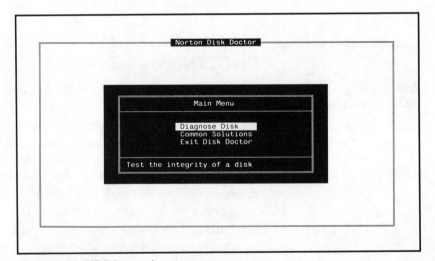

Figure 6.18: NDD's opening screen

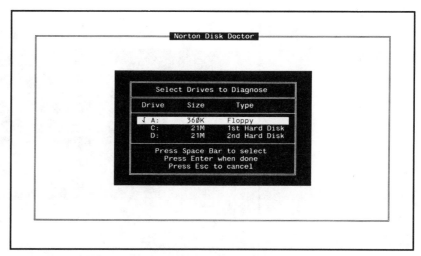

Figure 6.19: NDD's Select Drives to Diagnose screen

shown on the screen to indicate the progress of the test. If a bad data sector not in use by a file is found, it is marked as bad so that it will not be available for use in the future. If a bad data sector being used by a file is found, the file is copied to a safe location on the disk, and the sector is marked bad. NDD displays the names of any files moved. You must check the list afterwards to ensure that all your files are safe.

When the test is done, NDD displays the logical and physical data for the drive tested. It also lists the areas of the disk that were tested. An example of this screen is shown in Figure 6.20. NDD also generates a tabulated report suitable for printing or capturing as a file (see Figure 6.21).

FIXING DISK PROBLEMS WITH COMMON SOLUTIONS

Solutions to three of the most common disk problems are presented under this choice. These solutions, used alone or in combination, should solve most of the problems you are likely to meet in dealing with disks.

The menu selections are shown in Figure 6.22. Use the arrow keys to make your choice and press Enter to start the solution process.

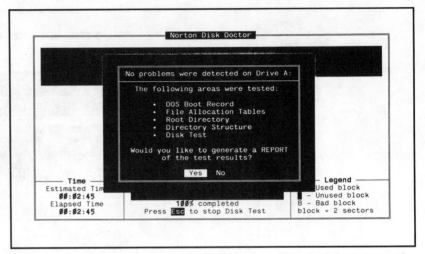

Figure 6.20: The Norton Disk Doctor screen at the end of the test run for drive A

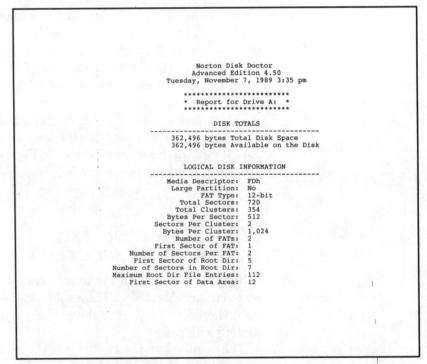

Figure 6.21: NDD's report for a 360K floppy disk

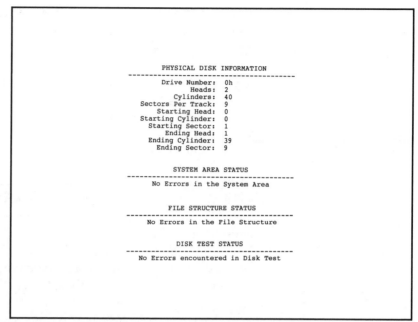

Figure 6.21: NDD's report for a 360K floppy disk (continued)

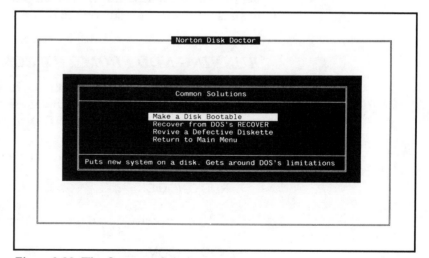

Figure 6.22: The Common Solutions menu screen

MAKING A DISK BOOTABLE   This selection does whatever is needed to make a disk bootable, including modifying the partition table if necessary. Use it with care.

RECOVERING FROM DOS'S RECOVER COMMAND The DOS RECOVER command attempts to recover data in a file after DOS reports a "bad sector" error message—all the data, that is, except the data contained in the bad sectors. You may use RECOVER to recover the data in the files minus the data in the bad sectors. If you use RECOVER on a disk that has bad sectors in the directory, each file recovered has the form

FILE*nnn*.REC

where *nnn* represents the order in which the files were recovered. You will have to rename each generic FILE*nnn*.REC file on the disk by looking at the contents of the file if you can and giving it a more meaningful name. You will also have to recreate the disk's directory structure. RECOVER does not restore deleted files. NDD allows you to restore your disk to the state it was in before you ran RECOVER. You can also use this option in the place of the DOS RECOVER command.

REVIVING A DEFECTIVE DISKETTE This option revives a floppy disk by reformatting it. The original data will not be lost during this reformat—it is still on the disk.

RUNNING NDD FROM THE COMMAND PROMPT

You can also run NDD from the DOS prompt with one of two switches: /COMPLETE tests each data sector on the disk as part of the tests, and /QUICK tells NDD to skip the lengthy, time-consuming test.

To run NDD on drive C without the data sector tests, type

NDD C: /QUICK

To run NDD on drive C with the data sector tests, type

NDD C: /COMPLETE

NDD finds and fixes most of the disk-related problems you are likely to encounter. It fixes bad or corrupted partition tables, bad or missing boot records, and a corrupted BPB (BIOS Parameter Block). In the area of file structure problems, NDD can repair bad or corrupted FATs, reconstruct cross-linked files, and fix physical problems having to do with reading directories or files.

You can use NDD on your hard disk every time you start up your computer if you include the line

    NDD C: /QUICK

in your AUTOEXEC.BAT file. This will do a short analysis of your hard disk every time you start your computer.

SUMMARY

In this chapter I concentrated on evaluating and improving the performance of your computer. Toward this end, I described the effects of fragmented files and how to use the Norton Utilities to remove them. You also examined several logical and physical disk problems, as well as the utilities used to isolate and deal with them.

- SI (System Information) makes a report detailing the hardware installed in your computer. SI also calculates three performance indices.

- NCC (Norton Command Center) allows you to control your computer's hardware functions, including the display mode, display colors, serial port settings, and keyboard rates.

- SD (Speed Disk) reorganizes the files and directories on your disk for optimum performance. SD also prepares a report of the fragmentation percentage of a file, a directory, or a disk.

- DT (Disk Test) checks your disk for bad clusters. It marks questionable clusters as bad and moves data out of these areas into good areas of the disk.

- NDD (Norton Disk Doctor) finds and fixes logical and physical errors on your disks. If DOS reports a disk-related error in booting your computer or in loading a file, run NDD Diagnose Disk to locate the problem. Next, fix the problem by using NDD's Diagnose Disk or Common Solutions.

SAFEGUARDING FILES AND IMPROVING DIRECTORY LISTINGS

THERE ARE MANY REASONS WHY YOU MIGHT WANT to protect a file from being changed or deleted. You might even want to hide a file so other people are not aware that it exists. If you are working with other users on a local area network, you may want to restrict access to files containing sensitive data, such as payroll information or personnel records. You may want to make important program files read-only so that you yourself cannot erase them accidentally.

You can provide some file protection by using DOS's ATTRIB command, but a much more complete and powerful set of capabilities are found in the Norton FA (File Attributes) utility.

Furthermore, as you have seen in earlier chapters, the DOS DEL command is by no means final when it comes to removing files. If you have to be absolutely certain that a file cannot be read after you have erased it, you can use the WIPEFILE utility to remove it. Similarly, you can make it impossible to restore all files on a disk by using the Norton Utilities WIPEDISK program.

This chapter also explains how to use the Norton Utilities to customize your directory listings. You can improve on DOS directories by creating listings that both present more information and convey it more clearly.

WHAT ARE FILE ATTRIBUTES?

File attributes are characteristics that you can establish for your files, as follows:

- A *read-only* file cannot be written to or erased by the normal DOS commands. However, you can use read-only files with other DOS commands. For example, you can print them.

They also appear in listings made by DIR. Very few commercial software packages use the read-only bit.

- *Hidden* files do not appear in listings made by DIR and can't be used with most DOS commands. Nonetheless, you can copy hidden files by using the DISKCOPY command, which makes a sector-by-sector duplicate of the original disk. To erase them from a floppy disk, you must resort to invoking the FORMAT command, which may not always be desirable.

- A *system* file is a hidden, read-only file that DOS uses and cannot be written to or erased. This attribute is often said to be a remnant from the CP/M operating system.

- The *volume label* identifies the disk and is an entry in the root directory.

- A *subdirectory entry* has an attribute that differentiates it from files, indicating that its entry in the directory is for another directory.

- The *archive bit* indicates whether a file has been changed since it was last backed up. If it has been changed or has just been created, the archive bit is set. After the file has been copied by the BACKUP command, its archive bit is turned off. In this way, BACKUP keeps track of the files it has backed up and those it has not.

RESTORE, XCOPY, and some third-party backup programs also use the archive bit.

THE ATTRIBUTE BYTE

A file's attributes are recorded in its *attribute byte*. The attribute byte is part of the file's directory entry, but unlike the other entries, the attribute byte settings are not displayed in the usual DIR listing. Each different attribute has an associated bit. An attribute is turned on, or set, if the value of its bit equals 1. Each bit in the byte may be set or reset individually without affecting the other bits. For example, a read-only file may also be archived.

Bits are like toggles—they are either off (equal to 0) or on (equal to 1). You can also think of them as being *set* (1) or *reset* (0). Another term for reset is *cleared*.

The numbers of the bits for each attribute are shown in Table 7.1. If none of the bits in the attribute byte is set, the file is a normal program or data file that can be read, written to, or erased. Almost all the files you will encounter are of this type.

Table 7.1: The Attribute Bits

ATTRIBUTE	BIT NUMBER
Read-only file	0
Hidden file	1
System file	2
Volume label	3
Subdirectory	4
Archive bit	5
Unused	6
Unused	7

USING THE DOS ATTRIB COMMAND

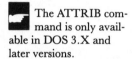 The ATTRIB command is only available in DOS 3.X and later versions.

To look at the status of a file's read-only and archive attributes with the DOS ATTRIB command, enter

ATTRIB MYFILE.TXT

Assuming MYFILE.TXT is a newly created file, DOS will return the current setting

A   C:\MYFILE.TXT

The A shows that the archive bit is set, indicating that the file will be backed up the next time BACKUP runs. The read-only bit is not set, which means the file can be read, updated, or deleted.

You can use the ATTRIB command to set or reset a file's read-only and archive bits. None of the other bits in the attribute byte are accessible from ATTRIB.

To manipulate the attribute bits using ATTRIB, you can specify the following parameters:

- + R makes the file read-only

- – R enables you to read and write to the file

- + A sets the archive bit
- – A resets the bit

For example, if you type

ATTRIB +R – A MYFILE.TXT

this will set the read-only attribute bit (turn it on) and reset the archive bit (turn it off). If you now use ATTRIB to look at the bits' settings by typing

ATTRIB MYFILE.TXT

the command will report

R   C:\MYFILE.TXT

As you can see, the read-only bit is set, but the archive bit is not.

USING FA TO DISPLAY FILE ATTRIBUTES

When you run FA without a file name it is the equivalent of typing FA *.*.

The FA (File Attribute) utility is a program that allows you to work with any of the attribute bits of a file. You can use FA to list all the files in the current directory and report the status of their attribute bytes by entering

FA

Figure 7.1 shows the FA listing for my root directory.

To use FA for the entire hard disk, including all subdirectories, type

FA /S/P

Pressing any key will also pause the display.

The /S switch extends the search to include all the subdirectories, and the /P switch pauses the display when the screen is full. To list only those files that have one or more attribute bits set, use the /U (unusual) switch.

```
C:\>FA
FA-File Attributes, Advanced Edition 4.5Ø, (C) Copr 1987-88, Peter Norton

 C:\
    ibmbio.com      Archive Read-only Hidden System
    ibmdos.com      Archive Read-only Hidden System
    sd.ini          Archive
    frecover.idx    Archive Read-only Hidden System
    command.com     Archive
    config.sys      Archive
    frecover.dat    Archive Read-only
    treeinfo.ncd    Archive
    frecover.bak    Archive Read-only
    autoexec.bat    Archive

    1Ø files shown
     Ø files changed

 C:\>
```

Figure 7.1: Listing the attribute status for the root directory's files

You can focus FA's directory listings further by telling it to list only those files that have specific bits set. For instance, to get a listing of any hidden files in the current directory, enter

FA /HID

In addition to /HID, you can specify

/A	for archive
/R	for read-only
/SYS	for system

These switches can be used together.

FA provides a short summary at the end of each directory, showing the number of files that meet the criteria you specified and the number of files for which the attribute byte has been changed (changing the attribute byte will be explained shortly). In Figure 7.1 ten files have at least one bit set, and no files were changed. If you want FA to display only these summary lines, use the /T (totals) switch.

USING FA TO CHANGE FILE ATTRIBUTES

Always place the attribute switches after the file specification and before other switches.

To change file attributes, you use the switches for the attributes (/A, /HID, /R, and /SYS), appending a plus sign to set the bit or a minus sign to clear or reset the bit. For example, if you want to make all your document files read-only files so that they cannot be deleted accidentally, enter

FA * .DOC /R +

(presuming, of course, that they have the extension .DOC). This sets the read-only bit for all .DOC files in the current directory. It is now impossible for anyone to change these files or to erase them using DOS's DEL or ERASE command.

If you want to reset all the attribute bits for certain files, use the /CLEAR switch.

Table 7.2 lists all the switches that you can use with FA.

Table 7.2: FA's Switches

SWITCH	FUNCTION
/A	Lists, sets, or resets archive attribute
/CLEAR	Removes all file attributes
/HID	Lists, sets, or resets hidden attribute
/P	Pauses the display after each screenful
/R	Lists, sets, or resets read-only attribute
/S	Tells FA to search through all subdirectories for files meeting file specification
/SYS	Lists, sets, or resets system attribute
/T	Shows totals only; doesn't list files individually
/U	Lists only files that have attributes set

SPECIAL CONCERNS WITH READ-ONLY FILES

Beware of making too many files read-only, as many commercial software packages' installation programs configure parts of the software to your system's hardware. These programs write the details of your hardware system back into their own files. If you alter these files to read-only and then reconfigure the program in some way, the program will attempt to update its files with the new information, find that they are now read-only, and report an error. Some programs are smart enough to produce a meaningful error message. For instance, if you try to use EDLIN on a read-only file, you will be told "File is READ-ONLY." dBASE III Plus, on the other hand, may give the more obscure message "File cannot be accessed."

SPECIAL CONCERNS WITH HIDDEN FILES

Some applications programs differ in their response to hidden files: WordStar will load a hidden text file, whereas WordPerfect will not. To edit a hidden file in WordPerfect, you will have to reset the hidden bit first to make the file visible.

Some commercial software packages use the hidden-file attribute as a part of their copy-protection scheme. If you do not remove the software properly, these hidden files may remain on your disk, occupying valuable space.

You should resist the temptation to make files hidden, as the saying "out of sight, out of mind" will become painfully evident. For example, there is no point in hiding batch files or program files since you will soon forget their names; when that happens, you will be unable to use them. If a directory is getting cluttered with files you do not use often, do not hide them by setting their hidden bits; instead, copy the files to another directory and add the directory's name to your PATH statement so that they will be available for the rare occasion that you do want to use them.

USING NU TO CHANGE FILE ATTRIBUTES

You can also edit a file's attribute byte with the NU (Norton Utility) program. To do this, you must use the directory byte editor.

Load the NU program by typing

NU

From the Main menu type E for Explore disk and then type C for Choose item. Next, type D for change Directory to display your directory structure. If the root directory isn't already highlighted, press the Home key to select it and press the Enter key to confirm your selection. Press Esc to return to the Explore menu and type E for Edit/display item. You will now see the directory format display shown in Figure 7.2.

The root directory's entry information is listed in the first six columns. As always, the file name, extension, file size, creation date and time, and starting cluster number are given. The last six columns refer specifically to the settings in the attribute byte. These columns are labeled: Arc, R/O, Sys, Hid, Dir, and Vol, for archive, read only, system, hidden, directory, and volume label. If a file's attribute bit is set, the attribute's label is repeated in the column. As you can see in Figure 7.2, many of the entries are subdirectories and there is only one volume label.

You can use the Tab key to move across the display, the arrow or PgUp and PgDn keys to move up and down in the display, and the Home and End keys to go from one end of the display to the other. If you use the Tab key to highlight one of the attribute settings, pressing the space bar toggles the attributes on and off again.

Any changes you make on this display are not saved to disk until you indicate that they should be. If you have made changes and then

```
┌─ Root dir ─────────────────────────────── Directory format ─┐
│ Sector 17 in root directory                   Offset Ø, hex Ø │
│                                                   Attributes   │
│ Filename Ext    Size    Date     Time   Cluster Arc R/O Sys Hid Dir Vol │
│                                                               │
│ IBMBIO   COM    7836   1-24-86  12:ØØ pm     2  Arc R/O Sys Hid │
│ IBMDOS   COM   27760   1-24-86  12:ØØ pm     3  Arc R/O Sys Hid │
│ BATCH           7-22-89   9:19 am   734               Dir │
│ SD       INI    2494  10-17-89   3:13 pm  1198  Arc          │
│ DOS             7-12-88   3:51 pm    13               Dir │
│ NORTON         11-Ø7-89  11:19 am  1118               Dir │
│ PCO             7-12-88   3:58 pm    79               Dir │
│ PFS             7-12-88   3:58 pm    12               Dir │
│ FRECOVER IDX     29   11-16-89   2:34 pm  2591  Arc R/O Sys Hid │
│ REFLEX          7-12-88   3:57 pm    1Ø               Dir │
│ WS4             7-12-88   3:57 pm    11               Dir │
│ DYSON          1Ø-Ø3-89   1:17 pm                        Vol │
│ COMMAND  COM   23210   1-24-86  12:ØØ pm     7  Arc │
│ CONFIG   SYS    128    9-24-89  10:Ø2 am   127  Arc │
│ FRECOVER DAT  38400   11-16-89   2:34 pm   117  Arc R/O │
│ TREEINFO NCD    267   11-16-89   2:45 pm   424  Arc │
│        Filenames beginning with 'σ' indicate erased entries │
│                 Press Enter to continue                       │
│ 1Help 2Hex 3Text 4Dir 5FAT 6Partn 7    8Choose 9Undo 10QuitNU │
└───────────────────────────────────────────────────────────────┘
```

Figure 7.2: NU's listing of the root directory

press F10, you are asked if you really want to return to DOS immediately. If you have made changes and press Esc, you will see the screen shown in Figure 7.3.

At this screen you can choose to save your changes (Write the changed data), return to the directory format display (Review the changed data), which gives you a second chance to make sure you have got it right, or quit without saving (Discard the changes). Choose the menu selection you want and then return to DOS.

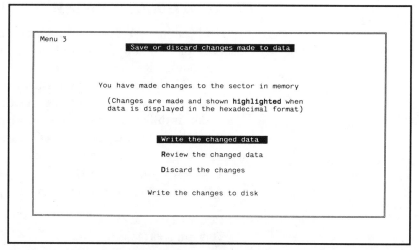

Figure 7.3: NU's Save or discard changes made to data screen

OTHER SECURITY ISSUES

If your job involves demonstrating a software package on a client's computer in her office, you will want to install the package on the hard disk to demonstrate the speed and efficiency of the program. However, suppose when it is time to leave, the client does not want to buy the package. You know that deleting the files using the regular DOS commands will only remove the entries from the FAT. With a good utilities package, your client could probably find and unerase the files quite easily. This is, of course, illegal.

Take another example: Let's say you have just finished working on a confidential project's documentation. You keep backup copies of your files in a safe place, but want to remove any traces of the original files from your hard disk.

In both cases, your solution is the Norton Utilities WIPEFILE program. Using this utility, or the WIPEDISK utility for an entire disk's contents, ensures that the deleted files are removed permanently. Not even the Norton Utilities' UnErase feature can recover files that have been overwritten by these programs.

USING WIPEFILE AND WIPEDISK

WIPEFILE and WIPEDISK are both used to eradicate files from a disk completely, not just erase them. They actually write new data into each of the files' sectors on your disk, overwriting any data that was there. The programs require that you specify their full names; they do not have two-character abbreviations like the other utilities. This makes it difficult to run them accidentally. The programs also have several checks and balances built into their startup dialog, further reducing the risk of accidental use.

To practice using the WIPEDISK program, first make a small test file on a blank floppy disk in drive A by typing

```
COPY CON A:MYFILE.TXT
This is a short test
```

Press F6 to end the file and then press Enter to return to the DOS prompt. This small file now exists on the floppy in drive A. Assuming that the disk is a newly formatted 360K floppy disk, sector 0 is the boot sector, sectors 1 to 4 contain the FAT, sectors 5 to 11 contain the root directory, and MYFILE.TXT should start in sector 12. You can use the NU main program to look at the hex display of the twelfth sector of the floppy disk to verify the file's location. From the Main menu type E for Explore disk and then C for Choose item. Next, type S for Sector and specify a range of sectors that includes sector 12 (you can simply enter 12 as the beginning and ending sector). Press Esc to return to the Explore menu and type E for Edit/display item. You will then see the hex byte-editor display shown in Figure 7.4. You can tell that this is a freshly formatted floppy disk since the remaining locations in the sector after the hex codes for the text, "This is a short test," contain F6 hex characters.

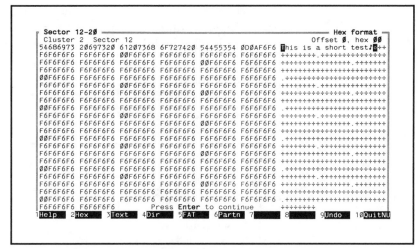

Figure 7.4: Hex display of MYFILE.TXT

Now leave the NU main program by pressing the F10 key and use WIPEDISK to clear the disk's contents. To do this, type

WIPEDISK A: /V69

The /V switch selects the character to be written to the disk; in this case, decimal 69 is an E character. This will write Es to all locations on the disk. If you do not specify a value with /V, WIPEDISK and WIPEFILE will use a value of zero.

As WIPEDISK is a powerful and irreversible process, proceed slowly. The program lists your selections on the screen and then prompts you to confirm that you want to continue. Double-check your selections and type Y for yes (see Figure 7.5).

As the program starts, it displays the message

Wiping the disk

It starts with the least used portion of the disk and works its way toward the most used section. You can interrupt WIPEDISK by pressing Ctrl-Break anytime. If you do interrupt WIPEDISK, some or all of the data may still be accessible on the disk. When WIPEDISK has finished, it displays the word

Done

If you interrupt WIPEDISK, you cannot predict what data has been wiped and what may be still recoverable.

If you now look at the floppy disk's sector 12 with NU, you will see
a completely different display. As you can see in Figure 7.6, the whole
sector is filled with Es. There is no sign of the original text message,
and if you use the DOS DIR command, DOS will tell you that the
disk is empty.

Both WIPEFILE and WIPEDISK meet the latest Department of
Defense 5220.22-M 116b(2) standards for media protection when

```
A:\>WIPEDISK A:/V69
WD-Wipe Disk, Advanced Edition 4.5Ø. (C) Copr 1987-88, Peter Norton

     Action:  Wipe the Entire disk
      Drive:  A:
Wipe count:  1
Wipe value:  69

DANGER! This will wipe-out the entire disk.
Proceed (Y/N) ? [Y]

During this operation, you may press
BREAK (Control-C) to interrupt Wipe Disk

Wiping the disk
Done

A:\>
```

Figure 7.5: WIPEDISK's startup dialog

```
┌─ Sector Ø-5Ø ──────────────────────────────────── Hex format ─┐
│ Cluster 2  Sector 12                              Offset Ø, hex ØØ │
│ 45454545 45454545 45454545 45454545 45454545 45454545 ▉EEEEEEEEEEEEEEEEEEEEEE │
│ 45454545 45454545 45454545 45454545 45454545 45454545 EEEEEEEEEEEEEEEEEEEEEEE │
│ 45454545 45454545 45454545 45454545 45454545 45454545 EEEEEEEEEEEEEEEEEEEEEEE │
│ 45454545 45454545 45454545 45454545 45454545 45454545 EEEEEEEEEEEEEEEEEEEEEEE │
│ 45454545 45454545 45454545 45454545 45454545 45454545 EEEEEEEEEEEEEEEEEEEEEEE │
│ 45454545 45454545 45454545 45454545 45454545 45454545 EEEEEEEEEEEEEEEEEEEEEEE │
│ 45454545 45454545 45454545 45454545 45454545 45454545 EEEEEEEEEEEEEEEEEEEEEEE │
│ 45454545 45454545 45454545 45454545 45454545 45454545 EEEEEEEEEEEEEEEEEEEEEEE │
│ 45454545 45454545 45454545 45454545 45454545 45454545 EEEEEEEEEEEEEEEEEEEEEEE │
│ 45454545 45454545 45454545 45454545 45454545 45454545 EEEEEEEEEEEEEEEEEEEEEEE │
│ 45454545 45454545 45454545 45454545 45454545 45454545 EEEEEEEEEEEEEEEEEEEEEEE │
│ 45454545 45454545 45454545 45454545 45454545 45454545 EEEEEEEEEEEEEEEEEEEEEEE │
│ 45454545 45454545 45454545 45454545 45454545 45454545 EEEEEEEEEEEEEEEEEEEEEEE │
│ 45454545 45454545 45454545 45454545 45454545 45454545 EEEEEEEEEEEEEEEEEEEEEEE │
│ 45454545 45454545 45454545 45454545 45454545 45454545 EEEEEEEEEEEEEEEEEEEEEEE │
│ 45454545 45454545 45454545 45454545 45454545 45454545 EEEEEEEEEEEEEEEEEEEEEEE │
│ 45454545 45454545 45454545 45454545 45454545 45454545 EEEEEEEEEEEEEEEEEEEEEEE │
│ 45454545 45454545 45454545 45454545 45454545 45454545 EEEEEEEEEEEEEEEEEEEEEEE │
│ 45454545 45454545          Press **Enter** to continue    EEEEEEEE │
│ 1Help  2Hex  3Text  4Dir  5FAT  6Partn  7    8    9Undo  1ØQuitNU │
└───────────────────────────────────────────────────────────────┘
```

Figure 7.6: Displaying the wiped sector 12

you include the /G switch. This switch specifies that a 0/1 pattern must be repeated three times, followed by a write of F6, followed by a verification of the last write. If you provide a number with the /G switch, as in /G4, the 0/1 pattern is repeated four times.

You can also run WIPEDISK to wipe only the erased or unused portion of a disk; in fact, this is probably one of its most frequent uses. Including the /E switch tells WIPEDISK to clear all unused clusters. This leaves current data files intact, obliterating everything else.

To delete individual files, however, use WIPEFILE. When you include the /N switch, WIPEFILE deletes the specified files without overwriting them, just like DOS's DEL or ERASE command. The advantage of this utility is that you can also use the /S switch to access all subdirectories—WIPEFILE will remove the specified files from the whole disk, whereas the DOS commands require you to work through each directory individually.

For example, suppose you have .BAK files cluttering up several directories. To delete these files from your disk with WIPEFILE, change to the root directory and type

> WIPEFILE \ *.BAK /S/N

By using WIPEFILE's /N switch, you may still be able to recover one of the deleted .BAK files if necessary. If you are positive you won't need any of the files you want to remove, you can omit the /N switch.

As a final cautionary word on WIPEFILE and WIPEDISK, however, do not forget that WIPEFILE without the /N switch and WIPEDISK actually write over files to destroy the original data. After this treatment, the original files cannot be recovered by utility programs, not even by programs as powerful as the Norton Utilities.

IDENTIFYING FILES BY THEIR TIME AND DATE

It is sometimes useful to reset the creation time and date for a group of files. By doing so, you can give the same date to a set of Lotus 1-2-3 budget proposal spreadsheets so that you can tell all the different revisions apart. Similarly, if you are working in a software development environment, you will be able to identify all the files in a

If you want to wipe all files that you have previously erased (that are still recoverable) without wiping files that have not been erased, use the /E switch.

When you use the creation dates and times to identify a group of files, remember to reset the date and time if you later modify one of them.

particular software release by their date and time. To change the date and time, you can use NU's directory editor.

USING NU TO CHANGE THE FILES' TIME AND DATE

If the root directory is not current when you load NU again, type E for Explore disk, C for Choose item, and D for change Directory. At the graphic display of your directory structure that then appears, press the Home key to select the root directory and press the Enter key to confirm your selection. Next, press Esc to return to the Explore menu and type E for Edit/display item. You will see the directory format display shown in Figure 7.2.

This time, use the Tab key to move to either the Date or Time column. You can now replace the date or time entry. NU provides the separating hyphen and colon characters between the entries. The space bar becomes a toggle key for changing between am and pm for the file's time entry.

After you have changed all the time and date entries you want, press Esc to leave the display. As you leave, you will be reminded to save, review, or abandon your changes before you return to DOS.

Another way of changing files' date and time throughout a directory is by using the FD program.

USING FD TO CHANGE THE FILES' TIME AND DATE

FD allows you to set or clear the date or time for an individual file or a group of files.

To use FD to reset the date for the MYFILE.TXT file, type

FD MYFILE.TXT /D*mm-dd-yy*

Both the date and time formats are determined by the COUNTRY code in your CONFIG.SYS file. The orders I list here are the default formats.

where *mm-dd-yy* represents the date format. If you don't specify a date, the date is set to the current system date. Not specifying a date is a quick way to reset the date. If you do this, make sure you change all the files that should have that system date on the same day.

To use FD to set the time for the previous example's file, type

FD MYFILE.TXT /T*hh:mm*

where *hh:mm* represents the time format. If you don't specify a time in the command line, the time entry for the file is set to the current system time.

You can tell FD to search subdirectories for the file by adding the /S switch, and you can pause the display by using the /P switch. Pressing any key also pauses the display. If you halt the display, press a key again to continue.

To reset the date and time for a whole directory at once with FD, use the DOS wildcard *.* specification in place of a file name. For example,

FD A:*.* D/10-30-69/T00:00

will set the dates and times of all the files in drive A's root directory to October 30, 1969, 00:00 hours.

MAKING MORE INFORMATIVE DIRECTORY LISTINGS

DOS allows eight characters for a file name and three more characters for the extension. This does not leave much room to make each file name both unique and meaningful. Some applications programs even take over the extension, attaching their own extensions for identification purposes. Lotus 1-2-3 and several word processors do this.

The FI (File Info) utility provides a way of attaching a comment to a file name. FI also allows you to view, edit, and delete the comments. Even if you don't use comments, FI provides better directory listings than the DOS DIR command.

COMPARING DOS'S AND FI'S DIRECTORY LISTINGS

Figure 7.7 shows the results from running the DIR command on my hard disk's root directory. File names and directory names are both uppercased, and the remaining space on the disk is given as a large, unpunctuated number.

Compare this to the listing presented in Figure 7.8, which displays the results of entering

FI

while in the same root directory. The file names and extensions are lowercased, while the directory names are uppercased. This makes it

```
C:\>dir

 Volume in drive C has no label
 Directory of  C:\

AUTOEXEC BAT       256     7-19-89   10:44a
NORTON         <DIR>       7-12-88    4:22p
TREEINFO NCD       315     7-19-89   10:58a
REFLEX         <DIR>       7-12-88    3:57p
PCO            <DIR>       7-12-88    3:58p
PFS            <DIR>       7-12-88    3:58p
DOS            <DIR>       7-12-88    3:51p
PROLOG         <DIR>       7-12-88    3:58p
WS4            <DIR>       7-12-88    3:57p
COMMAND  COM     23210     1-24-86   12:00p
C              <DIR>       7-12-88    3:58p
CONFIG   SYS       128     7-12-88    4:09p
BATCH          <DIR>       7-22-89    9:19a
        13 File(s)  14917632 bytes free

C:\>
```

Figure 7.7: A sample DIR listing of the root directory

```
FI-File Info, Advanced Edition 4.50, (C) Copr 1987-88, Peter Norton

 Directory of C:\

ibmbio   com      7,836     1-24-86   12:00p
ibmdos   com     27,760     1-24-86   12:00p
BATCH          <DIR>        7-22-89    9:19a
sd       ini      2,494    10-17-89    3:13p
DOS            <DIR>        7-12-88    3:51p
NORTON         <DIR>       11-07-89   11:19a
PCO            <DIR>        7-12-88    3:58p
PFS            <DIR>        7-12-88    3:58p
frecover idx         29    11-16-89    2:34p
REFLEX         <DIR>        7-12-88    3:57p
WS4            <DIR>        7-12-88    3:57p
command  com     23,210     1-24-86   12:00p
config   sys        128     9-24-89   10:02a
frecover dat     38,400    11-16-89    2:34p
treeinfo ncd        267    11-16-89    2:45p
frecover bak     38,400    11-16-89    2:34p
autoexec bat        256    10-05-89   11:14a

 17 files found   11,968,512 bytes free

C:\>
```

Figure 7.8: A directory listing produced by FI

easy to differentiate the two. FI also displays all hidden files present in a directory. At the end of the listing, the remaining space on the disk is punctuated to give a more readable number. If you want to include subdirectories in the listing, use the /S switch with FI.

Pressing Esc or F10 while FI is scrolling returns you to the DOS prompt.

If you want to pause an FI listing during scrolling, you have several options. You can press Enter once to stop the scrolling and then press it again to scroll the display one line at a time. Pressing any key (other than Enter, Esc, F10, or the space bar) will cause continuous scrolling to resume. If you want the display to pause when it fills the screen, press the space bar. When you press it again, the display will continue to scroll and then pause at the next screenful. Again, pressing any key (other than Enter, Esc, F10, or the space bar) will resume the continuous scrolling.

ADDING COMMENTS TO DIRECTORIES

When you use the interactive editor, each comment is limited to 65 characters (including spaces).

If you invoke FI with a file name and the /E switch, the comment box of the interactive editor will appear (see Figure 7.9). If you have not previously provided a comment for this file, the comment field will be empty. You enter text into the comment field using the WordStar-like key combinations listed in Table 7.3. When you use the interactive editor, each comment is limited to 65 characters (including spaces).

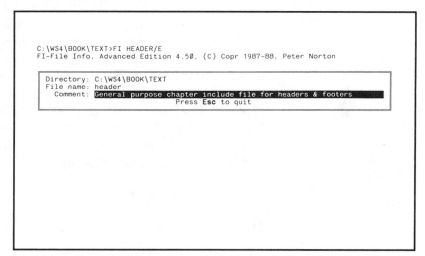

```
C:\WS4\BOOK\TEXT>FI HEADER/E
FI-File Info, Advanced Edition 4.50, (C) Copr 1987-88, Peter Norton

   Directory: C:\WS4\BOOK\TEXT
   File name: header
     Comment: General purpose chapter include file for headers & footers
                         Press Esc to quit
```

Figure 7.9: Comment box invoked by entering FI with the /E switch

Table 7.3: Cursor-Control Keys for FI

KEY	FUNCTION
Esc or F10	Aborts process
Ctrl-D or right arrow	Moves cursor right one character
Ctrl-F or Ctrl-right arrow	Moves cursor right one word
Ctrl-S or left arrow	Moves cursor left one character
Ctrl-A or Ctrl-left arrow	Moves cursor left one word
Home	Moves cursor to start of line
End	Moves cursor to end of line
Del	Deletes character under cursor
Backspace	Delete character to left
Ctrl-T	Deletes word to right
Ctrl-W	Deletes word to left
Ctrl-Y	Deletes complete line
Enter	Attaches comment to file entry

If you enter

FI /E

without typing a file name, FI will enter the interactive editor and display the name of the first file in the current directory and its attached comment if it has one. Press Enter if you don't want to provide or change a message. The name of the next file in the directory will then appear in the file name field, and you can enter a comment for that file. Press the Esc or F10 key to abort the message-entry process.

You can bypass the interactive editor to attach comments to a file or directory by using the following format:

FI *filename comment*

filename stands for any file or directory specification.

This method allows you to specify a comment longer than 65 characters.

⊙ If you enter FI /D
without a file name
you can delete all the
comments in a directory.

To delete a comment from a file or directory, type

FI *filename* **/D**

as shown in Figure 7.10. FI responds with a short progress message to show that the program has done what you asked it to do.

Figure 7.11 shows an FI directory listing I made after adding comments to several files in the PHOTO directory. As you can see, only the first 36 characters of a file's message are displayed. If the comment is longer, the remaining characters are truncated. However, you can display the complete message by entering

FI /L

FI then lists just the file names and comments, which allows more of the comment text to be displayed. An example of this display is shown in Figure 7.12.

On the other hand, if you type

FI /C

FI will list only those files that have messages attached to them (see Figure 7.13). As always, you can also pause the display by including

```
C:\WS4\BOOK\TEXT>FI HEADER /D
FI-File Info, Advanced Edition 4.5Ø, (C) Copr 1987-88, Peter Norton

 Directory of C:\WS4\BOOK\TEXT

header             128   7-19-89   1Ø:21a

1 comment deleted

C:\WS4\BOOK\TEXT>
```

Figure 7.10: Deleting a message attached to a file by invoking FI with the /D switch

```
C:\WS4\PHOTO>FI
FI-File Info, Advanced Edition 4.50, (C) Copr 1987-88, Peter Norton

  Directory of C:\WS4\PHOTO

  .                <DIR>      10-20-89   11:43a
  ..               <DIR>      10-20-89   11:43a
  fileinfo fi         291     11-16-89    5:19p
  miles    bob      5,632     11-13-89    2:30p   Enquiry on status of photographs for
  harrow            1,280     10-20-89    1:26p   Questions to The Harrowsmith Magazin

  5 files found    11,927,552 bytes free

C:\WS4\PHOTO>
```

Figure 7.11: File listing showing output from FI

```
C:\WS4\PHOTO>FI /L
FI-File Info, Advanced Edition 4.50, (C) Copr 1987-88, Peter Norton

  Directory of C:\WS4\PHOTO

  .
  ..
  fileinfo fi
  miles    bob   Enquiry on status of photographs for Raptors of Arizona
  harrow         Questions to The Harrowsmith Magazine

  5 files found    11,919,360 bytes free

C:\WS4\PHOTO>
```

Figure 7.12: Using /L with FI to display all the comment text

the /P switch with the FI command, and you can access the entire disk by using the /S switch.

All the comments you enter through FI for a directory's files are stored in a file called FILEINFO.FI in that directory. If you use FI a great deal, this file will grow and shrink accordingly. Because this leads to the file becoming fragmented, FI's response time will be slightly slower due to the extra searching on the disk required to find

```
C:\WS4\PHOTO>FI /C
FI-File Info, Advanced Edition 4.50, (C) Copr 1987-88, Peter Norton

 Directory of C:\WS4\PHOTO

miles    bob      5,632  11-13-89   2:30p  Enquiry on status of photographs for
harrow            1,280  10-20-89   1:26p  Questions to The Harrowsmith Magazin

2 files found    11,911,168 bytes free

C:\WS4\PHOTO>
```

Figure 7.13: Listing only files that have messages attached to them

all the pieces of the file. However, if you use the /PACK switch, the FILEINFO.FI file will be rewritten to disk as a single file of contiguous sectors. To do this, simply type

FI /PACK

IDENTIFYING YOUR DISKS WITH VOLUME LABELS

Each disk has a special entry in its root directory called the volume label. The DIR command shows the volume label at the start of the file listing, and it is most often used to add a global title to the contents of the whole disk. For example, you might call a disk containing word processing work "Memos," or a disk containing Lotus 1-2-3 worksheets "Budgets."

CREATING AND VIEWING VOLUME NAMES IN DOS

The volume label can have up to 11 characters, which are uppercased in DOS. To create a volume label, use the LABEL command. For example, enter

LABEL A: BUDGETS

to add the volume name BUDGETS to a floppy in drive A. You can also check a volume label by typing

LABEL A:

DOS will then reply

The exact wording of this message depends on the version of DOS that you are using.

Volume in drive A is BUDGETS
Type a volume label of up to 11 characters or
Press Enter for no volume label update:

You can add a volume label to a floppy disk immediately after you finish formatting it if you specify the /V switch with the FORMAT command. For example, type

FORMAT A: /V

and after the formatting process is finished, the following prompt appears:

Format complete
Volume label (11 characters, ENTER for none)?

You can now enter the volume label for the disk.
    You can also use the VOL command in DOS to look at the contents of the volume label. Type

VOL

and DOS will reply with

Volume in drive A has no label

if a volume label has not been specified for this disk, or it will report

Volume in drive A is BUDGETS

if the disk contains a label (BUDGETS, in this case).

CREATING BETTER NAMES WITH VL (VOLUME LABEL)

You can use the Norton Utilities' VL (Volume Label) program to look at or change the volume label. To start VL, type

VL

The interactive dialog that follows is shown in Figure 7.14.

If there is a label on the disk, VL displays it; if not, you are given the option of entering one. The eleven hyphens indicate how long the label can be and are replaced as you type the new label. The last line of the display confirms that VL is recording the new volume label on the disk. In this interactive mode, you can include a space character in the volume label by simply typing it as you enter the new label.

However, if you are using VL from the DOS prompt and want to include a space in your label, you must enclose the whole label in quotation marks. For instance, to set the volume label to be My Disk, enter

VL "My Disk"

Note that you can also use lowercase letters with VL; you are not restricted to uppercase letters as you are with DOS.

```
C:\>VL
VL-Volume Label, Advanced Edition 4.50, (C) Copr 1987-88, Peter Norton

Volume label in drive C: is now "          "

  Press Enter to leave old label unchanged, or
  Press Delete to remove old label, or
  Enter new label: DYSON------

Setting the new volume label to "DYSON          "

C:\>
```

Figure 7.14: VL displays the current volume label and allows you to enter another one.

SUMMARY

In this chapter I described security considerations and methods that make it easier to identify your files. In the process you worked with the following utilities:

- FA (File Attributes) allows you to examine and change the hidden, system, read-only, and archive bits of a file's attribute byte.

- NU (Norton Utility) also allows you to change these attribute bits through its byte editors.

- WIPEFILE eradicates a file from a disk so that it cannot be recovered.

- WIPEDISK eradicates the entire contents of a disk so that it cannot be recovered.

- FD (File Date) lets you change the time or date stamp on a file or a group of files. (You can also use NU's byte editors to do this.)

- FI (File Info) allows you to attach a comment to a file name or a directory. This way, you can make the file's description much more meaningful than the restricted 8-character DOS file name.

- VL (Volume Label) shows you the contents of the volume label and enables you to change it.

PROGRAMMING SIMPLE
BATCH FILES

CHAPTER 8

BATCH-FILES PROGRAMMING CAN AUTOMATE MANY of your daily computer tasks—a powerful tool that you may find indispensable once you know how to use it. *Batch*, a term that originated with mainframe computers, signifies a series of commands contained in a file that are invoked by running the file. In a DOS batch file you can include any of the DOS internal and external commands just as you would if you were using them at the command prompt. Batch files can also accomplish more complex tasks if they include elements of the DOS batch-programming language. This limited language allows for looping, conditional branching, prompting the user for input, and pausing.

The Norton Utilities provide several programs that extend the capabilities of this batch-programming language. These programs are grouped together into the BE (Batch Enhancer) program; they give you control of the screen, allow you to open and close windows, position text anywhere on the screen, and add capabilities to make truly interactive batch files.

All DOS batch files are ASCII text files, with a carriage return and a line feed at the end of every line. You cannot include any word processor formatting commands in them. Every batch file must have a unique name and .BAT as its name extension, so that DOS knows to invoke the batch-file processor. You do not have to type the .BAT extension when you run the file.

Each command in a batch file must be on its own line.

When you run a batch file, the DOS batch-file processor executes each of its commands in order. After DOS has run all of the batch file's commands, you are returned to the DOS prompt. Batch files can automate lengthy processes; for example, a batch file can set up your system automatically when you boot the computer, or it can simplify the procedure for backing up your hard disk.

HOW DO I MAKE A BATCH FILE?

There are several different ways to make a batch file. I do not describe how to make batch files with a particular program; instead I present the general method and explain the underlying principles so that you can then use whichever program you are comfortable with.

You can even use DOS's EDLIN program to make a batch file, or you can use your word processor, provided it has a feature for making straight ASCII text files. If you use a word processor that automatically adds its own extension to files, you will have to change the file's extension to .BAT.

USING COPY CON

I recommend against using COPY CON to make a large batch file; you will not be able to edit the file, which is often necessary after testing it the first time.

You can use the DOS COPY command to create short, simple batch files. Longer, more complex batch files will usually require some degree of editing, which COPY doesn't provide.

When you use the COPY command, you actually copy characters from the console (which is the monitor and keyboard) directly to a file. If the file you are writing to already exists on your disk, it will be overwritten by this process and the original contents will be lost.

To create a batch file with COPY, enter

```
COPY CON MYFILE.BAT
```

The DOS system prompt will disappear, and you can now enter your text directly from the keyboard, pressing Enter at the end of each line. When you have typed in all the text, press F6 and then Enter. MYFILE.BAT is now ready for use as a batch file.

To check the contents of the file, reverse the items in the COPY command by typing

```
COPY MYFILE.BAT CON
```

and pressing the Enter key. The commands contained in MYFILE-.BAT are then displayed on the screen just as you entered them.

STARTING
AND STOPPING A BATCH FILE

To run a batch file, just type the file name at the DOS prompt and press the Enter key. There is no need to specify its .BAT extension. Each command line in the batch file is executed just as if you had typed it at the DOS prompt. At the end of the batch file, execution stops, and the DOS prompt reappears.

To abort or interrupt a batch file while it is running, type Ctrl-C or Ctrl-Break. This sends a break character to DOS and usually results in the message:

Terminate batch job (Y/N)?

Typing Y stops the batch file completely and returns you to the DOS prompt. If you want to stop the current command's execution but continue with the next command in the batch file, type N. Some programs do not recognize the break character, and so will not stop when you press Break. Other programs may not be able to stop immediately.

USING A BATCH FILE TO RUN A PROGRAM

If you work primarily with your word processor, you can place its startup commands at the end of your AUTOEXEC.BAT file so that the program is automatically loaded every time you boot up your computer.

One common use of a batch file is to start a program quickly. For example, if you have the word processor PFS:Write installed on your hard disk in a directory called PFS, you must enter several commands to start the program. You can place these commands in a batch file and give the file a meaningful, easy-to-remember name. Running the batch file will then execute these commands automatically. In this case, suppose you create a batch file called PFSTART-.BAT and include in it the following commands:

```
CD \PFS
WRITE
```

When the batch file is run, the command CD \PFS makes the PFS directory current, and the command WRITE starts up the word processor. You can even name the batch file after yourself, the primary user of the word processor; then all you have to do is type your name after booting the computer.

USING A BATCH FILE
TO AUTOMATE A COMMON PROCESS

Another common use of a batch file is to automate a complex procedure, simplifying it to an easy-to-remember name. For instance, if you have an Epson- or IBM-compatible printer, you can create a batch file to put the printer into 132-column (compressed) mode. Simply include the line

MODE LPT1: 132

in a batch file called COMPRESS.BAT. If you make another batch file called NORMAL.BAT that includes the line

MODE LPT1: 80

you now have an easy way of setting and resetting your printer width. To choose compressed mode, type

COMPRESS

Any output you then send to the printer will be printed in 132 columns across the page. To return the printer to the normal mode, type

NORMAL

The printer will now print in the more usual 80-column width.

THE BATCH-PROGRAMMING
LANGUAGE

Although batch files can only contain commands, you can add a descriptive line to your batch file by prefacing the line with a colon. DOS will then ignore the line, and you will have a reference to check if you forget what the batch file does.

In this section I introduce DOS's batch-programming language, describing briefly the main commands you might require. Keep in mind that these commands can only be used in batch files; they cannot be used from the DOS prompt.

USING ECHO

Normally, DOS displays batch-file commands as the batch file executes them. If you don't want the commands to be displayed, place the line

ECHO OFF

at the beginning of the batch file. To turn the echoing to the screen on again, include the line

ECHO ON

You can also use ECHO to write short text on the screen to help you or other users follow the batch file's processing. To send a message to the screen with ECHO, use the form

ECHO *message*

The message will be displayed on the screen even if you included the ECHO OFF statement at the beginning of the batch file—the displayed message is the result of the command, not the command itself. For example, if you run a batch file that contains the line

ECHO This is a short message.

and ECHO is off, DOS will display

This is a short message.

However, if ECHO is on, the resulting display is

ECHO This is a short message.
This is a short message.

You see both the command and its execution.

Once you understand how ECHO works, it isn't so confusing; just be careful to turn ECHO on and off again in the appropriate places in the batch file.

In DOS 3.3 and later versions, there is another way to stop commands from being displayed. Simply add the @ character to the beginning of the batch-file command that you do not want displayed. Thus the statement

@ECHO OFF

will instruct DOS to execute this command without presenting it on the screen. (ECHO OFF, in turn, tells DOS to do the same for subsequent commands in the batch file.)

Another command that is often used in this way is the CLS (clear screen) command. If you use ECHO OFF followed by CLS, you will not see the ECHO OFF command as the screen will be cleared so quickly by CLS. You can start your batch files with the sequence

ECHO OFF
CLS

so that they start at the top of a clear screen.

INCLUDING REMARKS IN YOUR BATCH FILES

Use REM or a colon to create brief descriptions of the batch file's commands.

You can add comments or remarks to a batch file with the REM command. A REM statement is simply the word REM followed by any text. If ECHO is on, the REM statements are displayed, including the word REM. If you want to add comments to your batch file that are never displayed, regardless of whether ECHO is on or off, add a colon to the beginning of the comment line. Such comments help explain what the batch file is doing. Although this may be obvious to you when you write the batch file, you may forget some or all of the details in a year's time, particularly if the batch file executes complicated procedures.

PAUSING YOUR BATCH FILES

You can use the PAUSE command to halt a batch file's execution and give instructions to the user. For example, you can include the command

PAUSE Position Paper!

in a batch file that sends output to the printer. However, you must also use ECHO ON in the batch file to see the instruction, and this displays the whole command. A cleaner way of doing the same thing is with these lines:

```
@ECHO OFF
ECHO Position Paper!
PAUSE
```

When the batch file pauses, DOS displays the message:

Strike a key when ready...

After following the displayed instruction, press any key to continue executing the batch file.

CREATING BATCH FILES WITHIN BATCH FILES WITH CALL

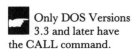 Only DOS Versions 3.3 and later have the CALL command.

By using the CALL command, you can have a batch file execute another batch file as part of its process; the second batch file is treated as a subroutine. After the subroutine has been called up and executed, the original batch file continues executing the rest of its commands. For example, if you want to write your name and your company address at the top of a page, you can call a batch file called ADDRESS.BAT from inside another batch file by including the command line

CALL ADDRESS

in the batch file. When ADDRESS.BAT has written out your name and the company address, control returns to the original batch file, which then executes the command following the CALL command. Having ADDRESS.BAT as a separate file enables you to use it in different batch files, without having to retype it for each file. This way, if you change your address, you only have to modify ADDRESS.BAT, not all the other batch files.

STARTING ONE BATCH FILE FROM ANOTHER BATCH FILE

You can also run a batch file from another batch file by invoking the second file in the last line of the first one.

If you invoke the second file before the last line of the first file, any remaining commands in the first file will not be executed because DOS passes control to the second file and does not return to the first batch file.

TESTING RESULTS WITH ERRORLEVEL

ERRORLEVEL is a variable within DOS that a DOS command, an application program, or a batch file can set. Several DOS commands, including BACKUP, FORMAT, and RESTORE, return an ERRORLEVEL code when they finish running, indicating whether they completed successfully or encountered an error. ERRORLEVEL can contain a number between 0 and 255. When used with IF and GOTO, ERRORLEVEL can help to make complex decisions.

CREATING ALTERNATIVE PROCEDURES WITH IF AND GOTO

IF allows conditional branching in a batch file. A *conditional branch* simply says

if a certain thing is true, do this; otherwise, do that.

With this capability you can create batch files to run increasingly complicated procedures. For example, you can use IF and GOTO with ERRORLEVEL codes to test your program or batch-file commands. When ERRORLEVEL reports no error, the file's execution would continue as intended. However, if there is an error, the GOTO statement would send control to lines that would deal with it in some way. GOTO allows a branch to a label in the batch file and passes control to the point in the program indicated by the label. In effect, it bypasses a section of the batch file. A *label* is just a name, of up to eight characters usually preceded by a colon (although the colon is optional in the GOTO statement), which identifies a section of code. The label indicates where execution should continue; it is not executable code. For example, when DOS encounters

GOTO :END

in a batch file, it jumps to the line

:END

(usually the last line in the file) and returns you to the DOS prompt.

USING REPLACEABLE PARAMETERS IN A BATCH FILE

You can set up placeholding variables in a batch file so that you can specify different parameters when you invoke the file. By doing so, you can run the batch file differently, to use it with different files, for example. There can be up to ten variables in a batch file, each identified by a percent sign followed by a number. Suppose you make a batch file called R.BAT that contains the statement

RENAME %0 %1

to run it, you would type

R FILE1 FILE2

DOS will replace the %0 with the first name, FILE1, and replace the %0 with the second name, FILE2. In other words, DOS's batch-file processor translates the sequence you typed to

RENAME FILE1 FILE2

The SHIFT command moves all the variables down one number; for example, %2 become %1, %3 becomes %2, and so on. The %1 variable is lost each time you use SHIFT. This allows batch files to handle more than ten replaceable parameters at a time.

THE CONFIG.SYS FILE

The CONFIG.SYS file resembles a batch file in that you create it and it can only contain DOS commands. However, CONFIG.SYS is loaded only when you boot the computer, and its commands are restricted to those that set up your system for DOS; other commands cannot be included in the file. If DOS doesn't find this file in the root directory of the disk used to boot the system, it provides default values for the system's setup. The contents of a typical CONFIG.SYS file are shown in Figure 8.1.

The commands in your CONFIG.SYS file configure your computer's hardware, allowing you to set certain internal DOS variables and load special device drivers. These commands each have the general form:

COMMAND = VALUE

Following is a discussion of the commands that you can use in your CONFIG.SYS file.

USING BREAK

Usually DOS operates with BREAK set to OFF, which means DOS will occasionally check for the Break key being pressed during standard input, output, or printing operations. If you include the command

BREAK ON

in your CONFIG.SYS file, DOS will check for the break key more often.

```
FILES = 20
BUFFERS = 20
DEVICE = C:\DOS\ANSI.SYS
DEVICE = C:\DOS\VDISK.SYS 64
```

Figure 8.1: A typical CONFIG.SYS file's contents

CREATING MEMORY BUFFERS

DOS creates several buffers in memory to store data that is read from or written to a disk temporarily. Each buffer uses 528 bytes of memory.

ESTABLISHING THE DATE AND TIME FORMAT

The COUNTRY command selects the format for the date and time commands. You can also use it to select the character sets for various countries. The COUNTRY command codes are based on the international telephone dialing codes. Table 8.1 lists the COUNTRY codes.

Table 8.1: COUNTRY Codes for DOS 3.3 and Later Versions

CODE	COUNTRY
001	United States
031	The Netherlands
032	Belgium
033	France
034	Spain
039	Italy
041	Switzerland
044	Great Britain
045	Denmark
046	Sweden
047	Norway
049	West Germany
061	Australia

ACCESSING MORE FILES WITH THE FCBS COMMAND

Many older applications programs use file control blocks (FCBS) instead of file handles when creating, opening, and closing files. If you use one of these programs on a network, you may have to increase the number of files that can be opened by FCBS from its default setting of 4.

ACCESSING MORE FILES WITH THE FILES COMMAND

The default setting of FILES allows up to 8 files to be open at one time. This number is often too small for modern applications programs. If you see the message

Too many files open

you should increase the FILES specification in CONFIG.SYS.

USING MORE THAN FIVE DRIVES

Because the highest drive letter that DOS can recognize is E, you must add a LASTDRIVE specification to your CONFIG.SYS file if you have more than five drives on your system. The general form is

LASTDRIVE = *n*

where *n* is a letter between A and Z.

LOADING SPECIAL DEVICE DRIVERS

DOS loads standard drivers for all devices, such as monitors, floppies, hard disks, and printers, during the bootup process. If, however, you need to install a nonstandard device driver, for a mouse, for example, you can do so with the DEVICE specification in the CONFIG.SYS file. Usually, the manufacturer of the special hardware supplies the device driver. DOS includes several device drivers; DISPLAY.SYS, PRINTER.SYS, DRIVER.SYS, ANSI-.SYS, and VDISK.SYS. In the next section I discuss ANSI.SYS and VDISK.SYS in more detail.

ANSI.SYS   ANSI.SYS is a device driver that allows you to set screen colors and attributes, as well as special key assignments. ANSI stands for American National Standards Institute. To take advantage of these features, the driver must be installed on your system by the CONFIG.SYS file's DEVICE command. For example, if the ANSI.SYS file is in the DOS directory on drive C, CONFIG.SYS should contain the line:

    DEVICE = C:\DOS\ANSI.SYS

Since several Norton Utilities programs use the facilities extended by the ANSI.SYS driver, make sure you always load ANSI.SYS.

For non-IBM computers the RAM disk device driver is often called RAMDRIVE-.SYS.

VDISK.SYS   DOS also has a device driver that creates a RAM disk. A RAM (random-access memory) disk is memory that is set aside to simulate the operation of a disk drive and, therefore, operates very quickly. Although files placed on this RAM disk are in memory, they can be lost if the computer's power is turned off before they are written to a real disk. To add a 64K RAM disk to your system, include the following line in your CONFIG.SYS file:

    DEVICE = C:\DOS\VDISK.SYS 64

In this example, the VDISK.SYS file is kept in drive C's DOS directory. VDISK.SYS creates and maintains the directory structure, FAT, and program and data files for the RAM disk.

You can create several RAM disks if you have sufficient memory by including a separate statement for each disk in the CONFIG.SYS file, as follows:

    DEVICE = C:\DOS\VDISK.SYS 64
    DEVICE = C:\DOS\VDISK.SYS 128

You can also use the /E switch to place the RAM disk in extended memory—extra memory above the one megabyte limit of conventional memory—if your system has this additional memory. To do this for the two RAM disks in the previous example, simply change the DEVICE specifications to

```
DEVICE = C:\DOS\VDISK.SYS 64 /E
DEVICE = C:\DOS\VDISK.SYS 128 /E
```

These RAM disks will now be loaded in extended memory. If you have a two floppy-disk/one hard-disk system, DOS will name the two new RAM disks D and E, respectively.

If you copy the Norton Utilities programs you use most frequently to your RAM disk, they will be loaded at blistering speed, as DOS will load them from memory rather than from disk. Use a batch file to copy the programs to the RAM disk since they will need to be reloaded each time you reboot your system. Assuming you have created a RAM drive D, the batch file to initialize the RAM disk might contain the statements

```
:batch file to load files to the RAM disk
COPY C:\NORTON\NU.EXE D: > NUL
COPY C:\NORTON\NCD.EXE D: > NUL
COPY C:\NORTON\DS.EXE D: > NUL
```

These lines will copy the Norton Utility, the Norton Change Directories, and the Directory Sort programs to the RAM disk. Remember to alter the PATH command to include this new device, putting drive D's specification before any reference to drive C in the PATH. For example, your PATH statement might include the following:

```
PATH D:\;C:\;C:DOS;C:\NORTON;C:\BATCH
```

This way, DOS will find and load the programs on the RAM disk, rather than the slower-to-load disk-based programs. You can initialize the RAM disk from a regular batch file that you run each time you want to use the RAM disk, or you can include the initializing commands in the AUTOEXEC.BAT file, which will be run automatically every time you start up your system. You can even make the AUTOEXEC.BAT file load the batch file for your RAM disk automatically by invoking it as the last command in AUTOEXEC.BAT.

When you copy program files to a RAM disk, you still keep a copy of them on your hard disk.

If you redirect the output from the COPY command to the device called NUL, you will not see any of COPY's messages written on the screen.

THE AUTOEXEC.BAT FILE

The AUTOEXEC.BAT file is similar in concept to CONFIG.SYS, but there is an important difference between the two files. AUTOEXEC.BAT can contain any DOS command you want to use every time you start up your computer, unlike CONFIG.SYS, which has only configuration commands. For example, it can load terminate-and-stay-resident programs, like SideKick, or start an application program.

Once DOS has booted itself, it looks for AUTOEXEC.BAT in the root directory of the disk it booted from. If the file is present, its contents are executed line by line until they have all been processed, just like any other batch file. Figure 8.2 presents the contents of a typical AUTOEXEC.BAT file.

Let's examine these commands more closely. Remember that you do not necessarily have to include all of them in your AUTOEXEC-.BAT file. On the other hand, your file may contain all these and more, depending on your needs.

SETTING UP THE DATE AND TIME

You can use the DATE and TIME commands to set or look at the date and time. Setting the correct date is important, because many programs use your system's date and time to track activity. To do this, you simply list the commands in your AUTOEXEC.BAT file individually, without any parameters. Once DOS has run AUTOEXEC.BAT, you will be prompted to enter the date and time.

Date is specified as *mm-dd-yy,* where *mm* is the month, numbered 01 to 12, *dd* is the day, numbered 01 to 31, and *yy* is the year, numbered 80 to 99 or 1980 to 1999. You can use periods, dashes, or slashes to

```
ECHO OFF
PROMPT = $e[37;44;1m$p$g
PATH = C:\;C:\DOS;C:\BATCH;C:\NORTON
DATE
TIME
```

Figure 8.2: A typical AUTOEXEC.BAT file

separate the date's entries. The order of the date's entries is set by the COUNTRY command in your CONFIG.SYS file.

Time is specified as *hh:mm:ss.xx*, where *hh* is the current hour in the 24-hour format, *mm* is the number of minutes, *ss* is the number of seconds, and *xx* is the number of hundredths of a second. You must use a colon to separate the TIME command's entries, except for hundredths of a second. You can enter seconds and hundredths of a second or not, as you wish. The order of the time's entries is also determined by the COUNTRY command.

ESTABLISHING A PATH

If you do not set up a PATH statement, DOS can only check the current directory for files when you give a command. The PATH command creates a list of directories for DOS to search through when it tries to locate a file. When you run a program or an external DOS command, DOS searches the PATH for the program file. Figure 8.2's PATH command,

```
PATH = C:\;C:\DOS;C:\NORTON;C:\BATCH
```

makes DOS first search through the entries in the root directory for the file you have requested. If DOS doesn't find the file, it next searches drive C's DOS directory, NORTON directory, and BATCH directory, in that order. (It doesn't matter which directory is current when you request the file.) The directory name's listed in the PATH specification must be separated by semicolons.

By including the names of the directories that contain the files you use most often in the PATH, you can work more efficiently; you won't have to specify long path names with each command, and DOS will find your files quickly.

To see what the PATH is, you can simply type

```
PATH
```

at the DOS prompt.

DOS will provide the current PATH if one has already been set up. If no PATH has been established, DOS will reply with the message

```
No path
```

To discontinue the PATH, type

>   **PATH;**

If you have included the PATH statement in your AUTOEXEC-.BAT file, running the file again will reset the PATH to its original setting.

USING THE PROMPT COMMAND

You can set or change the DOS prompt with this command. The general form is

>   **PROMPT** *string*

where *string* can be a simple or complex expression. It can contain straightforward text or metasymbols. *Metasymbols* are special IBM codes that stand for items to be included in the prompt. For example, if you type

>   **PROMPT $p**

the DOS prompt will list the name of the current directory. On the other hand, if you type

>   **PROMPT pg**

the prompt will be the name of the current directory and the > symbol. Table 8.2 lists all the PROMPT command metasymbols.

You can also add special display characters to the prompt by including a control sequence in the command statement or by using the Alt key with the numeric keypad. You can use this method to display most of the ASCII characters from 000 to 31 and 128 to 255. For example, to make your DOS prompt a happy face using the control sequence, type PROMPT, press Ctrl-A, and then press Enter. You can get the same result by typing PROMPT, pressing Alt-1 (using the numeric keypad), and pressing Enter. The prompt setting will stay in effect until you change it by typing another PROMPT sequence, or until you reboot your system and DOS loads the AUTOEXEC.BAT file, which resets it.

Table 8.2: The PROMPT Command's Metasymbols

SYMBOL	MEANING
$b	Vertical bar character (¦)
$d	Current date
$e	Esc character for an ANSI sequence
$g	> character
$h	Backspace one character
$l	< character
$n	Default drive specifier
$p	Current drive and path name
$q	= character
$s	Space character
$t	Current time
$v	DOS version number
$_	Inserts carriage return/line feed sequence

SETTING THE SCREEN'S COLORS AND ATTRIBUTES WITH PROMPT   If you include the ANSI.SYS driver in your CONFIG.SYS file, you can use the PROMPT command to manipulate the default colors on your color monitor. If you have a monochrome screen that can display different shades of its color, you can still use PROMPT to reset the screen. When you use the PROMPT command to define screen attributes, it takes the general form

    PROMPT $e[*nnnn*m

where *nnnn* defines the screen attributes or colors. The $e is the metasymbol for an Esc character. There is no limit to the number of attributes you can enter between the left bracket, [, and the terminating character, m. Note that the terminating character, m, cannot be uppercase. See Table 8.3 for a list of the colors that you can use and Table 8.4 for a list of the screen attributes you can use.

Table 8.3: Codes for Changing the Screen Colors

COLORS	FOREGROUND	BACKGROUND
Black	30	40
Red	31	41
Green	32	42
Yellow	33	43
Blue	34	44
Magenta	35	45
Cyan	36	46
White	37	47

Table 8.4: Codes for Changing the Screen Attributes

ATTRIBUTE CODES	EFFECTS
0	Turns all attributes off
1	Boldfacing
4	Underlining (on IBM-compatible monochrome monitors)
5	Blinking
7	Reverse video

To change your display to black characters on a white screen (in other words, to reverse video), type

PROMPT $e[7m

To reset the screen again, turning off all special attributes, type

PROMPT $e[0m

You can combine attributes and colors in a command line by separating the settings with semicolons. For instance, to make your screen a blinking, reverse video display, enter

PROMPT $e[7;5m

The reverse attribute is set with code 7, and blinking is set with code 5.

You can also combine screen attributes with metasymbols to produce eye-catching DOS prompts. For example, type

PROMPT $e[5m COMMAND $e[0m$p$g

The $e[5m sequence turns on the blinking screen attribute. COMMAND will be blinking text in the prompt because it is sandwiched between the commands that set and reset the blinking attribute. (The $e[0m sequence resets it.) The metasymbol $p displays the name of the current directory, and the metasymbol $g displays the > symbol.

Research has shown that white text on a blue background is the easiest to read. You can set your screen to this color combination by typing

PROMPT $e[37;44m

You may want to add the metasymbols for the name of the current directory, $p, and the > symbol, $g, to this PROMPT command, which results in the command

PROMPT $e[37;44m$p$g

Including these metasymbols makes it easy to identify the current directory.

Once you have decided which prompt and screen setup you prefer, you should include its PROMPT command in your AUTOEXEC.BAT file.

> You don't have to worry about running out of keys since you can reprogram up to 40 keys by using the function, Shift-function, Ctrl-function, and Alt-function keys.

REDEFINING KEYS WITH PROMPT AND ANSI.SYS

By using ANSI.SYS you can also program virtually any of the keys on the keyboard to type DOS commands. Like setting the screen attributes, assigning new meaning to keys requires the use of an Esc sequence. In this case, the sequence starts with $e[and continues with the ASCII value of the key you wish to use (if the key is a regular letter key), followed by a p character. The p terminates key assignment sequences, just like m terminates screen attributes sequences. If you want to assign a command to one of the function keys or function key combinations, you must use a zero followed by a special code to indicate which key. These special codes are listed in Table 8.5.

Table 8.5: Function Key Redefinition Codes

FUNCTION KEY	REDEFINITION CODE	FUNCTION KEY	REDEFINITION CODE
F1	59	Ctrl-F1	94
F2	60	Ctrl-F2	95
F3	61	Ctrl-F3	96
F4	62	Ctrl-F4	97
F5	63	Ctrl-F5	98
F6	64	Ctrl-F6	99
F7	65	Ctrl-F7	100
F8	66	Ctrl-F8	101
F9	67	Ctrl-F9	102
F10	68	Ctrl-F10	103
Shift-F1	84	Alt-F1	104
Shift-F2	85	Alt-F2	105
Shift-F3	86	Alt-F3	106
Shift-F4	87	Alt-F4	107
Shift-F5	88	Alt-F5	108
Shift-F6	89	Alt-F6	109
Shift-F7	90	Alt-F7	110
Shift-F8	91	Alt-F8	111
Shift-F9	92	Alt-F9	112
Shift-F10	93	Alt-F10	113

Suppose you want to assign the FORMAT command to a function key since you invoke this command frequently. To make the F5 key automatically type the command

FORMAT A:

enter

PROMPT $e[0;63;"FORMAT A:";13p

A semicolon separates each command.

The $e[alerts DOS that an ANSI escape sequence is starting, and the 0 indicates that the key to be redefined is a key on the extended keyboard. Code 63 stands for F5, and "FORMAT A:" is the command to be assigned to the F5 key. Code 13 represents a carriage return character, and p is the terminating character for the whole sequence.

SPECIFYING THE MODE

The MODE command selects the mode of operation for the parallel printers, modems, and display units. It can also redirect output and specify different character sets that you can use with various keyboards and printers.

VERIFYING COMMAND SETTINGS WITH SET

You can use SET to redefine operating parameters in the DOS environment that batch files or applications programs can use.

If you type

SET

at the DOS prompt, DOS will return the name and location of the command processor and the current setting of the PATH and PROMPT commands, as follows:

COMSPEC = C:\COMMAND.COM
PATH = C:\;C:\DOS;C:\NORTON
PROMPT = $e[37;44m$p$g

If a LASTDRIVE specification is in effect, it too will appear in this list of predefined reserved names. DOS's environment space is limited, so it is a good idea to remove any items that you no longer need. You remove these by typing

SET *Name* =

substituting the command name for *Name.*

AUTOMATICALLY LOADING TERMINATE-AND-STAY-RESIDENT PROGRAMS

Your AUTOEXEC.BAT file can load the TSR programs that you use routinely. Once TSR programs are loaded into memory, they stay there, remaining inactive until you use a particular key sequence to activate them. SideKick waits for you to press Ctrl-Alt, and Keyworks presents its menu when you press the large Plus key on the right side of the keyboard. You can call them up from inside other programs, and when you are finished with them, you are returned to your original program.

Memory-resident utilities are extremely fast; however, you pay for their speed dearly—you must devote a section of memory to them. This reduces the amount of memory available for your other applications.

Some TSR programs are extremely sensitive to the order in which they are loaded, and you should consult the documentation accompanying your TSR programs to determine the best sequence. As always, it is good practice to have a recent complete backup of your hard disk, just in case something should go wrong.

USING THE BE UTILITY TO PROGRAM YOUR BATCH FILES

The Norton Utilities BE program includes several older Norton Utilities programs, such as ASK, BEEP, and SA (Screen Attributes), that you can use to extend the scope of your batch programming. The BE (Batch Enhancer) utility provides more control over the screen colors and attributes than DOS's ANSI.SYS driver does. You can use its subprograms' routines to clear the screen, draw a box on the screen, open a window, position the cursor at a particular location on the screen, and write a character on the screen.

BE SA (SCREEN ATTRIBUTES)

BE SA requires that the ANSI.SYS device driver is loaded. Remember, you include the DEVICE command in your CONFIG.SYS file to do this.

BE SA allows you to set the screen colors and attributes either from the DOS prompt or from inside a batch file. You can specify the color names as BE SA's parameters, although when you become more familiar with them, you can abbreviate them to their first three letters. Table 8.6 shows the list of settings you can use with BE SA.

Table 8.6: BE SA's Attributes

SCREEN SETTING	CHOICES
Color (background and foreground)	Black Red Green Yellow Blue Magenta Cyan White
Intensity	Bright (Bold) Blinking
Text on screen	Normal Reverse Underline

Applications programs often set their own colors and attributes when they start running, and some programs are so well-behaved that they reset the screen again when they finish running. As other programs do not do this, however, you can make a batch file called RESET.BAT that contains the following BE SA command:

This command creates my favorite screen setup. You can substitute other parameters if you find another setup that you prefer.

    BE SA BRIGHT WHITE ON BLUE

To reset the screen quickly, all you then have to do is invoke this file.

You can also include BE SA in a batch file to change the screen and draw attention to whatever the batch file next executes. For example, the following BE SA command will get your attention no matter what you are doing:

BE SA REVERSE

BE SA settings will produce different results on different systems. Some monochrome screens can produce gradations of their color to correspond to the colors set by BE SA, while others cannot. You will have to experiment with BE SA to discover which settings you find the most appealing.

BE BOX

BE BOX draws a box on the screen of a specified size at a specified location. The general form for the command is

BE BOX *top left bottom right* [SINGLE or DOUBLE] *color*

The brackets around SINGLE or DOUBLE indicate that these are optional parameters. If you don't enter either one, BE will draw a single outline, which is its default. (Specify SINGLE to reset it after using DOUBLE.)

where *top* and *left* are the pair of screen coordinates defining the row and column position of the top-left corner of the box, while *bottom* and *right* similarly define the position of the bottom-right corner of the box on the screen. SINGLE or DOUBLE makes the box outline either a single line or a double line, and *color* specifies the color of the box's outline. In fact, you can even specify two colors for it. For example, if you enter

BE BOX *top left bottom right* GREEN ON BLUE

your box will have an attractive two-toned frame. See Table 8.6 for the list of colors you can use.

BE BOX draws a box anywhere on the screen. For example,

BE BOX 10 10 20 20 DOUBLE RED

draws a double-lined box from row 10 column 10 to row 20 column 20 using red for the box's outline.

BE CLS

BE CLS clears the screen and positions the cursor at the top-left corner, which is called the *home* position.

Using BE CLS is simple. To include it in a batch file, just add the line:

BE CLS

Place this command in batch files for drawing windows or boxes; preceding the drawing command with BE CLS ensures that you start with a fresh screen.

BE WINDOW

BE WINDOW is similar to BE BOX, except that two more parameters can be defined. SHADOW draws a drop shadow below and to the right of the window, and EXPLODE makes the window zoom to its full size. When you omit SHADOW, the window does not have a drop shadow, and when you omit EXPLODE, the full-sized window appears immediately; you will not see it enlarge on the screen.

In addition, BE WINDOW's *color* parameter, which has the same format as in BE BOX, operates differently. When you specify two colors, the first color becomes the window's outline and the second fills in as the background color.

The general form of BE WINDOW is:

BE WINDOW *top left bottom right color* **SHADOW EXPLODE**

If you give coordinates that position one window on top of another, the second window will overlay the first one, displaying the uncovered portion of the first window.

BE PRINTCHAR

BE PRINTCHAR can display a character a specified number of times at the cursor's current location. The general form of this command is

BE PRINTCHAR *character repetitions color*

where *character* is any character that you type, *repetitions* specifies how many times the character is to be repeated, and *color* gives the character's color.

BE ROWCOL

BE ROWCOL positions the cursor at a particular row and column location on the screen, displaying the specified text in the requested color. It takes the general form

BE ROWCOL *row column "text" color*

If you use ROWCOL with WINDOW, you can place text in windows. For example, the following batch file creates three windows, labeling them WINDOW 1, WINDOW 2, and WINDOW 3:

```
ECHO OFF
BE CLS
BE SA BRIGHT WHITE ON BLUE
BE WINDOW 4 4 14 64 SHADOW
BE ROWCOL 9 25 "WINDOW 1" YELLOW ON BLUE
BE WINDOW 8 8 18 68 SHADOW
BE ROWCOL 13 29 "WINDOW 2" YELLOW ON BLUE
BE WINDOW 12 12 22 72 SHADOW
BE ROWCOL 17 33 "WINDOW 3" YELLOW ON BLUE
```

Each window overlays part of the previous window.

Now that you have set up overlapping windows, you can reverse the order by having window 2 cover part of window 3 and window 1 cover part of window 2. To do this, add the following commands to the end of the batch file:

```
BE WINDOW 8 8 18 68 SHADOW
BE ROWCOL 13 29 "WINDOW 2" YELLOW ON BLUE
BE WINDOW 4 4 14 64 SHADOW
BE ROWCOL 9 25 "WINDOW 1" YELLOW ON BLUE
BE ROWCOL 24 0
:EXIT
```

The second and first windows are then redrawn, in that order. The last ROWCOL command sends the cursor to the last position on the screen and returns you to DOS.

By using this batch-file example as your guide, you construct a windowed menu system for loading applications programs or other batch files.

BE ASK

BE ASK provides an easy way to add conditional branching to a DOS batch file. It will stop the batch file during its execution and prompt you to choose the branch the batch file should then take. When you include a BE ASK command in a batch file, you need to specify which keystrokes are associated with the possible branches. You can also instruct BE ASK how long it should await a keystroke before returning a default value. You can specify what this default value will be.

After you have typed a key, BE ASK transfers control back to the batch file, passing along the ERRORLEVEL value that corresponds to the key you pressed. This is simply ASK's method of setting the value for the keystroke. For example, if you type the first key in the list, ASK generates an ERRORLEVEL value of 1. The IF statement then evaluates the value returned in ERRORLEVEL, and the GOTO command passes control to the branch of the batch file that is indicated by that value.

Let's take a branching batch file that contains two IF statements as an example. This file could be used to make a simple yes/no decision since it offers two branching choices. So that the batch file can evaluate these correctly, you need to list them in reverse order in the file; that is, the IF ERRORLEVEL 2 statement must precede the IF ERRORLEVEL 1 statement. The entire batch file might resemble this sequence:

```
ECHO OFF
BE CLS
BE ASK "Yes or No ? ( Press Y or N ) ", YN TIMEOUT = 30 DEFAULT = 2
        IF ERRORLEVEL 2 GOTO NO
        IF ERRORLEVEL 1 GOTO YES

    :YES
    GOTO END
```

```
:NO
GOTO END

:END
```

When you run this batch file, it turns ECHO off, clears the screen, and prompts:

Yes or No ? (Press Y or N)

BE ASK is not case sensitive; it treats the Y character and the y character the same.

If you answer Y for yes, BE ASK sets ERRORLEVEL to 1, which is then tested by the IF statement. Control passes to the subroutine labeled :YES, which in this simple example just ends the batch file.

If you answer N for no, BE ASK sets ERRORLEVEL to 2, which is then tested by the IF statement. Control passes to the subroutine called :NO, which also exits the file.

Set DEFAULT to the value for no, as it is usually the safest response to any yes or no prompt.

If you do not press any key before 30 seconds elapses, BE ASK returns the default ERRORLEVEL value, which is 2 in this example. (TIMEOUT and DEFAULT are the parameters that determine these settings.)

BE BEEP

You can use BE BEEP to play a single note from the DOS prompt or play a series of notes loaded in from an ASCII text file. You can specify the frequency and the duration of a note, the number of times a note is repeated, and the length of the wait period between notes.

BEEP relies on your system clock's ticks for a timer. Because the system clock ticks about 18.2 times a second, BEEP uses $1/18$ths of a second for notes' duration and wait periods. To specify the duration and wait periods, you can include the following switches in your BEEP command:

- /Dn gives the duration of the note in $1/18$ths of a second

- /Fn gives the frequency of the note in Hertz, or cycles per second

- /Rn tells BEEP how many times a note is to be repeated

- /W*n* establishes the length of the wait period between notes in $\frac{1}{18}$ths of a second

Remember that you replace *n* with the number you want.

To practice working with BEEP, enter

BE BEEP

at the DOS prompt. This should produce a single short tone. Entering

BE BEEP /F50/D18/R5/W18

plays five low notes a second apart. Each note is one second long.

BE BEEP /F3000/D1/R5/W9

plays five short duration high notes at half-second intervals.

When you specify a file name as input for BE BEEP, you can specify its path; however, you cannot use wildcards in the file name.

Say you want to create a file for BEEP, calling it BEEPTEST. Remember to include a comment line prefaced with a colon to describe what the file does. For example, BEEPTEST might contain the following:

```
:This creates three low, medium, and high notes
/F100/D9/R3/W18
/F500/D18/R3/W18
/F1000/D36/R3/W18
```

This file plays three low notes that are each half a second long, three middle notes that are one second long, and three high notes that are two seconds long. To invoke this file from the DOS prompt, type

BE BEEP BEEPTEST

By providing a file as input, you enabled BE BEEP to play a simple tune. Several files are included in the Norton Utilities package that will play tunes. For example, try entering the following at the DOS prompt with the appropriate disk in drive A:

BE BEEP A:MARY

This will play the children's nursery rhyme "Mary Had a Little Lamb."

Although you can use BE BEEP in a variety of ways, it is most convenient for signaling a batch file's completion of a process.

BE DELAY

BE DELAY allows you to specify a delay period in a batch file that must elapse before the batch file can continue executing.

To include BE DELAY in your batch file, add the line

BE DELAY *time*

in which *time* is specified in $\frac{1}{18}$ths of a second, as in BE BEEP. When the batch-file processor encounters a delay of $\frac{9}{18}$ths of a second, which is the command

BE DELAY 9

it waits a $\frac{1}{2}$-second before continuing with the next command in the file.

COMBINING NORTON AND DOS COMMANDS IN A MENU BATCH FILE

Now that you know what BE's subprograms can do, you can use them to make more complex batch files. For instance, you could make one that produces a menu system, calling it MENU.BAT. This file could put a menu on the screen and allow you to choose an application program to load from the selections presented in the menu. The batch file would then run the program of your choice, and when your selection stopped running, it would return you to the menu to await your next selection. The batch file you'll create here loads a word processor, a spreadsheet, or a database program. Once you understand how this batch file works, you can extrapolate the rules of selection and branching to create more elaborate menus.

To do all this, the batch file will use the BE CLS, WINDOW, ROWCOL, ASK, SA, and PRINTCHAR commands from the

Norton Utilities, along with the IF, GOTO, ECHO OFF, and ERRORLEVEL commands from DOS. Comments are included in the batch file to make things clearer; remember that a comment line must always begin with a colon character.

The first few commands in the file set up the screen:

```
:BE startup menu file

ECHO OFF
BE CLS

:set the screen colors

BE SA BRIGHT WHITE ON BLUE
```

ECHO OFF instructs DOS not to display the batch file's commands as they are executed; BE CLS clears the screen, and BE SA BRIGHT WHITE ON BLUE sets the screen colors and attributes to bold white text on a blue background.

To draw the menu window, enter the following lines to the MENU.BAT file:

```
:draw the menu window

BE WINDOW 05 10 17 30 BRIGHT WHITE ON BLUE SHADOW EXPLODE
     BE ROWCOL 07 12 "  --- MENU ---"


     BE ROWCOL 09 12 "1:" BRIGHT WHITE ON MAGENTA
     BE ROWCOL 09 14 "   Lotus 1-2-3" BRIGHT WHITE ON BLUE
```

The BE WINDOW command opens a window on the left side of the screen (row 5 column 10 to row 17 column 30). Its outline is bright white, with a black shadow, and it is filled in blue. The first BE ROWCOL command writes the text " --- Menu ---" at the top of the window using the default colors, bright white on blue. The next BE ROWCOL command moves the cursor two rows down and writes the bright white text "1:" into the window using a magenta background. This highlights the number in a different color, so that it will later be obvious that this number is what you enter to choose the

When using batch files to create screen displays, be careful to use spaces to position text properly.

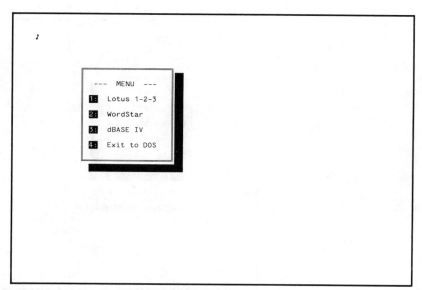

Of course, you can substitute other program names for the menu entries if you want to use this batch file on your system.

menu selection. The last BE ROWCOL command moves the cursor two columns over on the same row and adds the bright white text " Lotus 1-2-3" on a blue background. This sequence creates the first menu item.

Now repeat the last two BE ROWCOl commands for three more menu choices: WordStar, dBASE IV, and Exit to DOS. Space them two rows apart by changing the first parameter, 09, to 11, 13, and 15, respectively. Figure 8.3 shows what the MENU.BAT screen should look like so far.

Run your MENU.BAT file and compare the results with Figure 8.3. Once you have checked that your file is working correctly, add the following lines to it:

```
:draw the dialog box

BE WINDOW 19 10 21 30 BRIGHT WHITE ON BLUE SHADOW
BE ROWCOL 20 12 "Enter a Number     "
BE ROWCOL 20 28
BE PRINTCHAR " " 1 ON BLACK
BE ROWCOL 20 28
```

Figure 8.3: MENU.BAT's startup window

This creates a dialog box that prompts you to choose a menu item. The window opens below the menu and is also blue with a bright white outline. It contains the text "Enter a Number   ". The BE ROWCOL 20 28 command backspaces the cursor one space, and the BE PRINTCHAR " " 1 ON BLACK line prints a space character there. By printing a space with a black background, the batch file creates a box to display the character that you type to choose a menu item. Figure 8.4 shows what running the MENU.BAT file should produce now.

So that the batch file can evaluate what you type, include the following BE ASK sequence in it:

```
:evaluates menu selection
:if no key pressed in 30 secs, exit to DOS

BE ASK "", 1234 TIMEOUT = 30 DEFAULT = 4
    IF ERRORLEVEL 4 GOTO FOUR
    IF ERRORLEVEL 3 GOTO THREE
    IF ERRORLEVEL 2 GOTO TWO
    IF ERRORLEVEL 1 GOTO ONE
```

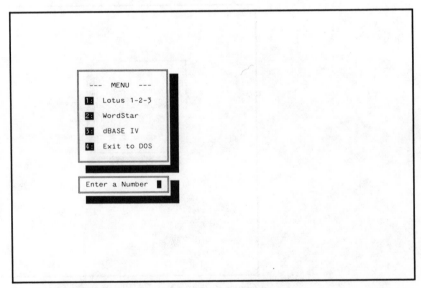

Figure 8.4: MENU.BAT now displays two windows.

Because the prompt is already displayed in the dialog box, the BE ASK command has no prompt string. The legal entries for BE ASK are 1, 2, 3, and 4. The TIMEOUT is set to 30 seconds; if this time elapses before a key is pressed, the DEFAULT parameter instructs the batch file to choose 4, the Exit to DOS menu item. If a key is pressed, one of the four IF statements pass control to one of four branches, depending on which key you press when the batch file prompts you.

At the moment, however, there aren't any branching sequences to go to; you need to add them. Each sequence must start with the labeled line its GOTO command indicated. For example, the Exit to DOS menu option's branch begins with

```
:FOUR
```

Since you need to list the IF statements in reverse order, order the branches the same way. Thus, to continue with the fourth menu item's branch, enter

```
BE ROWCOL 20 28 "4" BRIGHT WHITE ON MAGENTA
GOTO EXIT
```

The BE ROWCOL statement displays the key pressed in response to the prompt in the black space, turning it into a bright white on magenta character to indicate that the batch file has accepted the key you entered. The GOTO statement sends the batch-file processor to the end of the file and exits to DOS.

The remaining three branches share essentially the same sequence. Let's use the WordStar menu item's branch as an example. Enter

```
:TWO
BE ROWCOL 20 28 "2" BRIGHT WHITE ON MAGENTA
BE WINDOW 19 35 21 75 BRIGHT WHITE ON BLUE SHADOW
BE ROWCOL 20 37 "Loading WordStar, Please Be Patient"
CD \WS4
WS
CD \BATCH
MENU
```

Use this technique of echoing a character back to the screen for all data-entry processes; it confirms that the computer has accepted a person's input and is doing what it should be doing.

The selection is again echoed to the screen and another window opens to tell you which application program is being loaded. (This is done by the two command lines following the ROWCOL command.) Figure 8.5 displays the MENU.BAT screen that you should see at this point.

The last two commands

```
CD \BATCH
MENU
```

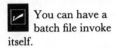 You can have a batch file invoke itself.

make the BATCH directory current and run MENU.BAT again. With this setup, you are always returned to the menu screen when you exit an application.

Use this example for your remaining applications and compare your batch file to Figure 8.6, which shows a complete listing of MENU.BAT.

If you add MENU.BAT to your AUTOEXEC.BAT file, you can make your system completely menu-driven. If the DOS programs are in a directory called DOS, the Norton Utilities are in a directory

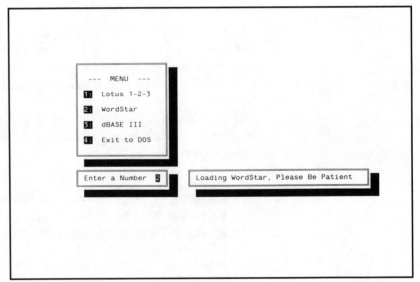

Figure 8.5: The MENU.BAT screen with all three windows open

```
:BE startup menu file

ECHO OFF
BE CLS

:set the screen colors

BE SA BRIGHT WHITE ON BLUE

:draw the window

BE WINDOW 05 10 17 30 BRIGHT WHITE ON BLUE SHADOW EXPLODE
BE ROWCOL 07 12 " ---  MENU  --- "

BE ROWCOL 09 12 "1:" BRIGHT WHITE ON MAGENTA
BE ROWCOL 09 14 "  Lotus 1-2-3" BRIGHT WHITE ON BLUE

BE ROWCOL 11 12 "2:" BRIGHT WHITE ON MAGENTA
BE ROWCOL 11 14 "  WordStar" BRIGHT WHITE ON BLUE

BE ROWCOL 13 12 "3:" BRIGHT WHITE ON MAGENTA
BE ROWCOL 13 14 "  dBASE IV" BRIGHT WHITE ON BLUE

BE ROWCOL 15 12 "4:" BRIGHT WHITE ON MAGENTA
BE ROWCOL 15 14 "  Exit to DOS" BRIGHT WHITE ON BLUE

:draw the dialog box

BE WINDOW 19 10 21 30 BRIGHT WHITE ON BLUE SHADOW
BE ROWCOL 20 12 "Enter a Number  "
BE ROWCOL 20 28
BE PRINTCHAR " " 1 ON BLACK
BE ROWCOL 20 28

:evaluates menu selection
:if no key pressed in 30 secs, exit to DOS

BE ASK "", 1234 TIMEOUT=30 DEFAULT=4
     IF ERRORLEVEL  4 GOTO FOUR
     IF ERRORLEVEL  3 GOTO THREE
     IF ERRORLEVEL  2 GOTO TWO
     IF ERRORLEVEL  1 GOTO ONE

:FOUR
BE ROWCOL 20 28 "4" BRIGHT WHITE ON MAGENTA
GOTO EXIT

:THREE
BE ROWCOL 20 28 "3" BRIGHT WHITE ON MAGENTA
BE WINDOW 19 35 21 75 BRIGHT WHITE ON BLUE SHADOW
BE ROWCOL 20 37 "Loading dBASE, Please Be Patient"
CD \DB4
DBASE
CD \BATCH
MENU

:TWO
BE ROWCOL 20 28 "2" BRIGHT WHITE ON MAGENTA
BE WINDOW 19 35 21 75 BRIGHT WHITE ON BLUE SHADOW
BE ROWCOL 20 37 "Loading WordStar, Please Be Patient"
CD \WS4
WS
CD \BATCH
MENU

:ONE
BE ROWCOL 20 28 "1" BRIGHT WHITE ON MAGENTA
BE WINDOW 19 35 21 75 BRIGHT WHITE ON BLUE SHADOW
BE ROWCOL 20 37 "Loading Lotus 1-2-3, Please Be Patient"
CD \123
CD \BATCH
MENU

:EXIT
BE WINDOW 19 35 21 75 BRIGHT WHITE ON BLUE SHADOW
BE ROWCOL 20 37 "Returning to DOS"
BE CLS

:reset screen colors for DOS

BE SA BRIGHT WHITE ON BLUE
```

Figure 8.6: The completed MENU.BAT file

called NORTON, and your batch files are in a directory called BATCH, your PATH setting might look like this:

PATH = C:\;C:\DOS;C:\NORTON;C:\BATCH

You can then add the line

MENU

to the end of your AUTOEXEC.BAT file, and the MENU.BAT file will be loaded automatically each time you boot up your computer. Now, you or other users won't even have to work in DOS to run your application programs. Including the Exit to DOS option in the menu, however, enables you to return to DOS to perform other important tasks necessary for managing and backing up your disks.

If you find that MENU.BAT runs too slowly, you can speed it up considerably by using two files instead of just one. To do this, place all the commands for drawing the menu window and the dialog box in a separate batch file, calling it MENU.TXT. This file will then be loaded by MENU.BAT at the appropriate point. The revised MENU.BAT file is shown in Figure 8.7, and MENU.TXT is shown in Figure 8.8. Note that in MENU.TXT, the BE statements at the start of each line have been removed, as they are no longer necessary. Their place is taken by the single command

BE MENU.TXT

in MENU.BAT. Because the MENU.TXT file is fed to BE all in one go, the number of separate calls made to BE are reduced. As a result the new MENU.BAT file executes about ten times faster than the original batch file.

If you plan to use the BE utility extensively, copy the BE.EXE program to your RAM disk by including another COPY command in the batch file that initializes your RAM disk. BE is then copied to the RAM disk automatically when you (or AUTOEXEC.BAT) invoke this batch file, and all the BE programs will run quickly, since they will be executing from memory.

```
:BE startup menu file

ECHO OFF
BE CLS

:set the screen colors

BE SA BRIGHT WHITE ON BLUE

:creates menu window and dialog box
:system runs faster when separated into two files; less calls to BE

BE MENU.TXT

:evaluates menu selection
:if no key pressed in 30 secs, exit to DOS

BE ASK "", 1234 TIMEOUT=30 DEFAULT=4
     IF ERRORLEVEL  4 GOTO FOUR
     IF ERRORLEVEL  3 GOTO THREE
     IF ERRORLEVEL  2 GOTO TWO
     IF ERRORLEVEL  1 GOTO ONE

:FOUR
BE ROWCOL 20 28 "4" BRIGHT WHITE ON MAGENTA
GOTO EXIT

:THREE
BE ROWCOL 29 28 "3" BRIGHT WHITE ON MAGENTA
BE WINDOW 19 35 21 75 BRIGHT WHITE ON BLUE SHADOW
BE ROWCOL 20 37 "Loading dBASE, Please Be Patient"
CD \DB4
DBASE
CD \BATCH
MENU

:TWO
BE ROWCOL 20 28 "2" BRIGHT WHITE ON MAGENTA
BE WINDOW 19 35 21 75 BRIGHT WHITE ON BLUE SHADOW
BE ROWCOL 20 37 "Loading WordStar, Please Be Patient"
CD \WS4
WS
CD \BATCH
MENU

:ONE
BE ROWCOL 20 28 "1" BRIGHT WHITE ON MAGENTA
BE WINDOW 19 35 21 75 BRIGHT WHITE ON BLUE SHADOW
BE ROWCOL 20 37 "Loading Lotus 1-2-3, Please Be Patient"
CD \123
123
CD \BATCH
MENU

:EXIT
BE WINDOW 19 35 21 75 BRIGHT WHITE ON BLUE SHADOW
BE ROWCOL 20 37 "Returning to DOS"
BE CLS

:reset screen colors

BE SA BRIGHT WHITE ON BLUE
```

Figure 8.7: The revised MENU.BAT file

```
:file for accessing BE all at once

WINDOW 05 10 17 30 BRIGHT WHITE ON BLUE SHADOW EXPLODE
ROWCOL 07 12 " ---  MENU  --- "

ROWCOL 09 12 "1:" BRIGHT WHITE ON MAGENTA
ROWCOL 09 14 "  Lotus 1-2-3" BRIGHT WHITE ON BLUE

ROWCOL 11 12 "2:" BRIGHT WHITE ON MAGENTA
ROWCOL 11 14 "  WordStar" BRIGHT WHITE ON BLUE

ROWCOL 13 13 "3:" BRIGHT WHITE ON MAGENTA
ROWCOL 13 14 "  dBASE IV" BRIGHT WHITE ON BLUE

ROWCOL 15 12 "4:" BRIGHT WHITE ON MAGENTA
ROWCOL 15 14 "  Exit to DOS" BRIGHT WHITE ON BLUE

WINDOW 19 10 21 30 BRIGHT WHITE ON BLUE SHADOW
ROWCOL 20 12 "Enter a Number  "
ROWCOL 20 28
PRINTCHAR " " 1 ON BLACK
ROWCOL 20 28
```

Figure 8.8: The MENU.TXT file's contents

Using batch files can make tedious, repetitive, or complex DOS operations much more straightforward. BE's subprograms are an important addition to the batch-programming language, as they allow you to create interactive conditional branching in a batch file, making complex screen handling and windowing easy to do.

UPDATING ASK, BEEP, AND SA

If you are using batch files that you made with an earlier version of the Norton Utilities, you can modify them by inserting the name BE before each occurrence of ASK, BEEP, and SA. This way, you can continue to use them. For example,

BEEP MARY

must now become

BE BEEP MARY

and

ASK "Option A or Option B", AB

now becomes

> BE ASK "Option A or Option B", AB

This simple change to existing batch files is all that is needed to update them.

OTHER USEFUL ADDITIONS TO YOUR BATCH FILES

You can invoke several utilities from a batch file to automate tasks that you want to run regularly. Two good candidates in this category are FR (Format Recover), which rescues the contents of your hard disk after it has been accidentally reformatted and TM (Time Mark), which allows you to keep track of how you use your computer.

USING FR IN A BATCH FILE

As you have learned in previous chapters, you should take steps to prevent an accidental reformatting from happening, as well as steps to recover from it if it does occur. As you may recall, FR enables you to recover an accidentally reformatted hard disk.

Using FR in a batch file is an excellent way to make sure it has made a new copy of the FRECOVER.DAT file, which it will use in the event your hard disk is accidentally reformatted. For example, you can run Format Recover from a batch file called SHUTDOWN-.BAT by including

> FR /SAVE

in it. Each time you run SHUTDOWN.BAT, FR will automatically update the FRECOVER.DAT file. Make a habit of running SHUTDOWN.BAT just before you turn your computer off to ensure that FRECOVER.DAT is as up-to-date as possible. An accurate, up-to-date FRECOVER.DAT file increases the chances of a complete recovery of all the files on your hard disk if it is reformatted.

Since you should always park your hard disk heads before turning off the power, have SHUTDOWN.BAT invoke your head-parking program as well. A completed SHUTDOWN.BAT file might contain the following statements:

```
:run shutdown.bat after every session

FR /SAVE
SHIPDISK
```

(Substitute the command for your head-parking program if it is not SHIPDISK.)

MAKING A TIME LOG WITH TM

In addition to displaying the current time and date on the screen, the TM (Time Mark) utility can start, stop, or reset up to four stopwatch timers from the DOS prompt or from inside a batch file. TM's output can also be formatted and sent to a printer or file.

If you want know what time it is, simply enter

```
TM
```

The system's current time and date will then be displayed on the right-hand side of the screen. If you type

```
TM /L
```

the display will appear on the left side of the display.

To start the first of the four timers in TM, type

```
TM START
```

and to stop it, type

```
TM STOP
```

In this example, not only are the time and date displayed on the screen, but the elapsed time between START and STOP is also given (Figure 8.9).

```
C:\>TM START
                                        5:20 pm, Thursday, September 28, 1989
C:\>TM STOP
                                        5:28 pm, Thursday, September 28, 1989
                                                       8 minutes, 18 seconds
C:\>
```

Figure 8.9: Timed output from TM

TM uses the first of the four stopwatches, unless you specify that you want to use one of the other three with the /C*n* switch, where *n* is the number of the stopwatch you want to start or stop.

For timing events that are external to the computer, you can also use the stopwatches in NCC (Norton Control Center). See Chapter 6 for more details.

If you want to time events related to your work on the computer, you can invoke TM from a batch file. For example, if you add TM to your AUTOEXEC.BAT and SHUTDOWN.BAT files, you can make TM report how many hours and minutes you have been using your computer. To do this, add the line

TM START

to your AUTOEXEC.BAT file and add the line

TM STOP

to SHUTDOWN.BAT so that it looks like this:

:run shutdown.bat after every session

FR /SAVE
TM STOP
SHIPDISK

The TM in AUTOEXEC.BAT will tell you when you started working on the computer, and the TM in SHUTDOWN.BAT will tell you when you ended, as well as the time you spent working in hours and minutes.

To create a time log of your computer use for later analysis, you can send the output from TM to a file by using DOS's redirection symbols. To do this, change the line in your AUTOEXEC.BAT file to read:

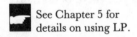 The comments inside the quotation marks are included to make the TIME.LOG file easier to read.

TM START "Started working at " /LOG >> TIME.LOG

The /LOG switch tells TM to prepare output in a form suitable for sending to a file, and the >> symbols send the output to the TIME-.LOG file.

Unlike the single > redirection symbol, which sends output to a file, overwriting any data the file may contain, the double >> symbol indicates that any output should be added to the end of the file if it already exists; if not, it tells DOS to create the file. Using the double redirection symbol allows you to collect information over a period of time in one file.

Now change the TM line in SHUTDOWN.BAT to read:

TM STOP "Stopped using the PC at " /LOG >> TIME.LOG

The TM STOP command will redirect the elapsed hours and minutes the computer has been running to the TIME.LOG file.

See Chapter 5 for details on using LP.

Since the TIME.LOG file is an ASCII text file, you can use the LP utility to print it.

SUMMARY

In this chapter I described DOS's batch-programming language, as well as the DOS commands in the two files used to set up your system: AUTOEXEC.BAT and CONFIG.SYS. You also explored programming batch files with the Norton Utilities programs. Here's a review of the programs you worked with:

- BE (Batch Enhancer) contains several subprograms that make screen handling and decision making easier from a batch file.

- BE SA sets the screen colors and attributes.

- BE BOX enables you to draw differently sized boxes on the screen.

- BE CLS clears the screen and returns the cursor to the home position at the top-left corner of the screen.

- BE WINDOW lets you draw windows on the screen, even including an optional drop shadow on them. You can also make the window zoom.

- BE ROWCOL moves the cursor to a specified location on the screen.

- BE PRINTCHAR display a character at the current cursor position. You can also repeat the character and define its color.

- BE ASK provides an easy way to include real-time conditional branching from a batch file.

- BE BEEP sounds a note on the computer's speaker. You can specify the note's pitch and duration, as well as wait periods between notes and repetitions. BE BEEP can also play the notes contained in a file.

- BE DELAY allows you to specify a wait period in a batch file that must elapse before the batch file continues executing.

- TM (Time Mark) controls up to four stopwatch timers that you can use from the DOS prompt or from inside a batch file.

This chapter also included examples of how you can combine these utilities with the DOS batch commands in your batch-file programming to make attractive and useful menu screens.

THE COMPLETE COMMAND REFERENCE
TO THE NORTON UTILITIES

APPENDIX A

IN THIS APPENDIX I LIST ALL THE NORTON UTILITIES programs alphabetically, giving a short description of each program. The syntax and possible switches for each utility are also provided. These are based on the Norton Utilities Version 4.5 Advanced Edition, which was released in 1988, but also apply to Version 4.5's Standard Edition. If you have an earlier version of the Norton Utilities, you will be able to follow the program descriptions here, but you will not have several major new programs and may want to seriously consider upgrading to Version 4.5.

To make the syntax easier to read, I have substituted categorical names for the parameters you can use for a particular command. The possible choices are then listed and described individually. Three of the most common parameters are

- *drive,* which should be replaced by the appropriate drive letter, followed by a colon.

- *filespec,* which should be replaced by a file's name (and path when necessary).

- *directoryspec,* which should be replaced by a directory's name (and path when necessary).

Keep in mind that, unless otherwise noted, a command's parameters are optional.

───────────────── *ASK* ─────────────────

Although ASK used to be a separate program, it is now a part of the BE (Batch Enhancer) program. See the section entitled "Subcommands" under BE for further details.

───────────────── *BE* ─────────────────

BE (Batch Enhancer) adds several important mechanisms for improved screen handling to the DOS batch-programming language. BE also enables you to create interactive decision-making in a batch file with its ASK subcommand.

Syntax

> BE *subcommand*

or

> BE *filespec*

Use

You can use BE followed by one of the subcommands listed here, or you can use BE with a file that contains all the subcommands and their parameters. When you group the subcommands together in a file and specify the file with BE, the commands will be executed much faster since BE is only invoked once instead of individually for every command. (See the examples in Chapter 8 for more information about improving batch-file screen handling.)

SUBCOMMANDS

Following is a list of the possible subcommands that you can include in a batch file.

BE ASK   This program provides a way to perform conditional branching from a batch file. The prompt you include in the command will be displayed on the screen when the batch file executes the command, and the answer given by the user tells the batch file which commands to execute next.

Syntax

BE ASK *"prompt" list* DEFAULT = *key* TIMEOUT = *n* ADJUST = *n* color

Description

The following list explains what each parameter can be:

"prompt"	is any text string, usually a question, that gives the user two or more choices. Also include a list of the keys that can be chosen, so the user knows which key to press.
list	tells BE ASK what the valid keystrokes are. If you don't specify anything for *list,* any keys will be accepted.
DEFAULT = *key*	indicates the key to use if no key is pressed before the allotted time has expired or Enter is pressed.
TIMEOUT = *n*	tells BE ASK how many seconds to wait for a keystroke after the *prompt* test has been displayed. If TIMEOUT equals zero or you do not include TIMEOUT in the command statement, BE ASK waits forever.
ADJUST = *n*	adjusts the return value by amount *n*.
color	specifies the color of the prompt text. See BE SA for a description of the available colors.

BE BEEP   This program plays a tone on the PC speaker. A single tone can be specified at the DOS prompt, or a series of tones can be played by loading a file.

Syntax

If you specify

BE BEEP *switches*

at the DOS prompt, a single tone will be played.

On the other hand, if you specify

BE BEEP *filespec*

all the tones specified by the switches in the file will be played. You can include a path name to specify a file in another directory, but wildcard characters may not be used.

Description

To create a single tone, you need to include the /Dn and /Fn switches in the command statement. You can also repeat the tone by adding the /Rn and /Wn switches to the same statement. Here is what each switch does:

/Dn	gives the duration of the tone in $^1/_{18}$ths of a second.
/Fn	specifies the frequency of the tone in Hertz (cycles per second).
/Rn	tells BE BEEP how many times to repeat the tone.
/Wn	provides the duration of the wait period between tones, in $^1/_{18}$ths of a second.

BE BOX   This program draws a box on the screen, according to your specifications.

Syntax

To run BE BOX, enter

BOX *top left bottom right outline color*

in your batch file.

Use BE BOX when you want to create a framed box. (Specifying two colors produces a two-toned frame for it.) Use BE WINDOW when you want to fill in the outline with color.

Description

To draw a box, you must include the *top, left, bottom,* and *right* parameters. The two remaining parameters are optional. Here is what all of these parameters stand for:

top   specifies the row of the top-left corner of the box.

left   specifies the column of the top-left corner of the box.

bottom specifies the row of the bottom-right corner of the box.

right   specifies the column of the bottom-right corner of the box.

outline specifying SINGLE draws a single-line outline for the box. Specifying DOUBLE draws a double-line outline for the box.

color   specifies the color of the box. See BE SA for a description of the color selections.

BE CLS   This program clears the screen and positions the cursor at the home position, which is the top-left corner of the screen.

Syntax

    BE CLS

BE CLS does not take any parameters.

BE DELAY   This program sets a specified time delay before executing the next command in the batch file.

Syntax

    BE DELAY counts

Description

You must specify the *counts* parameter when you invoke BE DELAY. You can use this program to create text in a window, displaying messages about the work in progress or prompting users with instructions.

The *counts* parameter determines how long (in $1/18$ths of a second) the batch-file processor will wait before continuing to execute the batch file.

BE PRINTCHAR   This program displays the specified character at the current cursor location.

Syntax

BE PRINTCHAR *character repetitions color*

Description

The definitions for PRINTCHAR's parameters are as follows:

character	selects the character for display.
repetitions	specifies the number of times the character will be displayed, up to a maximum of 80 repetitions.
color	chooses the color to be used for the character.

BE ROWCOL   This program moves the cursor to the specified place on the screen and displays the text.

Syntax

BE ROWCOL *row column text color*

Description

You don't have to specify *text* or *color* when you invoke BE ROWCOL.

row	selects the row to move the cursor to.
column	specifies the column to move the cursor to.
text	provides the optional text to be displayed at the new cursor location. If the text contains space characters, enclose the entire string in quotation marks.

color   specifies the color to be used for the text. See the description of BE SA for the colors available.

BE SA   This program enables you to set the screen foreground and background colors, and vary the intensity of the characters. The ANSI.SYS driver must be installed in your CONFIG.SYS file for BE SA to work properly. If ANSI.SYS is not installed, you will be given an error message that tells you ANSI.SYS is required.

Syntax

BE SA can be used in two ways. The first syntax is

BE SA *main-setting switches*

You use this syntax when you want to set up your screen's display of text.

Description

The *main-setting* parameter can be one of the following:

normal

reverse

underline

The *switches* you can include are

/N   does not set the border color. The EGA is a borderless display so using this switch with an EGA will have no effect; however, you can set the border for a VGA by omitting this switch.

/C   clears the screen after setting the color and screen attributes.

Syntax

The second syntax takes the form:

BE SA *intensity foreground* **ON** *background switches*

You use this command format to set the screen colors' attributes.

Description

The *switches* are the same ones you can use with BE SA's first syntax. The remaining parameters can be

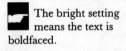

The bright setting means the text is boldfaced.

intensity	bright
	blinking
foreground	white
	black
	red
	magenta
	blue
	green
	cyan
	yellow
background	same as for *foreground*

You can abbreviate the color in the command statement by listing just the first three letters of their name. Therefore,

BE SA BRIGHT WHITE ON BLUE

can become

BE SA BRI WHI ON BLU

BE WINDOW   This program creates a window on the screen, according to your specifications.

Syntax

BE WINDOW *top left bottom right color switches*

Description

top	specifies the row location of the top-left corner of the window.
left	specifies the column location of the top-left corner of the window.
bottom	specifies the row location of the bottom-right corner of the window.
right	specifies the column location of the bottom-right corner of the window.
SHADOW	adds a drop shadow to the window.
EXPLODE	makes the window zoom.

BEEP

The Norton Utilities Version 4.5 includes BEEP as a subprogram of the BE (Batch Enhancer) program. See the section entitled "Subcommands" under BE for further details.

DI (DISK INFORMATION)

DI reads and displays technical information about a DOS disk.

Syntax for Full-Screen Mode

To run Disk Information in full-screen mode, enter

```
NU
```

From the menu that then appears, choose Disk information. You will be presented with the Disk information menu, which gives you the choice of mapping the disk's usage, displaying technical information, or returning to the Main menu. When you have finished viewing the information about the disk, press F10 to return to the DOS prompt.

Syntax for Command-Line Mode

To run DI directly from the DOS prompt, enter

DI *drive*

Description

The *drive* parameter tells DI which disk you want information on. For example, if you are working in a directory on your hard disk and want to check a floppy in drive A, you would enter

DI A:

DP (DATA PROTECT)

DP is part of the Norton Utilities Standard Edition Version 4.5, but not the Advanced Edition because it functions just like the Advanced Edition's FR program when you run it with its /SAVE switch. In other words, DP creates and updates the FRECOVER-.DAT file, storing in it disk information that makes it possible to recover data from the disk after it has been accidentally formatted, or after its files or directories have been inadvertently erased. The FRE-COVER.DAT may even enable you to unerase fragmented files.

Although you can't always recover erased or reformatted data, DP gives you a fighting chance when you use Quick UnErase, UnRemove Directory, or NU's UnErase feature.

You won't find DP in *The Norton Utilities Standard Edition Version 4.5* manual (1988), because it was added to the release too late to be included in the documentation. A summary explanation of this program can be found in the READ.ME file.

Syntax

To run DP, enter

DP *drive*

Description

The *drive* parameter tells DP which drive to protect. If you do not specify a drive letter when you run DP, it creates or updates the FRECOVER.DAT file for the current drive. To protect a floppy disk, simply place it in drive A and enter

DP A:

☑ If you have a batch file that you run to shut down your system, place the DP command there instead of in the AUTOEXEC.BAT file. For more information on how to create such a file, see Chapter 8.

To make sure that the FRECOVER.DAT file contains the most up-to-date information about your hard disk, include the command

DP C:

in your AUTOEXEC.BAT file. This way, DP will update the file each time you start up your system.

DS (DIRECTORY SORT)

DS provides several ways to sort a directory's contents. You can run the program in full-screen mode or from the DOS prompt.

If you are not sure how you want the directory to be sorted and want to see the effects of the different options, run DS in full-screen mode. However, if you know exactly what you want, run DS in command-line mode. You may find that you need to sort just a few files within the directory; in that case, run DS in full-screen mode and make the necessary changes manually.

Syntax for Full-Screen Mode

To run DS (Directory Sort) in full-screen mode, enter

DS

A window screen then appears, listing the current directory's contents on the left side and the Sort by and Order columns on the right. You can sort the directory's files by Name, Extension, Date, Time, or Size in ascending (+) or descending (−) order.

You can also enter

DS *directoryspec*

to work with a directory other than the current one in full-screen mode.

To set the screen attributes for DS's full-screen mode, use the following switches:

/D*n*   where *n* = 0 reestablishes the default setting for 100 percent compatibles.
              where *n* = 1 enables use with BIOS-compatible machines.

/BW   sets the color display to monochrome.

/NOSNOW   removes the flickering seen on some CGA cards.

Syntax for Command-Line Mode

To run DS from the DOS prompt, enter

DS *directoryspec sortkeys switches*

Description

The *directoryspec* parameter gives DS the name (including its path) of the directory to sort.

The *sortkeys* parameter can be one or more of the following letters, separated by spaces. To reverse the sort order (making it descending), simply add a minus sign after the sort-key letter in the command statement.

N   sorts alphabetically by file name.

E   sorts alphabetically by file extension.

T   sorts by time.

D   sorts by date.

S   sorts by file size (which is given in bytes).

DS can only take one switch: /S, which sorts all subdirectories. You do not need to specify a directory name if you want to sort the current directory and its subdirectories when you use this switch.

DT (DISK TEST)

DT checks a disk for bad areas—that is, areas that have been physically damaged and can't be read for data. It can attempt repairs of the bad areas and can move data from questionable areas of the disk to safer areas.

Syntax

To run DT, enter

DT *drive filespec switches*

Description

Your choices for DT's parameters are the following:

drive	indicates which *drive* should be checked.
filespec	tells DT which file to test. You can use wildcards to specify a group of files. When you give a file name, you don't need to include the /F switch.
/F	tests all files and directories on the chosen disk, but not erased or unused disk space or the system area.
/D	tests the whole disk by cluster, including the system area.
/B	is the same as using both the /F and /D switches. It performs a disk test and a file test.
/C*n*	marks cluster *n* as bad. DOS will no longer use this cluster once you have marked it.
/C*n*–	marks cluster *n* as good. DOS will now use this cluster when it is needed.
/LOG	formats the output from DT in a form suitable to send to a file or to the printer.
/M	moves data from areas of the disk identified as marginal to good areas of the disk and marks the original locations as bad.

/S   instructs DT to test files in subdirectories as well. To use this switch, you must specify a file name in the command.

EXPLORE DISK

Explore disk is part of the NU utility, so it can only be run in full-screen mode.

Syntax

To reach Explore disk, enter

    NU

Explore disk is the first selection on NU's Main menu. Press E or Enter to select it. You are then presented with the Explore disk menu, which offers a multitude of functions for examining and editing your disks. To specify what you want to look at, select Choose item. You can then select a drive, directory, file, clusters, or sectors.

Once you have selected an item, you are returned to the Explore disk menu. You can choose

- Information on disk to find out more about the selected item
- Edit/display item to view it in directory or hex format (what the item is determines which format is first shown)
- Search item/disk for data to locate information the item contains
- Write item to disk to copy an item before editing it

If you do edit the selected item, you will be prompted to save your changes before returning to NU's Main menu.

FA (FILE ATTRIBUTES)

FA allows you to display, set, or reset four of the bits in a file's attribute byte.

Syntax

To run FA, enter

FA *filespec attributes switches*

Description

Here is an explanation of FA's parameters:

filespec   tells FA which file to use. You must include a path name if the file is not in the current directory, and you can use wildcards to specify a group of files.

To set the file's attributes, use the following switches with a plus sign. To reset the file's attributes, you use the same switches but add a minus sign to turn off that attribute's bit.

/A   archives or unarchives the file.

/HID   hides or unhides the file.

/R   makes the file read-only or read-write.

/SYS   makes the file a system or nonsystem file.

For example, entering

FA *.TXT /R +

makes all your *.TXT files read-only. Conversely, entering

FA *.TXT /R –

enables anyone to modify them once again.

These next switches must follow the *attributes* switches and modify the entire command, not individual attribute settings.

/CLEAR   removes all file attributes.

/P	pauses display each time the data fills the screen.
/S	includes subdirectories in the search for *filespec*.
/T	shortens the listing, showing only the total number of files that are acted on, not their names.
/U	displays all files that have any attribute bits set.

FD (FILE DATE)

FF sets or clears a file's creation date or time. You can also change the date or time for a group of files all at once.

Syntax

To run FD, enter

FD *filespec switches*

Description

Following are descriptions of FD's parameters:

The format for the date and time is determined by the COUNTRY code in your CONFIG.SYS file if you change the format from its default of *mm-dd-yy* for the date and *hh:mm:ss.hh* for the time.

filespec	tells FD which files to modify.
/S	includes subdirectories in the search for *filespec*.
/P	pauses the display after each screenful.
/D*date*	sets the date of the file to *date*. If you don't include a date, the file's date is cleared. Make sure you use the correct format for *date*.
/T*time*	sets the time of the file to *time*. If you don't specify a time, the file's time is cleared.

To change the date and time for a group of files quickly, you can omit the /D*date* and /T*time* switches. The current system time and date will then be used for the files.

FF (FILE FIND)

FF searches a disk to find a file or a subdirectory. You can also use it to print a directory listing for a whole disk.

Syntax

To run FF, enter

FF *drive filespec switches*

Description

All of FF's parameters are optional:

drive	tells FF which drive to check. If no drive letter is given, FF uses the default drive.
filespec	specifies the file to be searched for. You can include wildcards. You do not have to specify a path if you use the /A switch.
/A	search for *filespec* on all drives.
/P	pauses the display after each screenful of data.
/W	lists data in a wide format.

For example, if you enter

FF A:

FF will list all files on the disk in drive A. To send this listing to the printer, simply modify the command to

FF A: > PRN

FI (FILE INFO)

FI provides a directory listing that is more complete than that offered by DIR. You can use its interactive editor to attach comments to each file and subdirectory.

Syntax

If you enter

FI

you generate a listing of the current directory, complete with the entries' attached comments if there are any.

On the other hand, if you enter

FI *filespec comments switches*

you can add, edit, or delete comments for a particular file or for each file in the directory, depending on which parameters you include.

Description

Here are the choices you have for FI's parameters:

filespec	provides the name of the file or directory to attach comments to. You can use DOS wildcard characters in this specification.
comments	provides the message to be attached to the file or subdirectory. You can specify up to 65 characters.
/C	only lists those files that have comments attached to them; it truncates the display of comments longer than 36 characters.
/D	deletes any comments attached to the file. If you don't include *filespec*, it deletes all comments in the current directory.
/E	invokes the interactive editor, enabling you to enter or edit a comment as prompted.
/L	displays the long format, which shows short file names and entire comments.
/P	pauses the display when it fills the screen.
/PACK	compresses and rewrites the FILEINFO.FI file.
/S	includes all subdirectories in the listing.

Although you can add comments directly from the DOS prompt, it is easier to use the /E switch, which allows you to edit what you enter.

FR (FORMAT RECOVER)

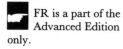

FR is a part of the Advanced Edition only.

FR recovers data and program files from a hard disk after it has been accidentally reformatted by the DOS FORMAT command. You should also use it daily so that it can record and update your system's information in its FRECOVER.DAT file, thereby making a complete recovery more feasible. (It can't recover what it doesn't know about.)

Syntax for Full-Screen Mode

To run FR in full-screen mode, enter

    FR

You can then use the menu selections that you need. Restore Disk Information recovers data from a reformatted disk that had an up-to-date FRECOVER.DAT file; UnFormat Disk recovers data from a reformatted disk that did not have a FRECOVER.DAT file (or the file was outdated); Save Disk Information creates or updates the FRECOVER.DAT file; and Exit Format Recover returns you to the DOS prompt.

The following switches are used to set the screen attributes for FR's full-screen mode.

/Dn	where n = 0 reestablishes the default setting for 100% compatibles. where n = 1 enables use with BIOS-compatible machines.
/BW	sets the color display to monochrome.
/NOSNOW	removes the flickering seen on some CGA cards.

Syntax for Command-Line Mode

To run FR directly from the DOS prompt, enter

FR *drive switches*

Description

drive	gives FR the hard-disk drive letter. If you omit the drive letter, FR uses the current drive.
/SAVE	creates or updates the FRECOVER.DAT file, which contains system information that FR will use to recover files after the hard disk has been accidentally reformatted.
/NOBAK	does not create the backup file FRECOVER.BAK.

FS (FILE SIZE)

FS gives information on a file's size and displays the percentage slack for the file. It can also determine whether a file will fit onto another disk.

Syntax

To run FS, enter

FS *filespec drive switches*

Description

Following are explanations of each parameter:

filespec	tells FS which file needs its size and percentage slack calculated. When you use wildcards, all files meeting the file specification will be checked.
drive	specifies the target drive's letter. When you provide a drive letter, FS checks the drive to determine whether it has room for *filespec*.

/P	pauses the display each time it fills the screen. You can also press the space bar to halt the display while the program is running.
/S	includes all subdirectories in the listing.
/T	displays the total size of *filespec,* without presenting data for the individual files.

For example, to check all files on the current disk, enter

FS /S

LD (LIST DIRECTORIES)

LD is a program that lists directory information in text or graphic form.

If you want to see a directory listing and change directories, use NCD.

Syntax

To run LD, enter

LD *drive directoryspec switches*

Description

LD's parameters can be the following:

drive	tells LD which drive to display.
directoryspec	provides a directory for LD to present. To specify a directory, you must include its full path. When you do not use this parameter, LD lists all directories on the disk.
/A	lists the directories of all drives.
/G	displays the directory structure in graphic form.
/N	stops the printing of the extended IBM graphics characters on non-IBM compatible printers. You only need to include this switch if you use the /G switch and send the command's output to this type of printer.

Pressing any key after the display has started will also pause it.

/P   pauses the display after each screenful.

/T   displays the total number and size of files in each directory.

For example, to see a listing of all directories on the current drive, simply enter

LD

LP (LINE PRINT)

LP prints text files, allowing a variety of options for formatting a document. You can also use LP to send a setup sequence to the printer to make sure that it is ready to print the text file. You can even send LP's output to a file for later printing.

Syntax

Enter

LP *filespec device switches*

to print a file according to your specifications.

Enter

LP *filespec filespec switches*

to store the file formatted for printing in another file so that you can print it later. You cannot use the wildcard characters in the target file name.

Description

Here is an explanation of LP's possible parameters:

filespec   tells LP which file to print. To print a file in another directory, include its path name. To print a group of files, use the wildcard characters.

device	specifies the printer to use. If you do not include this parameter, output is sent to the default printer, PRN.
/T*n*	establishes the number of lines for the top margin; the default is 3.
/B*n*	specifies the number of lines for the bottom margin; the default is 5.
/L*n*	establishes the number of spaces for the left margin; the default is 5.
/R*n*	specifies the number of spaces for the right margin; the default is 5.
/H*n*	tells LP how many lines to print per page; the default is 66.
/W*n*	sets the width of the page's text in columns; the default is 85.
/S*n*	specifies the line spacing; the default is 1, which is single spacing.
/P*n*	tells LP what the starting page number is; the default is 1.
/N	instructs LP to number the lines.
/80	sets 80-column mode, which is the default.
/132	sets 132-column mode.
/HEADER*n*	sets the type of header as follows:

n = 0:	does not print a header.
n = 1:	prints current time and date. This is the default.
n = 2:	print current time and date, and file's creation time and date.

/EBCDIC	prints an EBCDIC file.
/WS	prints WordStar files. (This means characters from the extended character set are not translated into ASCII standard characters.)
/SET: *filename*	sends the sequence contained in *filename* to the printing device.

When you use the /SET switch with a file name, the file can include these forms for its setup sequence:

nnn   where *nnn* is the decimal number for the printer code to send. All three characters are needed, so use leading zeros where necessary. To send the code 15 to set compressed mode, for example, enter \\015.

\\C   where \\C is the control character to send.

C   where C is any character you want to send.

NCC (NORTON CONTROL CENTER)

NCC controls the computer's hardware, including its display, keyboard, serial ports, and battery-powered clock boards. You can run it in full-screen mode to use its organized menu and graphic display window, or you can run it directly from the DOS prompt if you have saved settings in a file or know which switch you want to use. If you haven't saved settings in a file and need to adjust several hardware settings, you may find it quicker and easier to run NCC in full-screen mode.

Syntax for Full-Screen Mode

When you enter

NCC *switches*

you are presented with a window containing the Select Item menu and a graphic display of the menu selection you choose. Your choices are Cursor Size, DOS Colors, Palette Colors, Video Mode, Keyboard Rate, Serial Ports, Watches, and Time and Date.

Description

You can work with as many of these menu items as you like. If you make changes to a particular setting that you do not want to keep, press Esc to leave it without saving the changes; you will be returned to the Select Item menu. You can also press * to reset the menu choice to its default settings.

Once you have set everything you want, you can save all the settings to a file by pressing F2. When you press F2, a dialog box appears, prompting you to specify the name of the file. You can then later use this file to run NCC directly from the DOS prompt. For example, you can save your preferred hardware setup in it, and then anytime you change the settings temporarily, you can run NCC with the file to restore your system to your normal setup.

You can use any of the following as the *switches* parameter. They set the display attributes for NCC's full-screen mode.

/Dn	where $n = 0$ reestablishes the default setting for 100 percent compatibles. where $n = 1$ enables use with BIOS-compatible machines.
/BW	sets the color display to monochrome.
/NOSNOW	removes the flickering seen on some CGA cards.

Syntax for Command-Line Mode

You can control some aspects of your screen display by entering

NCC *quick switches*

Description

Following is a list of the switches that can be used for the *quick switches* parameter:

APP. A

/BW80	sets the display mode to monochrome, 25 lines by 80 columns.
/CO80	sets the display mode to color, 25 lines by 80 columns.
/25	sets the display mode to 25 lines by 80 columns.
/35	sets the display mode to 35 lines by 80 columns for EGA monitors.
/40	sets the display mode to 40 lines by 80 columns for VGA monitors.
/43	sets the display mode to 43 lines by 80 columns for EGA monitors.
/50	sets the display mode to 50 lines by 80 columns for VGA monitors.
/FASTKEY	sets the keyboard rate to the fastest rate.

☞ Use the /25 switch if you want the color display to be 25 lines long—it has the same effect as the /CO80 switch but requires less typing.

Syntax for Command-Line Mode

To run NCC directly from the DOS prompt after you have run it in full-screen mode and saved settings to a file, enter

NCC *filespec switches*

Description

The *filespec* parameter tells NCC which file contains the settings for your system's hardware. By including switches with *filespec* in the command statement, you can specify that only the switches' respective settings in the file are used.

The possible switches that you can use with *filespec* to run NCC directly from the DOS prompt are the following:

/COM*n*	sets the serial port configuration specified by *n* in *filespec*.
/CURSOR	sets the cursor configuration saved in *filespec*.
/DISPLAY	sets the video mode configuration saved in *filespec*.

/DOSCOLOR	sets the DOS colors saved in *filespec*.
/KEYRATE	sets the keystroke rate saved in *filespec*.
/PALETTE	sets the color configuration saved in *filespec*.
/SETALL	sets all the configuration settings contained in *filespec*.

NCD (NORTON CHANGE DIRECTORY)

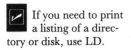 If you need to print a listing of a directory or disk, use LD.

Run from the DOS prompt, NCD allows you to change to another directory without having to type the complete path for the directory. NCD also has a full-screen mode that allows you to create, change, delete, or rename directories.

When you first run NCD, it creates a file called TREEINFO.NCD for that disk's directory structure. From then on, NCD refers to that file whenever you run it—it updates the directory structure information and checks it to find the file or directory that you specify in abbreviated form.

Syntax for Full-Screen Mode

To run NCD in full-screen mode, enter

NCD *switches*

NCD then displays the complete graphic listing of the current drive. To work with a particular directory, simply scroll to it and press F6 to rename it, F7 to make a subdirectory under it, or F8 to delete it. The directory that is highlighted when you exit NCD becomes the current directory.

Description

You can use the following as the *switches* parameter:

/R rereads the directory structure on the disk.

/N instructs NCD to ignore the changes made—to not write them to the TREEINFO.NCD file.

These next switches are used to set the display attributes for NCD's full-screen mode:

/Dn	where $n = 0$ reestablishes the default setting for 100 percent compatibles. where $n = 1$ enables use with BIOS-compatible machines.
/BW	sets the color display to monochrome.
/NOSNOW	removes the flickering seen on some CGA cards.

Syntax for Command-Line Mode

To create a directory directly from the DOS prompt, enter

NCD MD *directoryspec*

Similarly, you enter

NCD RD *directoryspec*

to remove a directory without running NCD in full-screen mode. You can also run NCD by entering

NCD *directoryspec switches*

This makes *directoryspec* current.

Description

directoryspec	tells NCD which directory to create, remove, or change to. You do not specify the directory's path; instead, you provide just enough of its name to make it unique so that NCD can identify it.
/R	rereads the directory structure on the disk. You include this switch only when you have used

DOS's MD, CD, or RD commands since the last time you ran NCD.

/N   instructs NCD to ignore the changes made—to not write them to the TREEINFO.NCD file.

NDD (NORTON DISK DOCTOR)

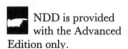
NDD is provided with the Advanced Edition only.

NDD finds and corrects physical errors on hard or floppy disks. You can run NDD in either full-screen or command-line mode. Each mode enables you to test the disk thoroughly or partially.

Syntax for Full-Screen Mode

When you enter

NDD *switches*

NDD's Main menu appears. You can choose between the Diagnose Disk and Commons Solutions selections for fixing your disk.

Description

If you know what is wrong, choose Common Solutions. You are then presented with four choices: Make a Disk Bootable, Recover from DOS's RECOVER, Revive a Defective Diskette, and Return to Main Menu. Be careful when using Make a Disk Bootable; it will erase whatever is in the system area to make room for the system files. It also copies the COMMAND.COM file to the disk. Revive a Defective Diskette reformats the disk without overwriting the original data.

Recover from DOS's RECOVER requires some explanation. In fact, when you choose this menu selection, a window containing a discussion of this feature appears. If you use RECOVER on a damaged disk, files are copied to the root directory and given generic names. In other words, the disk's directory structure is erased. Invoking Recover from DOS's RECOVER simply restores the directory structure and renames the files.

The following switches are used to set the display attributes for NDD's full-screen mode.

/D*n*	where *n* = 0 reestablishes the default setting for 100 percent compatibles. where *n* = 1 enables use with BIOS-compatible machines.
/BW	sets the color display to monochrome.
/NOSNOW	removes the flickering seen on some CGA cards.

Syntax for Command-Line Mode

To run NDD directly from the DOS prompt, enter

NDD *drive drive switches*

Description

These parameters modify the NDD command as follows:

drive	selects the drive to be tested. You can select more than one drive for testing at the same time if you separate each drive letter from the next by a space.
/QUICK	omits the test for bad data sectors on the disk.
/COMPLETE	includes the test for bad data sectors on the disk.
/R:*filename*	sends the NDD report to the file specified by *filename*.
/RA:*filename*	adds or appends the NDD report to *filename*.

NI (NORTON INTEGRATOR)

The Norton Integrator is a shell program for running the other utilities. If you are unsure of which commands to use, run this program and then select the program you want from its menu. When you highlight a program in the menu, information about it is displayed on the right side of the screen. Included in this information is a line telling you to get help on an individual program by selecting it and entering a question mark. The command syntax for the program will then be displayed on the screen. If you press F1 for help, you will see information about running NI, not about the other programs.

Syntax

> NI *switches*

Description

The following switches are used to set the display attributes for NI:

/D*n*	where *n* = 0 reestablishes the default setting for 100 percent compatibles. where *n* = 1 enables use with BIOS-compatible machines.
/BW	sets the color display to monochrome.
/NOSNOW	removes the flickering seen on some CGA cards.

NU (NORTON UTILITY)

The NU program is the heart of the Norton Utilities. The program provides access to all areas of your system's disks. You can recover deleted files with it. You can also edit directories, the FAT, and the partition table, all through NU's full-screen mode.

Syntax for Full-Screen Mode

To run NU in full-screen mode, enter

> NU *switches*

Its Main menu then appears, offering you these menu selections:

- Explore disk
- UnErase
- Disk information
- Return to DOS

To learn how to use the first three features, see the sections entitled "Explore Disk," "UnErase," and "Disk Information (DI)" in this appendix. Choosing Return to DOS ends NU and exits you to the DOS prompt.

Description

The following switches are used to set the display attributes for NU's full-screen mode:

/Dn where $n = 0$ reestablishes the default setting for 100 percent compatibles.
where $n = 1$ enables use with BIOS-compatible machines.

/BW   sets the color display to monochrome.

/NOSNOW   removes the flickering seen on some CGA cards.

Syntax for Command-Line Mode

To run NU directly from the DOS prompt, enter

NU *drive filespec switches*

Description

Once you have become familiar with NU's menu selections, you can include the following parameters to bypass some of the selection steps and run NU more quickly:

drive   tells NU which drive to use. If you do not specify a drive letter, NU uses the current drive.

filespec   specifies the file to use with NU. If you give the name of an existing DOS file, NU automatically runs Explore disk, opening the appropriate editor on the file. If you specify an erased file by using a question mark for its initial character, NU runs the UnErase feature for this file.

/M   runs NU in maintenance mode to bypass the initial scan of the DOS directory structure. You may use this switch when the directory structure has been lost or badly damaged.

/EBCDIC   tells NU that the file is in EBCDIC format. To toggle this switch on and off in NU, press Alt-F5.

/WS   toggles WordStar format (7 bits per character) on and off. When this switch is active, characters from the IBM extended character set are not displayed. To toggle this switch on and off in NU, press Alt-F6.

/P   displays text characters only, suppressing the display of IBM graphics characters. To toggle this switch on or off, press Alt-F2.

/X:*drives*   excludes the specified drives from absolute-sector processing. If you are having difficulty running NU in absolute-sector mode, use this switch to exclude allocated but nonexistent drives from the processing.

When you include the /P switch, you can use PrtSc in NU to generate a screen dump of the screen.

Zenith DOS always allocates drives D, E, and F even though they may not exist on your system. If you have a Zenith system, use the /X switch to exclude them.

QU (QUICK UNERASE)

QU automatically recovers deleted files, provided you have not written to the disk since the files were erased. If the erased file was on a floppy disk, you may even be able to use QU successfully after writing to the disk. It can't hurt to try using QU whenever you want to recover erased files; if it doesn't work, you can use NU's UnErase feature.

Although QU does not have a full-screen mode, it does have interactive and automatic modes. In interactive mode, QU lists information about the erased files it finds, prompts you to confirm that you want to restore each file individually, and asks you to provide the missing letter in the file's name. In automatic mode, QU tries to recover every erased file that matches the file specification and assigns the first letter that will make the recovered file's name unique.

Syntax

QU *filespec switches*

Description

Following is an explanation of QU's parameters:

filespec gives QU the name of the file to be recovered. When you include wildcards, QU tries to recover all files matching the specification. If you do not specify a name, QU will consider the command to be for all files (which is the same as using the *.* specification).

/A Unerases the file automatically.

SA (SCREEN ATTRIBUTES)

The Norton Utilities Version 4.5 includes the SA program in the BE (Batch Enhancer) utility. See the section entitled "Subcommands" under BE for further details.

SD (SPEED DISK)

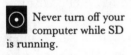
Never turn off your computer while SD is running.

SD generates a report on disk fragmentation. You can also use it to rewrite files to eliminate fragmentation and increase the disk's performance. To accomplish this, it minimizes the necessary movement of the read-write head by reorganizing the layout of the files and directories on the disk. You can even have some say in how this reorganization takes place, specifying where certain files and directories are placed.

You should run SD on your hard disk periodically—the disk will then run faster and you will prevent any unnecessary tie-ups of your machine later (SD can take a long time to complete when a disk hasn't been optimized recently). How often you need to run SD depends on the speed of your system and your needs, among other factors. To keep track of the hard disk's fragmentation, check SD's report frequently.

Syntax for Full-Screen Mode

When you enter

SD *switches*

a window appears, containing a dialog box that prompts you to select the drive to optimize, a menu in the lower-left corner that is currently inaccessible, a Status box, and a Legend box.

Description

When you select a drive, the dialog box closes and SD reads the disk information, presenting a graphic map of the disk when it has finished. The first selection in the menu, Optimize Disk, also becomes highlighted.

To invoke a complete optimization of the selected disk, simply press Enter. However, if you decide you want to optimize another disk, choose Change Drive from the menu. To see information about the disk and its usage, select the Disk Statistics menu item.

If you want to modify SD's operation, select Set Options instead. The Set Options menu will then be displayed. You can choose from seven selections: Optimization method, Directory order, Files to put first, Unmovable files, Show static files, Verify is OFF, and Exit and save options.

The following switches are used to set the display attributes for SD:

/Dn where $n = 0$ reestablishes the default setting for 100 percent compatibles.
                      where $n = 1$ enables use with BIOS-compatible machines.

| /BW | sets the color display to monochrome. |
| /NOSNOW | removes the flickering seen on some CGA cards. |

Syntax for Command-Line Mode

To run SD directly from the DOS prompt, enter

SD *drive directoryspec filespec switches*

Description

Back up your entire hard disk before optimizing it with SD for the first time.

Each of these parameters are optional. However, if you include the *drive* parameter, you cannot use the *directoryspec* or *filespec* parameter and vice versa—SD can take only one of the three. Following are descriptions of all of SD's parameters:

drive	instructs SD to use this drive.
directoryspec	provides the directory for SD to analyze or optimize.
filespec	provides the file for SD to analyze. You must include the /REPORT switch with this parameter so that SD can give its fragmentation report.
/REPORT	generates a disk fragmentation report but does not rewrite any of the files. You can abbreviate this switch to /R and get the same result.
/A	runs SD in automatic mode, which means *drive* (or the current drive if you omit a drive specification) is completely optimized. You cannot include the *directoryspec* or *filespec* parameter when you use this switch.
/P	pauses the display after each screenful.
/S	includes files in subdirectories in the report.
/T	gives totals only rather than a detailed report.
/C	selects complete optimization of the disk.

/D	selects directory optimization only. The disk is not entirely unfragmented, and unused areas are not collected together at the end of the disk.
/Q	selects the quick compression. Files are made contiguous, with no unused space in between. All new files will now be written at the end of the current files.
/U	partially unfragments files. Some files are left alone, and unused space will remain between some files.
/V	turns Verify on to ensure that the disk is read after each time SD writes to it.

For example, to have SD report on your hard disk's fragmentation, enter

SD C: /R

To compress the files on a floppy in drive A, enter

SD A: /Q

SF (SAFE FORMAT)

SF provides a faster, safer alternative to the DOS FORMAT command, making it easier to recover an accidentally reformatted disk. This is because SF does not overwrite existing data on the disk when it formats it. If you realize you need a file that was on the disk you just formatted, you can recover it with Quick UnErase or NU's UnErase feature if you formatted the disk with SF, whereas you cannot recover the file if you used DOS's FORMAT command.

Syntax for Full-Screen Mode

To run SF in full-screen mode, enter

SF

A window will then appear, containing statistics on the disk and a dialog box that prompts you to select the drive to format.

Description

After you choose the drive to format, you can select any of the menu items listed on the left side of the screen: Begin Format, Drive, Size, System Type, Volume Label, Format Mode, and Quit. By using these menu selections, you can tailor the format to the type of disk you have and label it.

The following switches are used to set the display attributes for SF:

/Dn   where $n = 0$ reestablishes the default setting for 100 percent compatibles.
where $n = 1$ enables use with BIOS-compatible machines.

/BW   sets the color display to monochrome.

/NOSNOW   removes the flickering seen on some CGA cards.

Syntax for Command-Line Mode

To run SF directly from the DOS prompt, enter

SF *drive switches*

Note that if you substituted SF for the DOS FORMAT command when you installed the Norton Utilities, you can also enter

FORMAT

to run SF.

Description

Following are the parameters you can use to specify a particular format for a disk from the command prompt:

drive   specifies which drive contains the disk to be formatted.

You can include SF with the /A switch in batch files to make formatting disks an efficient process.

/A	selects automatic mode, which means the disk is formatted without losing any of its data, the system files are not added to it, and no volume label is added. It will also format the disk to match the drive type.
/S	copies the DOS system files to the disk.
/B	leaves space on the disk for the DOS system files so you can add them later.
/V:*label*	adds the volume label specified by *label*.
/1	selects single-sided formatting.
/4	formats a 360K floppy disk in a 1.2Mb disk drive.
/8	formats 8 sectors per track.
/N*n*	selects the number of sectors per track, where *n* can equal 8, 9, 15, or 18 sectors per track.
/T*n*	selects the number of tracks, where *n* can equal 40 or 80 tracks.
/*size*	selects the size of the floppy disk. For example, use /720 for a 720K floppy disk.
/Q	selects the quick format. This just places a new system area on the disk, leaving everything else intact.
/D	selects the DOS format, which means all data is erased.
/C	selects the complete format for floppy disks. Any bad sectors are automatically reformatted. (Data is not erased though.)

SI (SYSTEM INFORMATION)

The SI program displays a report on your system's configuration and calculates several performance indicators.

Anytime you need to know how much memory you have available, run SI and check its report. For example, if you use many TSRs or buffers, run SI before you load them and then run it after you load them to find out how much memory they require.

Syntax

If you enter

SI

SI generates its entire report on the current drive.
On the other hand, if you enter

SI *drive switches*

you can instruct SI to modify the report.

Description

Following are explanations of the parameters you can use with SI:

drive	tells SI which drive to check. If you do not specify a drive letter, SI uses the current drive.
/A	runs SI in ANSI mode and skips certain BIOS-specific routines.
/N	skips the live memory test, which will require you to reboot if it fails.
/LOG	prepares the report in a form suitable for sending to a printer or to a file.

TM (TIME MARK)

TM records and reports elapsed time from up to 4 separate timers. This is handy for keeping track of your work on the computer. You can even include TM commands in batch files so that the time information is automatically recorded daily. For more information on how to do this, see Chapter 8's discussion of TM.

Syntax

To run TM, enter

TM START STOP *comment switches*

Description

Here is an explanation of TM's parameters:

START   resets the stopwatch, displaying the time and date with which it begins.

STOP   displays the time since the last TM START command was given and does not reset the stopwatch.

comment   provides the text the TM utility displays when the command is executed. If *comment* contains spaces, enclose it in quotes. Include this switch when you run TM from batch files and send the commands' output to a file. This way, you will be able to differentiate the output from the separate TM commands.

/C*n*   selects stopwatch *n*, where *n* is between 1 and 4. If you do not specify a number, the first stopwatch is used.

/L   displays TM information in the upper-left corner of the screen. If you omit this switch, TM's information is displayed in the top-right corner of the screen.

/LOG   prepares the output of TM in a form suitable for printing or for redirecting to a file.

/N   instructs TM to suppress the display of the current time and date, showing elapsed time intervals only.

Always include comments when you are running more than one stopwatch from batch files—you will then be able to keep the watches straight.

TS (TEXT SEARCH)

TS can locate specified text in one or more files. You can also use it to search across a disk or limit your search to a disk's erased file space.

Syntax

If you enter

TS

TS will prompt you to specify where to search and what to search for.
To provide these instructions directly from the DOS prompt, enter

TS *filespec "search string" switches*

Description

Here is an explanation of what these parameters do:

filespec	selects the file or files to be searched. You can use the DOS wildcard characters.
"search string"	specifies text to be searched for. If *"search string"* contains spaces, it must be enclosed in quotes. Because TS is not case sensitive (unless you use the /CS switch), you may get more matches than you anticipated.
/A	automates the search process, continuing to look for more matches until it does not find any.
/CS	forces the TS search to be case sensitive.
/EBCDIC	tells TS that the files being searched are in EBCDIC form rather than ASCII.
/LOG	prepares the output of TS in a form suitable for printing or redirecting to a file.
/WS	excludes the ASCII characters from 128 to 255 from the search.

When searching files, you can use the following switches:

/S	includes subdirectories in the search.

/T   lists the names of the files that contain text matching the search string. It does not display the context of the match.

When searching the disk or the erased file space, you can include these switches:

/D   searches the whole disk.

/E   searches the erased data space of the disk.

/C*n*   starts the search at cluster *n*.

UD (UNREMOVE DIRECTORY)

UD recovers erased directories and attempts to recover the files that were previously in the directory.

Syntax

If you enter

UD

UD assumes that you want to recover all subdirectories that were erased from the current directory. If it can't find any, it will give you a message stating that no directories were found. If it does find a removed directory, it displays information about the directory and prompts you to specify the first letter of its name.

You can also enter

UD *drive directoryspec*

to run UD for specific directories.

Description

The parameters that you can use with UD are the following:

drive   tells UD to check the specified drive's root directory. If you do not specify a drive letter, UD checks the current drive.

directoryspec   provides UD with the complete path name of the removed directory to recover. If you omit this switch, UD will try to recover all removed directories in the current directory.

After UD has recovered the directories, it recovers the directory's listing—the erased files it used to have. It presents the erased files' entries a group at a time, allowing you accept or reject each group's recovery.

UNERASE

UnErase is a part of the NU utility, so you must run NU in full-screen mode to use it. UnErase enables you to make partial recoveries of files that have had some of their data overwritten. You can use this feature when the Norton Utilities QU program does not work. You may not always be able to salvage your erased files, but UnErase provides the surest method of recovery.

Syntax

To reach Unerase, enter

    NU

The Recover erased file menu then appears. Make sure you are in the drive and directory that contained the erased file. If you are not, use the Change drive or directory menu selection to move there. Otherwise, press Enter to choose Select erased file. Notice that the unerase menu choice is unavailable since you haven't yet specified a file.

Description

When you choose the Select erased file menu selection, you are prompted to choose one of the files listed on the screen (if there are any). If the file you want is listed, highlight it and provide its missing initial letter. You will then see more information about the erased file, including the likelihood of its recovery. If you don't see the file in the list, select Create file. You will then be prompted for the file's name.

After specifying a file, you are returned to the Recover Erased file menu. Choose Erase menu to display the Find erased file's data screen. This window screen contains two menus, offering all sorts of means to recover files. If UnErase told you previously that the file could probably be recovered, press Tab to move to the right-hand menu and select All clusters automatically. The remaining selections on this menu enable you or UnErase to specify the erased file's location more exactly.

You can use the selections on the left-hand menu once you have specified the location. If the necessary number of clusters are found, which you can determine from the Clusters added to file line, choose Save erased file. You can then leave NU safely; the file will have been restored.

VL (VOLUME LABEL)

VL allows you to view, add, change, or delete a disk's volume label. The volume label can be up to 11 characters long, include spaces, and have lowercase as well as uppercase letters.

Syntax

If you enter

VL

you will be shown the current label (if there is one) and prompted to edit it. To include a space in the new label when you are running VL in this prompted mode, simply press the space bar—you do not need to enclose the label in quotes.

However, if you enter

VL *drive text*

and *text* contains spaces, you must enclose it in quotes.

Description

You can use the following parameters when you want to bypass the text-entry prompt and enter the label directly from the DOS prompt:

drive   tells VL which drive to label. If you do not specify a drive letter, VL uses the current drive.

text   specifies the text for the volume label. If *text* contains spaces, it must be contained in quotes.

WIPEDISK

WIPEDISK overwrites the erased and unused parts of a disk with a special code to ensure that old data on the disk can never be recovered. Use this program when you need to get rid of an entire disk of confidential data. Be very careful though—this program overwrites every part of the disk, and nothing can be done to reverse its effects.

Syntax

If you enter

WIPEDISK

you are told that you must specify a drive and are returned to the DOS prompt.

When you enter

WIPEDISK *drive switches*

WIPEDISK lists the current setting for its operation and prompts you to confirm that you want to proceed.

When you interrupt WIPEDISK before it has completed its operation (by pressing Ctrl-Break), some or all of the data may be preserved.

Description

Here are the choices you have for WIPEDISK's parameters:

drive   specifies the drive letter.

If you regularly use WIPEDISK with its /E switch, be careful that you don't omit or mistype the /E switch. One preventive method is to include the command in a batch file and verify that you have typed the command correctly before you run it. By running the command from a batch file, you will never lose hours of work from a simple typo.

/E   specifies that only the erased or unused data space should be overwritten. Your current files will not be wiped when you include this switch.

/Gn   selects a government-specified algorithm for wiping, where n determines the number of times the wipe operation is performed. (The default is 3.)

/LOG   formats the output of WIPEDISK for printing or redirecting to a file.

/Rn   sets the repeat factor for the number of times the data will be overwritten; the default is 1.

/Vn   sets the value to be used for overwriting and can be any number from 0 to 255. The default is 0 unless you have included the /G switch, in which case /Vn equals 246 or F6 hex.

If you use the /G switch, the overwritten disk will need to be reformatted before it can be used again.

WIPEFILE

WIPEFILE overwrites selected files so that they cannot be read or recovered. Use this program to erase confidential data files when they are mixed in with other files that you want to keep. Because WIPEFILE overwrites both the specified files' data spaces and entries, you cannot use Quick Unerase or NU's Erase feature to recover wiped files.

If you run WIPEFILE to remove hidden, system, and read-only files, WIPEFILE will automatically stop to ask you to confirm that you want to remove them.

Syntax

If you enter

WIPEFILE

you are told that you must specify a file (or files) and are returned to the DOS prompt.

To run WIPEFILE, enter

WIPEFILE *filespec switches*

WIPEFILE will stop for confirmation before it executes your command.

Description

The parameters you can include with WIPEFILE are as follows:

filespec   selects the file for WIPEFILE. You can include wildcards.

/G*n*   selects a government-specified algorithm for wiping, where *n* establishes the number of times the data is overwritten; the default is 3.

/LOG   formats the output of WIPEFILE for printing or redirecting to a file.

/N   does not wipe the file. Instead it erases it, just like the DOS ERASE or DEL command would.

/P   asks for confirmation before deleting and wiping each file.

/R*n*   sets the repeat factor for the number of times the data will be overwritten; the default is 1.

/S   extends the operation to subdirectories.

/V*n*   sets the value to be used for overwriting, which can be any number from 0 to 255. The default is 0 unless you have specified the /G switch in which case /V*n* equals 246 or F6 hex.

APPENDIX *B*

DOS, WHICH IS SHORT FOR DISK OPERATING SYSTEM, is the operating system most commonly found on PCs. When I refer to DOS in this book, I mean the disk operating system used by IBM microcomputers and the range of IBM-compatible machines. An *operating system* is simply a collection of software and firmware computer programs that makes the computer's hardware usable. Hardware provides computing power, but it is the operating system that provides access to this power. Other operating systems, such as XENIX or Concurrent DOS, can also run on PC hardware, but they are nowhere near as prevalent as DOS.

You can think of the operating system as a resource manager, acting as a go-between for you and your system's hardware. It performs many useful functions such as defining the user interface, detecting and recovering from errors, managing storage and input and output devices, and organizing data traffic to and from the microprocessor.

THE ORGANIZATION OF YOUR COMPUTER'S RESOURCES

The main task of any computer operating system is to manage the resources of the computer to achieve good performance. The computer has three main components: hardware, software, and firmware. Hardware is the computer itself—the screen, the keyboard, the hard and floppy disks, and the microprocessor. Software consists of computer programs that run on the hardware. For example, operating systems, word processors, spreadsheets, and language compilers are all software. The definition of firmware is less precise. It is usually considered to be software that executes from a very high speed hardware-storage device that is not a disk drive or RAM (random-access memory). Commonly used firmware programs are burned onto ROM (read-only memory) or PROM (programmable read-only memory). For example, your hard-disk controller has a considerable amount of firmware on it, which enables it to do its job properly. Your computer also contains a boot-ROM, a ROM that contains a short program used to load the operating system when you turn on the machine. As this program is written into nonvolatile ROM, it is not lost when power is removed; it is always available.

A SHORT HISTORY OF DOS

There were several operating systems available for small computers before DOS, of which CP/M is probably the best known. CP/M was the standard operating system for 8-bit computers, but all that changed with the arrival of the IBM PC, which contained a 16-bit Intel 8088 central processing unit (CPU). We can use DOS Version 1.0 as the starting point for this overview of DOS.

VERSION 1.X

The first version of DOS was nowhere near as powerful as DOS is today; however, since it relied on a FAT to keep track of a disk's files, it ran significantly faster than CP/M. DOS 1.0 was released in 1981, a joint venture between IBM and Microsoft. It was designed to work with single-sided floppy disks and could not support hard disks. Each disk could hold a maximum of 112 files. A file was only date-stamped, not time-stamped. The TIME and DATE commands were external programs instead of part of the COMMAND.COM user interface. BASIC contained several bugs that were fixed in Version 1.05.

VERSION 2.X

DOS 2.0, which was introduced in 1983, was a significant improvement over Version 1.X. Its most notable features were its hard-disk support and hierarchical directory structure. Many new commands were also added to DOS to help deal with hard disks, such as FDISK to partition the hard disk for different operating systems, and BACKUP and RESTORE to save and reload the contents of the hard disk. The new hierarchical structure allowed files to be grouped together in a single logical unit called a *directory*. Directories, which remain in force in modern DOS versions, could contain other directories or subdirectories as well as files. Files could be moved between directories, and directories could be created with MKDIR or removed with RMDIR. DIR /P made directory listings that paused when the screen is full, and DIR /W made a wide listing of file names.

Many of Version 2.X's new features were borrowed from UNIX, the operating system that was written at Bell Laboratories by a small group of programmers in the early 1970s. Concepts such as the standard input device (the keyboard) and the standard output device (the screen), hierarchical directory structures, pipes, and filters all originated in UNIX.

The concept of using the CONFIG.SYS file to configure the PC hardware automatically at startup was also first introduced in Version 2.X; the programmers at Microsoft came up with this idea so that all types of devices could be used with DOS without becoming part of DOS's programming, which would make DOS too large to manage.

Because Version 2.0 incorporated so many new features and drastically increased Version 1.X's disk-storage capacity, it was riddled with bugs. IBM released several new 2.X versions to remedy these errors and provide some support for international time, date, keyboard, and currency formats.

VERSION 3.X

Version 3.0 was introduced in 1984, providing the first legitimate 16-bit-system, the PC/AT. In addition to establishing 1.2Mb floppy disks, Version 3.0 provided a new device driver to make a portion of memory work like a disk drive. Its subsequent versions, 3.1, 3.2, and 3.3, all added specific features to support new hardware.

Version 3.1 contained enhancements to several commands that made them compatible with local-area networks. Two new commands were also introduced: JOIN, which allows a drive to act like a subdirectory, and SUBST, which allows a directory to act as a drive.

You can think of XCOPY as an evolved form of the COPY command: it runs faster and can duplicate directory structures, creating copies of the subdirectories automatically when you copy the parent directory.

Version 3.2 added support for the 3½-inch 720K disk drives that were used in several lap-top computers. Two new copying features were introduced: REPLACE, which allows files to be copied selectively, and XCOPY, which copies files and entire directories selectively.

DOS 3.3, released with IBM's new PS/2 series of computers in 1987, added many commands for the new hardware. New files were distributed to work with the new VGA screens. Support became available for the 3½-inch 1.44Mb disks, and the MODE command supported up to four communications ports at rates of up to 19,200 baud. Previous versions of DOS only supported two ports at rates of up to 9,600 baud. DOS 3.3's BACKUP and RESTORE commands also ran faster.

As the operating system has expanded with each release, the accompanying technical documentation has also improved dramatically. IBM now provides excellent documentation, although a lot of the material is of primary interest to those who want to write programs.

VERSION 4.X—THE LATEST VERSION

DOS Version 4.0, released in the U.S. in 1988 and slightly earlier in Europe, adds another layer to the operating system with its new shell, which can be invoked from a batch file. The DOS shell makes it easier to manage file and directories, and can be customized to handle all your applications on a menu-driven system. DOS 4.0 supports the Lotus/Intel/Microsoft 4.0 Expanded Memory Specification, allowing the memory used for BUFFERS and FILES to be taken from expanded memory. Applications not specifically written for EMS still cannot use expanded memory. The new MEM command reports on the amount of conventional, expanded, and extended memory it can find. Many other DOS commands have been enhanced, including FORMAT, CHKDSK, APPEND, MODE, TIME, and GRAPHICS.

ARE THERE ANY OTHER DIFFERENCES?

Generally speaking, an application program that is written to run on a particular DOS version will run on that version and all later versions. However, the program will not be able to take advantage of the new features available in the later versions. Likewise, there is no guarantee that a program written for a more recent version of DOS will run on an earlier version.

The DOS programs themselves are usually not compatible with those of other DOS versions. For example, if you try to use the external programs from DOS 2.X with DOS 3.X's COMMAND.COM program, you will probably get an error message indicating that you are using the wrong version of DOS. Each version of COMMAND.COM and the system files have particular requirements, and the external commands are designed to match these characteristics precisely.

The DOS version supplied with your computer may differ slightly from the standard MS-DOS release, depending on the company that manufactured your computer. Some manufacturers add features not found elsewhere, while other manufacturers do not implement the full set of commands. Still other manufacturers choose to stay with a particular DOS version and will not upgrade their products. If you are in doubt as to which DOS release runs on your machine, consult your local dealer or the manufacturer of your computer for more details.

If this brief review has piqued your interest in the workings of DOS, consult the *DOS User's Desktop Companion* by Judd Robbins (SYBEX, 1988). This book covers all aspects of DOS with lots of solid, up-to-date information.

WHERE DO THE NORTON UTILITIES FIT IN?

As no system is perfect, users were not entirely content with DOS. Programmmers, in particular, were quick to fault its shortcomings— and more important, to invent solutions of their own to remedy them. The Norton Utilities has evolved from one such programmer's ingenuity. Initially, Peter Norton presented the UnErase feature, becoming the first to provide a means of retrieving what was permanently lost in DOS. This program was released in 1982 (when DOS 1.X was on the market) and quickly caught on, establishing the base of the first version of the Norton Utilities. In subsequent releases the Norton Utilities provided workable solutions to other DOS oversights; for example, NCC contains graphics settings for an EGA monitor (DOS still hasn't offered adequate settings with its MODE command.)

In addition to filling DOS's unmet needs, the Norton Utilities gradually acquired more features that duplicated (or improved on) equivalent commands in DOS. Having these features in Norton makes it more efficient to use—you no longer have to switch between DOS and Norton as often. Instead you can run the Norton Utilities and accomplish most of your daily tasks.

BACKING UP AND RESTORING FILES

APPENDIX C

THROUGHOUT THIS BOOK I REMIND YOU TO MAKE A backup copy of your entire system as a preliminary step for some operations. For example, before running the SD (Speed Disk) utility on your hard disk for the first time, I suggest you back it up. A *backup* is an up-to-date copy of all your files that you can use to reload your system in the event of an accident. This is purely insurance against anything untoward happening to the hundreds or possibly thousands of files you might have on your hard disk. If the unthinkable did occur—you lost all of your system's data and didn't have backup copies of it—it could take you weeks or even months to recreate your system, if indeed it could be recreated.

In this appendix I describe in detail how to use several DOS commands to back up your files so that this never happens to you. These commands all perform specific copying operations, and you can choose the command that best suits your needs. When I employ the term *backup copies,* I generally mean any file duplicates that you keep on hand in the event of a loss of data. When I refer to backup copies made with the BACKUP command, the term takes on a more precise meaning; the BACKUP command creates files in such a way that they can't be used as is—you must first copy them back to your system with DOS's RESTORE command, and then they become usable.

WHEN TO BACK UP

You should get into the habit of backing up your system regularly so that you are never required to do any extra work as a result of damaged or missing files. How often you should make a backup depends on how much work you do on the computer. For example, a computer programmer creates a lot of data during a week and stands to lose a lot of work in the event of an accident. Because of this, she will back her files up on a daily basis, perhaps even twice a day. A person running what-if financial analyses might back up his work every two or three days because the amount of data generated in three days could be easily recreated if necessary. A person who writes only the occasional memo can probably get by with backing up his system once a week. Think of it this way:

- You should make a backup copy of your files just before the point where recreating that data is going to create a considerable amount of extra work for you.

There are several other occasions when you should back up your entire system. If you are going to move your computer, you should first make a complete backup of the hard disk. You should do this even if you are only moving to the office next door, as your hard disk may not survive the trip. Similarly, if you are sending your computer in for any kind of service work, including work on the disk drives, verify that you have a complete system backup first. Some large service companies resort to issuing you another computer or disk drive. Imagine not getting your hard disk back again and not having an up-to-date copy of its contents.

Whenever you need to remove any directories and their files because you are running out of space on your hard disk is another time you should back it up completely. Make a backup before making the deletions and carefully note the date you made it. You may need these files again sometime. Similarly, if a person leaves your company after using a computer for some time, a complete backup is a good way to preserve that person's work, allowing the replacement person to start work without any anxieties about the files on his disk.

Finally, if you are going to run a program like the Norton Utilities Speed Disk, which optimizes your hard disk's file layout by rewriting all your files, be sure to back up your entire hard disk before you start running the program. There is always that slim possibility that your hard disk and the optimizing program are incompatible. Furthermore, power outages and brownouts can occur at anytime, even during the optimization itself (which would be tragic).

If you have only a small number of files on your system or you work strictly with floppy disks, you can use DISKCOPY, COPY, or XCOPY to make backup copies of your files. In the next sections I describe how to use each of these commands.

USING DISKCOPY TO BACK UP FLOPPY DISKS

 You cannot use DISKCOPY to copy hard disks.

The DOS DISKCOPY command makes an exact duplicate copy of your original floppy disk's contents. DISKCOPY copies the low-level data of your disk sector by sector, rather than file by file. For example, if your original disk is a system disk, your copy will be also. You don't even have to format the destination disk; DISKCOPY takes care of it for you during the copy process. I recommend that you use unformatted disks with DISKCOPY to save time. This way, you will avoid copying a nonsystem disk to a system disk, which changes it to a nonsystem disk, and having to format another system disk, as you are short one.

If drive A is current and you type

DISKCOPY

without specifying a drive letter, DISKCOPY will prompt you to change source and target disks in and out of drive A during the copy process (see Figure C.1).

```
C:\>DISKCOPY

Insert SOURCE diskette in drive A:

Press any key when ready . . .

Copying 40 tracks
9 Sectors/Track, 2 Sides

Insert TARGET diskette in drive A:

Press any key when ready . . .

Copy another diskette (Y/N)?NO

C:\>
```

Figure C.1: Using just one floppy-disk drive with DISKCOPY

If DISKCOPY encounters an area of the destination disk that it cannot read, it displays a message showing where the error is, continues with the copy process, and when it has finished copying, it tells you that the destination disk may not be usable. At the end of a successful copy, DISKCOPY asks if you want to make another disk. Answer Y for yes when you have several floppy disks to copy and have a stack of blank disks ready to continue the process. If you had just the one disk to copy, answer N for no.

The DISKCOPY command works best for floppy disks that contain lots of unfragmented data; the COPY command would take too long to copy this type of disk. Note, however, that you wouldn't want to use DISKCOPY for disks whose files are very fragmented, as it will duplicate the disk's contents exactly.

If you have two floppy-disk drives, you can also speed up the DISKCOPY operation by eliminating the switching of disks necessary for using just one drive. For example, enter

> Use the SD (Speed Disk) utility to unfragment your files.

    DISKCOPY A: B:

to copy the contents of the disk in drive A to the disk in drive B without changing any disks.

You can compare the disk made by DISKCOPY with the source disk and verify the readability of the new disk by running the DISK-COMP command.

To compare the disk in drive B to the disk in drive A that you just copied, enter

    DISKCOMP B: A:

DISKCOMP reads the disk's data track by track and reports any errors it finds in terms of side and track number.

You can also compare the source disk when you have only one floppy-disk drive by entering

    DISKCOMP A: A:

You will be prompted to insert the second disk into drive A when DISKCOMP is ready.

Although DISKCOPY is faster than COPY, it does have several drawbacks. Most important, it can copy data to bad areas on the destination disk, which means you have to redo the copying operation with another disk or fix the damaged disk with the NDD utility.

You also cannot use DISKCOPY with

- hard disks
- network drives
- differently sized source and destination disks

To copy files from one disk type to another, use the COPY command.

USING COPY TO MAKE BACKUPS

If you want to back up files selectively, choosing a few files from a disk or a directory from your hard disk, you can use the COPY command. COPY copies files by name rather than making a duplicate copy of the original disk. As always, you need to verify that the destination disk has enough space available on it for the files you want to copy. If you are using a disk that already contains data, you need to check it. You can use the FS (File Size) utility to do this. For instance, to determine whether your .BAT files will fit on the used disk in drive B, enter

```
FS *.BAT B:
```

from the directory your batch files are in. When copying files to disks containing files, you need to be careful that you don't overwrite the disk's existing files. That is, if you are making a backup copy of a directory to a disk that holds the directory's previous backup, all files with matching names will be overwritten by the new copies. When you want to keep your backup versions separate, the easiest thing to do is use different disks.

Once you have chosen the correct disk for the destination disk, you can run the COPY command and name the files individually.

You can also specify the DOS wildcard characters instead of complete file names. For example, to copy all the files in the BATCH directory on drive C to the disk in drive A, make BATCH the current directory and type

COPY *.* A:

During the copy process your files are read file by file and then rewritten to the disk in drive A, as shown in Figure C.2. This means that the COPY command eliminates file fragmentation; the backup files' clusters are written consecutively for each file.

```
C:\BATCH>COPY *.* A:
BU.BAT
MENU.BAT
PCOBU.BAT
TEST.BAT
MENU.TXT
        5 File(s) copied

C:\BATCH>
```

Figure C.2: COPY displaying the name of each file copied

USING XCOPY TO BACK UP FILES

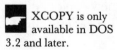 XCOPY is only available in DOS 3.2 and later.

The XCOPY command is even more powerful and faster than the COPY command. XCOPY uses as much free memory in the computer as possible during the copy process. Instead of reading a file, writing it to disk, and then reading the next file (as COPY does), XCOPY reads as many files as it can into memory and then writes them to disk. As with the COPY command, you must ensure that there is enough space on the destination disk for all the files you want to back up with XCOPY.

Although many DOS users automatically invoke COPY from habit when duplicating files, XCOPY is the better command. The only time you should use COPY (unless you have a DOS version earlier than 3.2) is when you are copying just one file— you'll have one less letter to type.

XCOPY also has several switches associated with it that make it more flexible. These switches are shown in Table C.1. In particular, running XCOPY with its /S switch is invaluable for backing up your hard disk. For example, if you enter

XCOPY *.* A: /S

when drive C's root directory is current, your entire hard disk is copied since /S tells XCOPY to copy all subdirectories of the root. When you run out of space on the floppy in drive A, insert a new, blank floppy and rerun the command. XCOPY will not recopy the files it already copied.

On the other hand, when you want to back up most files in a large directory, XCOPY's /P switch comes in handy. Supposing the directory you want to back up is current, you can enter

XCOPY *.* A: /P

Table C.1: XCOPY's Switches

SWITCH	FUNCTION
/A	Copies only those files whose archive bit is set.
/D	Copies only those files whose date is the same or later than the date specified.
/E	Creates corresponding subdirectories, including empty ones, on the destination disk when used with the /S switch.
/M	Copies files whose archive bit is set and clears the bit.
/P	Prompts you before copying each file.
/S	Copies files in subdirectories.
/V	Forces DOS to check that all files have been written correctly.
/W	Prompts you for a keystroke before copying, allowing you to insert a new disk.

and XCOPY will prompt you for each file to confirm that you want to copy it. You can then instruct XCOPY not to duplicate the few files that you don't want to back up.

Copying files with the command

XCOPY *.* A: /M

creates backups of only those files that have been modified since the last time you copied them (with XCOPY or BACKUP). To back up only those files that have been modified and not instruct XCOPY to reset their archive bit, which shows that they have been copied, enter

XCOPY *.* A: /A

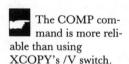

The COMP command is more reliable than using XCOPY's /V switch.

You can use the COMP command to compare the results of a COPY or XCOPY operation to ensure that the files are the same and that the copied file is readable. To compare two files, enter

COMP A:MYFILE.TXT B:MYFILE.TXT

This compares the contents of the original MYFILE.TXT on drive A with the copy of MYFILE.TXT on drive B. To compare a set of files on drives A and B, enter

COMP A:*.* B:

This compares each file by name on the source disk with its copy on drive B. Some versions of DOS also provide the command FILCOMP for comparing files.

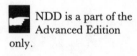

NDD is a part of the Advanced Edition only.

If COMP does report errors, run the Norton Utilities' NDD program to check the destination disk. If it has lots of bad sectors, you may want to use NDD's Revive a Defective Diskette feature, or you may deem it safer to throw out the disk and repeat the copying operation to a fresh disk.

BACKING UP HARD DISKS

As you have seen, DISKCOPY and COPY have limited usefulness when it comes to backing up your files. XCOPY, on the other hand, can duplicate your entire hard disk quite easily. The only drawback to using this command is that it can easily require an enormous quantity of floppy disks. One alternative is to use the DOS command designed for backing up hard disks, the BACKUP command. BACKUP condenses the files, requiring less disks for storage and the RESTORE command to make the backup files usable again.

USING THE BACKUP COMMAND

BACKUP allows you to copy a file or a group of files to floppy disks (or to another hard disk) for archival purposes. The BACKUP command keeps track of which file is where on the backup floppy disks for you.

The general syntax of the BACKUP command is

BACKUP *source destination switches*

If you do not use any of the optional parameters, BACKUP will back up all the files in the current directory. (You must always specify the destination drive.)

To back up all the files in your word processing directory, specify the directory, including its path, as the first parameter. If you do not specify any files, DOS copies all the files in the directory to the backup disk. For example, enter

BACKUP C:\WS4 A:

DOS responds with the message

Insert Archive Diskette 01 in Drive A:

WARNING! All Files Will Be Deleted!
Press Any Key to Continue, Control-C To Abort

The exact wording of the BACKUP prompts depends on the version of DOS you are using.

This short warning gives you the chance to confirm that you have inserted the right disk in drive A before DOS overwrites everything on the disk. Pressing the Enter key starts the backup process. DOS lists the complete path name of each file on the screen as it is written to the backup disk. If you have more files to back up than will fit on a single disk, DOS prompts you to load another disk with the message

Insert Archive Diskette 02 in Drive A:

These steps are shown in Figure C.3. As you can see, DOS again warns you that the contents of the disk BACKUP is writing to will be overwritten.

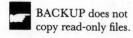

BACKUP does not copy read-only files.

During the BACKUP process, DOS will continue to ask for more disks until the entire directory has been backed up. You should carefully order and label each disk with its disk number, the date of the backup, a note of any switches you used, and the total number of disks in this backup. All this is necessary because when you restore the backup copies to your hard disk, the disks must be loaded in exactly the same order in which you made them.

With versions of the BACKUP command before DOS 3.3, you had to ensure that you had a sufficient number of formatted disks available before you invoked BACKUP—it used to abort the entire backup when it encountered an unformatted disk. In DOS 3.3 and later versions, you can include the /F switch to make the BACKUP command format the disk before backing it up. This useful switch can save you a lot of time, as you don't have to calculate how many backup disks you will need before you start the process. The DOS FORMAT command must be available via the current PATH setting for the /F switch to work.

```
C:\WS4>BACKUP C:\WS4 A:

Insert Archive Diskette Ø1 in Drive A:
WARNING: All Files Will Be Deleted!
Press Any Key To Continue, Control-C To Abort

  1-15-87  8:12a    325330   C:\WS4\WFBG.SYN
  7-19-89 10:35a     78336   C:\WS4\WS.EXE

Insert Archive Diskette Ø2 in Drive A:
WARNING: All Files Will Be Deleted!
Press Any Key To Continue, Control-C To Abort
```

Figure C.3: The BACKUP command prompts you for another disk when the first is full.

Do not have the DOS commands SUBST, JOIN, APPEND, or ASSIGN active when you use BACKUP, or you may not be able to restore the files properly.

When BACKUP copies a file to the destination disk, it clears the archive bit in the original file's attribute byte. By doing so, it indicates that the file has been archived (backed up). BACKUP and RESTORE will check the archive bit's status when they perform certain operations. For example, BACKUP refers to it when you include the /M switch in its command. If the archive bit is still clear, the /M switch tells BACKUP to ignore this file. If you have modified the file, which will set the archive bit again, the /M switch tells BACKUP to copy the file. RESTORE also uses the archive bit to make sure that it doesn't overwrite a new version of the file with an old version. (We'll examine these situations in more detail shortly.)

The files made by BACKUP are not simple reproductions of the original files. When you use the BACKUP command in DOS 3.3 or later, all your files are combined into one single file called BACKUP.*nnn* on each disk, where *nnn* corresponds to the disk number. The first disk's files have the extension 001, the next has the extension of .002, and so on. A second file CONTROL.*nnn* contains the actual file names and lengths, as well as a description of their directory structure. This set of files on each disk contain a complete description of all the files you have backed up. The RESTORE command refers to these files to tell the backup disks apart.

To differentiate your sets of backup files easily, label them with their disk number and creation date, storing each set separately.

You cannot use the DOS DEL or ERASE commands to delete files made by BACKUP because the command makes these files read-only when it creates them. Since BACKUP does this by setting the read-only bit in the attribute byte, you could erase them if you first reset their attribute bits. (See Chapter 7 for a complete discussion of attributes.) You can also recover the disk space used by these files by reformatting the disk with the SF utility or the DOS FORMAT command. (Only do this when you no longer need the files.)

Because some application programs don't work well after they have been backed up and restored with DOS's BACKUP and RESTORE commands, you may find it easier to back up these applications by duplicating the original program disks with DISKCOPY or COPY and keeping the copied set in a safe place, separate from the safe place for the original disks. (This is what I recommended you do in Chapter 1 for the Norton Utilities disks.) If anything ever happens to your hard-disk versions of these programs, you can then reinstall them from their duplicate sets.

BACKING UP SELECTED FILES

You do not have to back up a complete directory every time; you can also back up a part of a directory, simply by specifying the appropriate file names. You can also use the DOS wildcard characters. To back up all the *.EXE files in the NORTON directory, for example, make the NORTON directory the current directory and enter

    BACKUP C:\NORTON*.EXE A:

DOS will now copy the files that match this specification to your backup disk in drive A, as shown in Figure C.4.

Keep in mind that backing up selectively means you will have to restore all your files selectively if anything happens to your whole disk—this could be very time-consuming.

USING SWITCHES WITH BACKUP

There are several useful switches you can use with the BACKUP command, and these are shown in Table C.2.

```
C:\NORTON>BACKUP C:\NORTON\*.EXE A:

Insert Archive Diskette 01 in Drive A:
WARNING: All Files Will Be Deleted!
Press Any Key To Continue, Control-C To Abort

10-16-88  4:50p    44244   C:\NORTON\FR.EXE
10-16-88  4:50p   116276   C:\NORTON\NDD.EXE
10-16-88  4:50p   140616   C:\NORTON\NU.EXE
10-16-88  4:50p    36000   C:\NORTON\DS.EXE
10-16-88  4:50p    21080   C:\NORTON\DT.EXE
10-16-88  4:50p     9020   C:\NORTON\FF.EXE

Insert Archive Diskette 02 in Drive A:
WARNING: All Files Will Be Deleted!
Press Any Key To Continue, Control-C To Abort
```

Figure C.4: Specifying which files in the NORTON directory are to be backed up

Table C.2: BACKUP's Switches

Switch	Function
/A	Adds files to a backup disk.
/D:*date*	Backs up files by date.
/F	Formats the destination disk if required.
/L	Creates a log file.
/M	Backs up modified files.
/S	Backs up subdirectories.
/T:*time*	Backs up files by time on date specified by /D. Specify a for a.m. or p for p.m.

ADDING FILES TO AN EXISTING BACKUP DISK   Sometimes it is useful to be able to add files to an existing backup disk. Usually the BACKUP command erases the original contents of the disk before starting to make the backup. By including the /A switch, you can add your new files to the end of the first backup, and the original files from the first backup will not be overwritten.

To add more word processing files from the WS4 directory to an existing backup disk, enter

    BACKUP C:\WS4 A: /A

and DOS will add the new files to the BACKUP.001 and CONTROL.001 files.

BACKING UP SUBDIRECTORIES   You can run BACKUP with the /S switch to back up files in a directory's subdirectories as well as its own files. For example, to back up all the files in the WS4 directory's BOOK directory and the files in its subdirectories, enter

    BACKUP C:\WS4\BOOK A: /S

Supposing BOOK has a subdirectory called TEXT, you might get the results shown in Figure C.5.

```
C:\>BACKUP C:\WS4\BOOK A:/S

Insert Archive Diskette 01 in Drive A:
WARNING: All Files Will Be Deleted!
Press Any Key To Continue, Control-C To Abort

 1-19-89 11:58a     25600   C:\WS4\BOOK\TEXT\CHAPTER.1
11-18-89 12:18p     56832   C:\WS4\BOOK\TEXT\CHAPTER.2
11-19-89  3:43p     59136   C:\WS4\BOOK\TEXT\CHAPTER.3
11-16-89  4:56p     46464   C:\WS4\BOOK\TEXT\CHAPTER.4
11-15-89  3:44p     77056   C:\WS4\BOOK\TEXT\CHAPTER.5
11-20-89  3:25p     33408   C:\WS4\BOOK\TEXT\CHAPTER.6
11-16-89 11:48a     81152   C:\WS4\BOOK\TEXT\CHAPTER.7

Insert Archive Diskette 02 in Drive A:
WARNING: All Files Will Be Deleted!
Press Any Key To Continue, Control-C To Abort
```

Figure C.5: Backing up files in subdirectories

USING /S TO BACK UP AN ENTIRE HARD DISK   You can
also use the /S switch to back up your complete hard disk. To do this,
enter

> BACKUP C:\ /S

You could also enter

> BACKUP /S

if drive C's root directory was current.

BACKING UP NEW OR MODIFIED FILES   When you are
actively adding and changing files in a directory as a normal part of your
work, it is often convenient to back up just those work-in-progress files,
provided you have already made a complete backup of your hard disk.
Copying only the files that have been added or modified since you
backed up your entire disk keeps your backup current without recopy-
ing all the files that have remained unchanged. To do this with the
BACKUP command, use the /M switch. For example, if you have only

The first time you
run BACKUP for
your hard disk, back up
everything. After that, you
can choose to back up only
new or modified files.

worked with your WS4 directory since you last backed up, entering

BACKUP C:\WS4 A: /M

Keep each backup made with the /M switch on separate disks that are clearly labeled and file the disks in order. This way, restoring all the bits and pieces of your backup won't be as difficult.

updates your backup. Remember to back up any directory that you have worked in. One way to make sure that you copy all new or modified files on your hard disk is simply to run the command

BACKUP C:\ A: /M /S

The /M switch instructs DOS to back up only those files that have their archive bit set, and the /S switch tells it to look for these files in drive C's root directory and all of its subdirectories.

The format of the date and time entry depends on the country code entry in your CON-FIG.SYS file.

BACKING UP BY DATE AND TIME   As an alternative method for backing up your new or modified files, you can specify a date with the /D switch or a time with the /T switch. If you use the /D switch, all the files that have been altered on or after the date specified will be backed up. If you also include the /T switch, the files that have been altered on or after the specified time will be backed up. (You wouldn't want to use the /T switch without /D since unmodified files with earlier dates could also be backed up if their time fit the /T switch's specification.) With the /T switch you can specify a time in the morning by adding the letter a (for a.m.) or the letter p (for p.m.) to the end of the time entry.

If you always back up your system on a Friday afternoon, set the date in the /D switch to the previous Friday's date, and all the files you have created or modified during the week will be backed up for you automatically; you won't have to know which ones they are. For example, enter

BACKUP C:\ /S /D:11/17/89

to back up files that have been charged or added to your hard disk since Friday, November 17, 1989.

Backing up your files by date requires that you always date your files accurately. If your system automatically assigns a date when you boot up, using this method to update your backup is fine. However, if you have to set the date manually each day, you may forget to set the date, and files created on that day would not be backed up. In this case, you might want to back up your files selectively by using the /M switch instead, especially if several people use the computer. This guarantees that all new or modified files are copied, regardless of their dates.

CREATING A LOG FILE OF THE BACKUP   The remaining switch you can use with BACKUP is the /L switch, which creates a log file in the root directory of the drive being backed up. In this file BACKUP stores the backup date and time, as well as the disk number of each backup file and the file's full path name. This information is essential if you have to restore your files back onto your hard disk again and something goes wrong. Because it keeps track of the backup files' disk numbers, it is also helpful if you have to restore individual files.

When you run the command

BACKUP C:\BATCH A: /L

DOS creates a file called BACKUP.LOG in the root directory of your hard disk. If you want to give this file another name, specify the file name after the switch as follows:

BACKUP C:\BATCH A: /L:OCT30.LOG

If your file name includes a date, you can refer to it to remember when this particular backup set was made. If you don't want the log file in your root directory, you can specify where DOS should put the log file by specifying a complete path name, such as

BACKUP C:\BATCH A: /L:\BATCH\OCT30.LOG

In this example the file is written into the BATCH directory (see Figure C.6).

When this log file is made during the backup, DOS displays the message

Logging to file BATCH\OCT30.LOG

The contents of the OCT30.LOG file are shown in Figure C.7.

```
C>BACKUP C:\BATCH A: /L:OCT3Ø.LOG

Source disk is Non-removable

Insert backup diskette Ø1 in drive A:

Warning! Files in the target drive
A:\ root directory will be erased
Strike any key when ready

*** Backing up files to drive A: ***
Diskette Number: Ø1

\BATCH\BU.BAT
\BATCH\MENU.BAT
\BATCH\PCOBU.BAT
\BATCH\TEST.BAT
\BATCH\MENU.TXT
\BATCH\OCT3Ø.LOG

C>
```

Figure C.6: Telling DOS exactly where to put the log file for the backup

```
C:\WS4\BOOK\SCREENS>TYPE OCT3Ø.LOG
[11-14-1989 1Ø:43:1Øa]
        1    /BATCH/BU.BAT
        1    /BATCH/MENU.BAT
        1    /BATCH/PCOBU.BAT
        1    /BATCH/TEST.BAT
        1    /BATCH/MENU.TXT
        1    /BATCH/OCT3Ø.LOG

C:\WS4\BOOK\SCREENS>
```

Figure C.7: Contents of the log file OCT30.LOG

RESTORING FILES FROM A BACKUP DISK

RESTORE always restores files to the directories in which they were located when they were backed up.

You can use the RESTORE command to restore files made by the BACKUP command back onto your hard disk again. You can restore single files, complete directories and their subdirectories, or the entire disk. The syntax for RESTORE command takes the general form

RESTORE source destination switches

Because the files made by BACKUP have a special format, you cannot use COPY or XCOPY to load them onto your hard disk.

Remember that because these backup files are special files, you cannot use COPY or XCOPY to accomplish this task.

When you use RESTORE, if the current directory is not the directory into which you want to restore files, you must specify the complete paths of those files. If you do not specify a complete path and the files you have specified for restoration were not backed up from the current directory, you will receive the potentially misleading error message "Warning! No files were found to restore".

You can use the /S switch (discussed below) to avoid having to specify complete paths when you want to restore files to subdirectories.

The RESTORE command has several optional switches you can use, which are summarized in Table C.3.

RESTORING SELECTED FILES

To restore a single file, specify its name and complete path. For example, entering

RESTORE A: C:\MYFILE.DOC

will restore MYFILE.DOC to the root directory of drive C.

To restore all the *.DOC files in the WS4 directory, type

RESTORE A: C:\WS4*.DOC

If WS4 was the current directory, you could simply enter

RESTORE A: C:*.DOC

to accomplish the same thing.

Table C.3: RESTORE's Switches

SWITCH	FUNCTION
/A:*mm-dd-yy*	Restores files that were modified on or after *mm-dd-yy*.
/B:*mm-dd-yy*	Restores files that were modified on or before *mm-dd-yy*.
/E:*hh-mm-ss*	Restores files that were modified earlier than *hh-mm-ss*.
/L:*hh-mm-ss*	Restores files that were modified later than *hh-mm-ss*.
/M	Restores files that have been changed or erased since the last backup was made.
/N	Restores files that no longer exist on the destination disk.
/P	Prompts you before restoring a file if it has been modified since it was backed up.
/S	Restores files in subdirectories.

This ability to restore single files when necessary can speed up operations, as only the files you need are restored.

The /M switch only restores files that have been deleted or changed since they were backed up, and the /N switch restores files that are no longer on the hard disk. For example, suppose you have an up-to-date backup of your hard disk and accidentally delete a group of files while working in your WP directory. To restore these files, place the correct backup disk in drive A and enter

RESTORE A: C:\WP /M

Since you are not concerned here with files that have been modified, entering

RESTORE A: C:\WP /N

would also accomplish this file restoration.

RESTORING SUBDIRECTORIES

Use the /S switch when you are completely restoring a hard disk.

To restore files to subdirectories on your hard disk, use the /S switch. This switch ensures that the backup files are restored back into their proper subdirectories. If the directory structure on your hard disk differs from the structure established on the backup disks, for instance, if directories on the hard disk have been deleted or you are loading files onto a new disk that doesn't have the original directory structure on it, DOS will create any directories that don't exist on the destination drive and then copy the appropriate files into the newly created (or recreated) directories.

For example, entering

RESTORE A: C: /S

restores to drive C drive A's backup files for the current directory on drive C and its subdirectories. If you enter

RESTORE A: C:\ /S

the files in drive A will be restored to the root directory and all subdirectories on drive C, regardless of what the current directory is.

RESTORING FILES BY DATE

If you are not exactly sure when you backed up your hard disk and want to avoid overwriting files that may have been modified since the backup was made, use the RESTORE command with the /P switch.

The /P switch asks you for permission to restore a file if the file on the hard disk is newer than its backup file. You can then choose to keep the current version of the file and not restore the backup file. Backup files that do not have newer versions on the hard disk will be restored automatically. For example, if you enter

RESTORE A: C:\WS4*.DOC /P

and there is a NEW.TXT file in drive C's WS4 directory dated 12/13/89 whose backup file is dated 06/13/89, you will be prompted to choose whether you want to restore its backup.

Two other switches, /A and /B, also rely on the files' dates. They both restore files based on a date that you specify. The /A switch restores files that were modified on or after the specified date, and the /B switch restores files that were modified on or before the date specified.

Similarly, the /E and /L switches restore files based on a specified time. The /E switch restores files that were modified at the specified time or earlier, and the /L switch restores files that were modified at the time specified or later.

OTHER BACKUP DEVICES

Although floppy disks are the most common media for storing backup files, other types of media are also available.

Magnetic tape cartridges are often used for backing up vast quantities of data, particularly in a business or scientific environment. These tape drives are fast; some can store more than a megabyte a minute. A tape drive can be added to most computer systems easily as an internal or external drive, requiring only a single circuit board and some connecting cables. These drives often cost less than $1,000, and the tapes themselves are cheap and easy to store. You can even use a video cassette recorder as a backup device. Remember to include the special device driver supplied with the recorder in your CONFIG.SYS file.

You can also use a second hard disk as a backup device. Make sure that there is enough room on the backup drive for all the data from the first disk before you start the backup process. If you run out of space during the backup, the backup copy will be invalid and unusable.

UNDERSTANDING DOS'S REDIRECTION CAPABILITIES

APPENDIX *D*

IN PREVIOUS CHAPTERS I OCCASIONALLY REFERRED to redirection symbols and used them in a few command examples. Here, I explain redirection in more detail, showing how these symbols work and presenting related DOS features that also take advantage of redirection, although their official names are pipes and filters.

WORKING WITH REDIRECTION SYMBOLS

Being able to redirect a command's input or output is one of the things that gives DOS so much power. The concept of redirection, as well as the programming structure that makes redirection possible, was borrowed from the UNIX operating system. Usually, the PC receives information from the standard input device, which is the keyboard, and displays any results on the standard output device, which is the screen. However, you can make DOS redirect its output to another device or even to a file. DOS considers device names and file names functionally equivalent, so you can interchange them in commands that require you to specify a source or destination name.

The three symbols used to redirect input or output are

> Sends the output of a command to the device or file specified after the symbol. (If the file already exists, its data is overwritten by this output.)

>> Adds the output of a command to an existing file, or creates a new file if the specified file does not already exist.

< Directs input to a command from the source specified after the symbol.

Let's examine each of these symbols in order.

REDIRECTING OUTPUT

As you know, when you enter

DIR

a listing of the current directory's contents is displayed on the screen. You can use redirection to sent the output to the printer instead by typing

DIR > PRN

where PRN is the device name of the printer.

To send the output from DIR to a file, simply enter

DIR > DIR.LST

(DIR.LST can be replaced with another file name.)

This sequence will create the ASCII file DIR.LST if it does not already exist, or overwrite the existing file with the output from the DIR command. You will not see the DIR output on the screen since you have redirected it to the DIR.LST file.

If DIR.LST already exists and you want to add the output from DIR to the end of it instead of overwriting its contents, enter

DIR >> DIR.LST

The double redirection symbol > > tells DOS to add the DIR listing to the file. If you had not yet created the file, DOS would do so, just as it does with the single redirection symbol.

Redirecting to files comes in handy in a variety of situations. For example, if you are in a hurry, you can collect output from a lengthy process into a file that you can examine later at your leisure. Alternatively, when you do not want to modify the data but need to see a copy of it, you can send the output directly to the printer.

You can also set up your printer by creating and using a batch file that contains the ECHO command in the form

ECHO *control sequence* > PRN

Use the DOS TYPE command to view the file containing the redirected output or load your word processor to edit the file.

For example, to put an Epson printer into near-letter-quality mode, use a batch file with the command

    ECHO ESC X1 >PRN

To select draft mode again, use ESC X0. See your word processor manual for details on how to enter the escape sequences correctly.

DOS has one more device that you can access by redirection: NUL. You can think of it as an empty file or an invisible device. When you send output to NUL, it just disappears from your system—you will not see it on the screen, on the printer, or in any file. For example, if you redirect the COPY command's output to NUL, you will not see the list of files as they are being copied. By redirecting output from a batch file's commands to NUL, you can prevent the output from cluttering up the display and interfering with prompts or other screen features that the batch file produces.

REDIRECTING INPUT

You may not need to redirect input as often as you redirect output, but there are several circumstances where it is particularly useful for programmers. When you redirect input, it must come from a file rather than the keyboard. You can redirect input from a file to any DOS command that requires input. You cannot use redirection to provide input to a batch file, and you cannot use redirection to supply parameters to a command. Be careful when you are creating a file that will supply input. When you try to send input to a command from a file that is not constructed properly, your computer may freeze; to get it back, you will have to reboot.

A common use for redirecting input is to speed up the operation of an interactive DOS command that stops its execution to wait for a key from the keyboard before continuing. To indicate that the keystrokes are coming from a file rather than the keyboard, use DOS's redirection symbol with the file name, as follows:

    command < filename

A well-known example of this type of input redirection is using a file that contains the keystrokes required to automate the DOS FORMAT command. These characters are a carriage return to respond to the prompt

Insert new diskette for drive A:
and strike ENTER when ready

and an N character, followed by another carriage return, to tell DOS that you only want to format one disk.

After you enter these characters into a file using COPY CON, EDLIN, or your word processor's nondocument mode, you can include a command statement in your batch file that redirects the file's input to FORMAT. Suppose that you named the file containing the three characters STROKES. The line to include in your batch file would then be

FORMAT < STROKES

When you run the batch file, the response characters will be sent from the STROKES file to the FORMAT command in the correct sequence.

USING PIPES

Another concept borrowed from the UNIX operating system is that of the pipe. A *pipe* sends the output of one command to another command, becoming that command's input. By using the redirection symbols described previously, you could achieve the same result. To do this, you would redirect a command's output to a file and then use the same file as input to another command. Using a DOS pipe is simply quicker; it keeps track of the input and output for you (it relies on temporary files to do this). In other words, the pipe is another kind of redirection tool.

You create a pipe with the ¦ symbol, the vertical bar. For example, to send the output from COMMAND1 to COMMAND2 as input, enter

command1 ¦ command2

You can also combine several programs or commands together with pipes to create complex operations. In more complex command statements, pipes are often used with special DOS commands that are classified as filters.

WORKING WITH FILTERS

There are three external DOS commands that function as filters: MORE, SORT, and FIND. A *filter* is a program that takes output from another program and modifies it in some way. Filters can be used with pipes to create long, complex processes that would otherwise require a great deal of programming to accomplish.

WHEN TO USE MORE

You can use MORE to display data a screenful at a time. This gives you a chance to review all the data at a leisurely pace. For example, if you type

    DIR ¦ MORE

for a directory that contains more than 23 entries, you will see the first screen of the directory's listing, which also contains the message

    -- MORE --

at the bottom of the screen. This is displayed to let you know that the command is still running and that there is more output for you to review. Press any key to continue the display. An example of a DOS directory listing that has been piped through MORE is shown in Figure D.1.
If you type

    MORE < *filename*

or

    TYPE *filename* ¦ MORE

```
      .              <DIR>       7-12-88    3:51p
      . .            <DIR>       7-12-88    3:51p
COMMAND   COM       23210       1-24-86   12:00p
MODE      COM        5386       1-24-86   12:00p
GWBASIC   EXE       70704       1-24-86   12:00p
BASIC     COM         686       1-24-86   12:00p
BASICA    COM         686       1-24-86   12:00p
GRAPHICS  COM        6481       1-24-86   12:00p
FORMAT    COM        9390       1-24-86   12:00p
FDISK     COM        5652       1-24-86   12:00p
SYS       COM        3008       1-24-86   12:00p
CHMOD     COM        6704       1-24-86   12:00p
SIZE      COM        4800       1-24-86   12:00p
ASSIGN    COM         864       1-24-86   12:00p
RAMDISK   DEV         768       1-24-86   12:00p
COMP      COM        2845       1-24-86   12:00p
ANSI      SYS        2510       1-24-86   12:00p
PRINT     COM        7043       1-24-86   12:00p
TREE      COM        8955       1-24-86   12:00p
DISKCOMP  COM        4074       1-24-86   12:00p
-- More --
```

Figure D.1: A DIR listing of the DOS directory using the MORE filter

the specified file will be displayed a screenful at a time. The first command sends the file's contents directly to MORE, while the second command takes the output of TYPE (the display of *filename*) and sends it to MORE.

WHEN TO USE SORT

Remember, DOS defines a single column as the width of one character.

The SORT filter sorts the information in a text file. It can sort any column you specify. Because it sorts by column, use it for rearranging tabular data. An example of tabular data is a directory listing. To display a directory sorted by file name, which starts in the first column, you can use the DIR command and pipe its output to the SORT filter by typing

    DIR ¦ SORT

When I invoked this command for the DOS directory, the listing shown in Figure D.2 appeared.

The first column of the listing, the file name, is the default, so you don't need to specify a column number for this sort. To make SORT

```
                    <DIR>        7-12-88    3:51p
                    <DIR>        7-12-88    3:51p
ANSI     SYS         2510        1-24-86   12:00p
ASSIGN   COM          864        1-24-86   12:00p
AUTOEXEC BAT            3        1-24-86   12:00p
BACKUP   COM        15728        1-24-86   12:00p
BASIC    COM          686        1-24-86   12:00p
BASICA   COM          686        1-24-86   12:00p
CHKDSK   COM         9435        1-24-86   12:00p
CHMOD    COM         6704        1-24-86   12:00p
COMMAND  COM        23210        1-24-86   12:00p
COMP     COM         2845        1-24-86   12:00p
DEBUG    COM        15552        1-24-86   12:00p
DISKCOMP COM         4074        1-24-86   12:00p
DISKCOPY COM         4665        1-24-86   12:00p
EDLIN    COM         7261        1-24-86   12:00p
EXE2BIN  EXE         2816        1-24-86   12:00p
FC       EXE        14576        1-24-86   12:00p
FDISK    COM         5652        1-24-86   12:00p

C:\DOS>_
```

Figure D.2: A sorted DIR listing of the DOS directory

work on any column in the file, you use the /+ switch along with the starting column number for the sort. For instance, you can sort the listing by file name extension rather than file name by specifying the tenth column. To do this, enter

DIR ¦ SORT / + 10

Similarly, to sort by file size, specify the fourteenth column. As you can see in Figure D.3, I resorted the DOS directory by this column.

You can also reverse the sort order with the /R switch. To do so, enter

DIR ¦ SORT /R

The listing will be displayed in reverse alphabetical order. If you want to print this listing, you can combine this filter with redirection by entering

DIR ¦ SORT /R > PRN

```
        AUTOEXEC BAT       3   1-24-86  12:00p
        MORE     COM     282   1-24-86  12:00p
        BASIC    COM     686   1-24-86  12:00p
        BASICA   COM     686   1-24-86  12:00p
        RAMDISK  DEV     768   1-24-86  12:00p
        ASSIGN   COM     864   1-24-86  12:00p
        SORT     EXE    1664   1-24-86  12:00p
        ANSI     SYS    2510   1-24-86  12:00p
        EXE2BIN  EXE    2816   1-24-86  12:00p
        COMP     COM    2845   1-24-86  12:00p
        LABEL    COM    2889   1-24-86  12:00p
        SHIP     EXE    3003   1-24-86  12:00p
        SYS      COM    3008   1-24-86  12:00p
        RECOVER  COM    4050   1-24-86  12:00p
        DISKCOMP COM    4074   1-24-86  12:00p
        DISKCOPY COM    4665   1-24-86  12:00p
        SIZE     COM    4800   1-24-86  12:00p
        MODE     COM    5386   1-24-86  12:00p
        FDISK    COM    5652   1-24-86  12:00p
        FIND     EXE    6403   1-24-86  12:00p
        GRAPHICS COM    6481   1-24-86  12:00p
        CHMOD    COM    6704   1-24-86  12:00p

        C:\DOS>
```

Figure D.3: A directory listing sorted by file size (the 14th column)

You can even join SORT with other filters by using pipes. For example, to display a sorted directory listing a screenful at a time, enter

DIR ¦ SORT ¦ MORE

In this case DIR sends its listing to SORT, which arranges it by file name (the default). MORE then displays the results of the sort a screenful at a time.

WHEN TO USE FIND

FIND is the last of DOS's three filters. It too can be used with pipes and redirection. You can invoke FIND to locate a particular string of text in a file. For example, to locate all the lines in a directory listing that contain EXE, type

DIR ¦ FIND "EXE"

The DIR command sends the entire listing of the directory to FIND, which chooses all lines that include EXE and displays them only, ignoring the rest of the DIR listing.

To sort this output from FIND by file name, enter

DIR ¦ FIND "EXE" ¦ SORT

The results I got when I ran this command sequence on the DOS directory are shown in Figure D.4. Note that the AUTOEXEC-.BAT file entry is listed since the letters EXE occur in the word AUTOEXEC, while the remaining file entries are included because their file extension is .EXE.

If you want to print this sorted FIND listing, reenter the command as

DIR ¦ FIND "EXE" ¦ SORT >PRN

You can also use FIND to locate all lines in a file that do not match the search string by using the /V switch. If you rerun the previous example with this switch, only those lines (file entries) not containing the characters "EXE" would be passed on to the SORT filter. To do this, enter

DIR ¦ FIND /V "EXE" ¦ SORT

```
        AUTOEXEC BAT       3    1-24-86   12:00p
        EXE2BIN  EXE    2816    1-24-86   12:00p
        FC       EXE   14576    1-24-86   12:00p
        FIND     EXE    6403    1-24-86   12:00p
        GWBASIC  EXE   70704    1-24-86   12:00p
        JOIN     EXE   15971    1-24-86   12:00p
        LINK     EXE   38422    1-24-86   12:00p
        SHARE    EXE    8304    1-24-86   12:00p
        SHIP     EXE    3003    1-24-86   12:00p
        SORT     EXE    1664    1-24-86   12:00p
        SUBST    EXE   16611    1-24-86   12:00p

        C:\DOS>
```

Figure D.4: Locating and sorting all occurrences of "EXE" in the DOS directory

The results of using this command sequence in the DOS directory
are shown in Figure D.5.

```
          BASIC     COM       686    1-24-86   12:00p
          BASICA    COM       686    1-24-86   12:00p
          CHKDSK    COM      9435    1-24-86   12:00p
          CHMOD     COM      6704    1-24-86   12:00p
          COMMAND   COM     23210    1-24-86   12:00p
          COMP      COM      2845    1-24-86   12:00p
          DEBUG     COM     15552    1-24-86   12:00p
          DISKCOMP  COM      4074    1-24-86   12:00p
          DISKCOPY  COM      4665    1-24-86   12:00p
          EDLIN     COM      7261    1-24-86   12:00p
          FDISK     COM      5652    1-24-86   12:00p
          FORMAT    COM      9390    1-24-86   12:00p
          GRAPHICS  COM      6481    1-24-86   12:00p
          LABEL     COM      2889    1-24-86   12:00p
          MODE      COM      5386    1-24-86   12:00p
          MORE      COM       282    1-24-86   12:00p
          PRINT     COM      7043    1-24-86   12:00p
          RAMDISK   DEV       768    1-24-86   12:00p
          RECOVER   COM      4050    1-24-86   12:00p
          RESTORE   COM     21232    1-24-86   12:00p
          SIZE      COM      4800    1-24-86   12:00p
          SYS       COM      3008    1-24-86   12:00p
          TREE      COM      8955    1-24-86   12:00p

          C:\DOS>
```

Figure D.5: Using FIND's /V switch to locate lines that do not contain the
search string

BECOMING PROFICIENT WITH
ASCII AND BINARY FILES

APPENDIX *E*

THROUGHOUT THIS BOOK I HAVE REFERRED TO ASCII and program files. As you can work with both types of files when you run the Norton Utilities, acquiring a better understanding of what these file types are and the numbering systems they rely on will enable you to enhance your productivity. As you may know, ASCII files are often called text or nondocument (this last term comes from word processors) files. Program files are actually binary files.

BINARY FILES

Binary files contain instructions and data (encoded as numbers) that your system's processor can decode and act on. Such files are specific to the microprocessor or microprocessor family they will execute on. For instance, a binary file prepared for an Intel microprocessor will not run on a Motorola microprocessor, and vice versa, without special software.

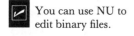 You can use NU to edit binary files.

You cannot read or edit binary files with a word processor. Programmers initially write programs in human-readable computer languages, which are then *compiled, interpreted,* or *assembled* by the computer into binary files.

ASCII FILES

ASCII files are text files. ASCII (pronounced ''as-key'') stands for the American Standard Code for Information Interchange. ASCII codes represent letters, punctuation symbols, numbers, mathematical symbols, and so on. When you type a character, what the computer actually ''reads'' is the ASCII code for that character. You can also employ ASCII codes to control devices (such as monitors and printers).

The standard ASCII codes use seven of the eight bits in a byte.

In ASCII each character is represented by a unique integer value, which is commonly referred to as a *decimal value*. The values 0 to 31 are used for control codes, and the range of 32 to 127 is used to represent the letters of the alphabet and common punctuation symbols. The entire set of 0–127 is called *standard* ASCII. All computers that use ASCII characters can understand the standard ASCII set, although not all can work with the *extended character set,* which are the values 128 to 255. These values encode uncommon symbols and punctuation marks, for example, Greek letters. (We'll examine this set shortly.)

ASCII CONTROL CHARACTERS

The *control code* characters (0 to 31) are reserved for special purposes that usually have to do with controlling devices or communications.

Codes 1–4 are generally not used in modern microcomputer communications.

Codes 1 to 4, which stand for SOH, STX, ETX, and EOT, are used in communications to indicate the start and end of both the transmission (codes 1 and 4) and its text (codes 2 and 3). Other codes are used to control the flow of transmitted data; for example, ACK (acknowledge) and NAK (negative acknowledge) indicate whether the data was received successfully, and ENQ (enquire), SYN (synchronize), ETB (end-of-transmission block), and CAN (cancel) are also used to control the flow. Additional codes punctuate the flow of information; FS (file separator), GS (group separator), RS (record separator), and US (unit separator) all fall into this category.

The VT sequence is rarely used to control devices.

Several codes are used to control peripheral devices, particularly printers. The CR (carriage return), LF (line feed), FF (form feed, which is sometimes referred to as new page), HT (horizontal tab), BS (backspace), and VT (vertical tab) sequences all find uses in device control. For a complete listing of the control codes, see Table E.1.

Ctrl-S is often called X-OFF, and Ctrl-Q is often referred to as X-ON.

Ctrl-S and Ctrl-Q are often used as pause and restart commands, and Ctrl-[produces the Esc character. An escape sequence, comprising the Esc character, followed by one or more other characters in a set order, is a common way of controlling complex devices such as terminals and printers that have more capabilities than can be controlled by the individual ASCII control characters alone. See your printer manual for more details.

Table E.1: The ASCII Control Codes

DECIMAL VALUE	HEX VALUE	KEYS TO PRESS	NAME
000	00	Crtl-@	NUL (nul character)
001	01	Ctrl-A	SOH (start of header)
002	02	Crtl-B	STX (start of text)
003	03	Ctrl-C	ETX (end of text)
004	04	Ctrl-D	EOT (end of transmission)
005	05	Ctrl-E	ENQ (enquire)
006	06	Ctrl-F	ACK (acknowledge)
007	07	Ctrl-G	BEL (bell)
008	08	Ctrl-H	BS (backspace)
009	09	Ctrl-I	HT (horizonal tab)
010	0A	Ctrl-J	LF (line feed)
011	0B	Ctrl-K	VT (vertical tab)
012	0C	Ctrl-L	FF (form feed or new page)
013	0D	Ctrl-M	CR (carriage return)
014	0E	Ctrl-N	SO (shift out)
015	0F	Ctrl-O	SI (shift in)
016	10	Ctrl-P	DLE (data link escape)
017	11	Ctrl-Q	DC1 (X-ON)
018	12	Ctrl-R	DC2 (tape)
019	13	Ctrl-S	DC3 (X-OFF)
020	14	Ctrl-T	DC4 (no tape)

Table E.1: The ASCII Control Codes (continued)

DECIMAL VALUE	HEX VALUE	KEYS TO PRESS	NAME
021	15	Ctrl-U	NAK (negative acknowledge)
022	16	Ctrl-V	SYN (synchronize)
023	17	Crtl-W	ETB (end of transmission block)
024	18	Ctrl-X	CAN (cancel)
025	19	Ctrl-Y	EM (end of medium)
026	1A	Ctrl-Z	SUB (substitute)
027	1B	Ctrl-[	ESC (escape)
028	1C	Ctrl-/	FS (file separator)
029	1D	Ctrl-]	GS (group separator)
030	1E	Ctrl-^	RS (record separator)
031	1F	Ctrl-_	US (unit separator)

THE EXTENDED CHARACTER SET

255 is the largest decimal value that can be represented by using all eight of the bits in one eight-bit byte.

The IBM extended character set starts where the standard ASCII set leaves off. The next available decimal code is 128, and the extended set runs from 128 to 255. Its characters, which include the PC line-drawing set, mathematical symbols, and graphics characters, are not standard on computers that are not compatible with IBM's microcomputers. Word processing programs have different ways of allowing you to use the characters in the extended ASCII set. In WordStar, for example, you can display these characters by simultaneously pressing the Alt key and typing the decimal value of the appropriate character on the numeric keypad (you cannot use the regular number keys for this purpose). Printers vary in their ability to print these characters.

Because different languages (for example, Norwegian and Portuguese) use different characters and keyboard layouts, there are a number of language-specific ASCII tables. These tables use decimal codes 128–255 for necessary characters that are not provided by the standard ASCII set. Each of these tables is called a *code page*.

Table E.2 lists the standard and IBM extended ASCII characters and their decimal and hexadecimal values.

Table E.2: The Standard and Extended ASCII Sets

Character	Decimal Value	Hex Value	Character	Decimal Value	Hex Value
	000	00	♫	014	0E
☺	001	01	☼	015	0F
☻	002	02	►	016	10
♥	003	03	◄	017	11
♦	004	04	↕	018	12
♣	005	05	‼	019	13
♠	006	06	¶	020	14
•	007	07	§	021	15
◘	008	08	▬	022	16
○	009	09	↨	023	17
◙	010	0A	↑	024	18
♂	011	0B	↓	025	19
♀	012	0C	→	026	1A
♪	013	0D	←	027	1B

Table E.2: The Standard and Extended ASCII Sets (continued)

CHARACTER	DECIMAL VALUE	HEX VALUE	CHARACTER	DECIMAL VALUE	HEX VALUE
∟	028	1C	.	046	2E
↔	029	1D	/	047	2F
▲	030	1E	0	048	30
▼	031	1F	1	049	31
	032	20	2	050	32
!	033	21	3	051	33
"	034	22	4	052	34
#	035	23	5	053	35
$	036	24	6	054	36
%	037	25	7	055	37
&	038	26	8	056	38
'	039	27	9	057	39
(	040	28	:	058	3A
)	041	29	;	059	3B
✹	042	2A	<	060	3C
+	043	2B	=	061	3D
,	044	2C	>	062	3E
—	045	2D	?	063	3F

Table E.2: The Standard and Extended ASCII Sets (continued)

CHARACTER	DECIMAL VALUE	HEX VALUE	CHARACTER	DECIMAL VALUE	HEX VALUE
@	064	40	R	082	52
A	065	41	S	083	53
B	066	42	T	084	54
C	067	43	U	085	55
D	068	44	V	086	56
E	069	45	W	087	57
F	070	46	X	088	58
G	071	47	Y	089	59
H	072	48	Z	090	5A
I	073	49	[	091	5B
J	074	4A	\	092	5C
K	075	4B	]	093	5D
L	076	4C	^	094	5E
M	077	4D	_	095	5F
N	078	4E	`	096	60
O	079	4F	a	097	61
P	080	50	b	098	62
Q	081	51	c	099	63

Table E.2: The Standard and Extended ASCII Sets (continued)

CHARACTER	DECIMAL VALUE	HEX VALUE	CHARACTER	DECIMAL VALUE	HEX VALUE
d	100	64	υ	118	76
e	101	65	ʍ	119	77
f	102	66	x	120	78
g	103	67	y	121	79
h	104	68	z	122	7A
i	105	69	{	123	7B
j	106	6A	¦	124	7C
k	107	6B	}	125	7D
l	108	6C	~	126	7E
m	109	6D	△	127	7F
n	110	6E	Ç	128	80
o	111	6F	ü	129	81
p	112	70	é	130	82
q	113	71	â	131	83
r	114	72	ä	132	84
s	115	73	à	133	85
t	116	74	å	134	86
u	117	75	ç	135	87

Table E.2: The Standard and Extended ASCII Sets (continued)

CHARACTER	DECIMAL VALUE	HEX VALUE	CHARACTER	DECIMAL VALUE	HEX VALUE
ê	136	88	ü	154	9A
ë	137	89	¢	155	9B
è	138	8A	£	156	9C
ï	139	8B	¥	157	9D
î	140	8C	₧	158	9E
ì	141	8D	ƒ	159	9F
Ä	142	8E	á	160	A0
Å	143	8F	í	161	A1
É	144	90	ó	162	A2
æ	145	91	ú	163	A3
Æ	146	92	ñ	164	A4
ô	147	93	Ñ	165	A5
ö	148	94	ª	166	A6
ò	149	95	º	167	A7
û	150	96	¿	168	A8
ù	151	97	⌐	169	A9
ÿ	152	98	¬	170	AA
ö	153	99	½	171	AB

Table E.2: The Standard and Extended ASCII Sets (continued)

Character	Decimal Value	Hex Value	Character	Decimal Value	Hex Value
¼	172	AC	┛	190	BE
¡	173	AD	┐	191	BF
«	174	AE	└	192	C0
»	175	AF	┴	193	C1
░	176	B0	┬	194	C2
▒	177	B1	├	195	C3
▓	178	B2	─	196	C4
│	179	B3	┼	197	C5
┤	180	B4	╞	198	C6
╡	181	B5	╟	199	C7
╢	182	B6	╚	200	C8
╖	183	B7	╔	201	C9
╕	184	B8	╩	202	CA
╣	185	B9	╦	203	CB
║	186	BA	╠	204	CC
╗	187	BB	═	205	CD
╜	188	BC	╬	206	CE
╝	189	BD	╧	207	CF

Table E.2: The Standard and Extended ASCII Sets (continued)

CHARACTER	DECIMAL VALUE	HEX VALUE	CHARACTER	DECIMAL VALUE	HEX VALUE
⊔	208	D0	Γ	226	E2
⊤	209	D1	π	227	E3
π	210	D2	Σ	228	E4
⊔	211	D3	σ	229	E5
⊦	212	D4	µ	230	E6
⊧	213	D5	τ	231	E7
π	214	D6	Φ	232	E8
╫	215	D7	θ	233	E9
‡	216	D8	Ω	234	EA
⌐	217	D9	δ	235	EB
⌐	218	DA	∞	236	EC
█	219	DB	ø	237	ED
▄	220	DC	∈	238	EE
▌	221	DD	∩	239	EF
▐	222	DE	≡	240	F0
▀	223	DF	±	241	F1
α	224	E0	≥	242	F2
β	225	E1	≤	243	F3

Table E.2: The Standard and Extended ASCII Sets (continued)

CHARACTER	DECIMAL VALUE	HEX VALUE	CHARACTER	DECIMAL VALUE	HEX VALUE
⌠	244	F4	·	250	FA
⌡	245	F5	√	251	FB
÷	246	F6	ⁿ	252	FC
≈	247	F7	²	253	FD
°	248	F8	■	254	FE
•	249	F9		255	FF

EBCDIC FILES

EBCDIC uses an 8-bit code to define 256 characters, and as it used more bits than ASCII did at that time, it was described as an *extended code.* This was established long before the PC arrived on the computing scene. EBCDIC is the character set commonly used on large IBM mainframe computers. Most such computers have their own ASCII-to-EBCDIC and EBCDIC-to-ASCII converting programs, but if you forgot to convert the file before downloading it from the mainframe, several of the Norton Utilities utilities have an / EBCDIC switch that allows you to continue working with the file in its original form.

Any standard typewriter character can be represented in either ASCII or EBCDIC, although each method uses a different bit pattern in the byte to represent it. In ASCII the lowercase letters follow the uppercase letters after a short set of punctuation symbols. In EBCDIC, however, the numbering of the letters of the alphabet is discontinuous (see Table E.3). There is no direct character-to-character match when converting from ASCII to EBCDIC. Some characters exist in one character set but not in the other, and vice versa. Although regularly used ASCII characters, such as the alphabet and common punctuation symbols, can be translated into EBCDIC, some of the control characters cannot. Some EBCDIC devices also support a variety of characters in addition to those shown here.

Table E.3: The EBCDIC Character Set

NAME/CHARACTER	DECIMAL VALUE	HEX VALUE
NUL	000	00
SOH	001	01
STX	002	02
ETX	003	03
PF	004	04
HT	005	05
LC	006	06
DEL	007	07
GE	008	08
RLF	009	09
SMM	010	0A
VT	011	0B
FF	012	0C
CR	013	0D
SO	014	0E
SI	015	0F
DLE	016	10
DC1	017	11
DC2	018	12
TM	019	13
RES	020	14

Note that EBCDIC does not provide characters for all the possible decimal and hex values; these have been omitted from the table.

Table E.3: The EBCDIC Character Set (continued)

NAME/CHARACTER	DECIMAL VALUE	HEX VALUE
NL	021	15
BS	022	16
IL	023	17
CAN	024	18
EM	025	19
CC	026	1A
CU1	027	1B
IFS	028	1C
IGS	029	1D
IRS	030	1E
IUS	031	1F
DS	032	20
SOS	033	21
FS	034	22
BYP	036	24
LF	037	25
ETB	038	26
ESC	039	27
SM	042	2A
CU2	043	2B
ENQ	045	2D
ACK	046	2E
BEL	047	2F
SYN	050	32
PN	052	34

Note that EBCDIC does not provide characters for all the possible decimal and hex values; these have been omitted from the table.

Table E.3: The EBCDIC Character Set (continued)

NAME/CHARACTER	DECIMAL VALUE	HEX VALUE
RS	053	35
UC	054	36
EOT	055	37
CU3	059	3B
DC4	060	3C
NAK	061	3D
SUB	063	3F
SP	064	40
¢	074	4A
.	075	4B
<	076	4C
(	077	4D
+	078	4E
|	079	4F
&	080	50
!	090	5A
$	091	5B
*	092	5C
)	093	5D
;	094	5E
¬	095	5F
-	096	60
/	097	61
¦	106	6A
,	107	6B

Note that EBCDIC does not provide characters for all the possible decimal and hex values; these have been omitted from the table.

Table E.3: The EBCDIC Character Set (continued)

NAME/CHARACTER	DECIMAL VALUE	HEX VALUE
%	108	6C
–	109	6D
>	110	6E
?	111	6F
:	122	7A
#	123	7B
@	124	7C
'	125	7D
=	126	7E
''	127	7F
a	129	81
b	130	82
c	131	83
d	132	84
e	133	85
f	134	86
g	135	87
h	136	88
i	137	89
j	145	91
k	146	92
l	147	93
m	148	94
n	149	95
o	150	96

Note that EBCDIC does not provide characters for all the possible decimal and hex values; these have been omitted from the table.

Table E.3: The EBCDIC Character Set (continued)

NAME/CHARACTER	DECIMAL VALUE	HEX VALUE
p	151	97
q	152	98
r	153	99
~	161	A1
s	162	A2
t	163	A3
u	164	A4
v	165	A5
w	166	A6
x	167	A7
y	168	A8
z	169	A9
{	192	C0
A	193	C1
B	194	C2
C	195	C3
D	196	C4
E	197	C5
F	198	C6
G	199	C7
H	200	C8
ˎ	201	C9
⌐	204	CC
⊔	206	CE
}	208	D0

Note that EBCDIC does not provide characters for all the possible decimal and hex values; these have been omitted from the table.

Table E.3: The EBCDIC Character Set (continued)

NAME/CHARACTER	DECIMAL VALUE	HEX VALUE
J	209	D1
K	210	D2
L	211	D3
M	212	D4
N	213	D5
O	214	D6
P	215	D7
Q	216	D8
R	217	D9
\	224	E0
S	226	E2
T	227	E3
U	228	E4
V	229	E5
W	230	E6
X	231	E7
Y	232	E8
Z	233	E9
⊣	236	EC
0	240	F0
1	241	F1
2	242	F2
3	243	F3
4	244	F4
5	245	F5

Note that EBCDIC does not provide characters for all the possible decimal and hex values; these have been omitted from the table.

Table E.3: The EBCDIC Character Set (continued)

NAME/CHARACTER	DECIMAL VALUE	HEX VALUE
6	246	F6
7	247	F7
8	248	F8
9	249	F9
|	250	FA
EO	255	FF

Note that EBCDIC does not provide characters for all the possible decimal and hex values; these have been omitted from the table.

A NOTE ON
DIFFERENT NUMBERING SCHEMES

As you have seen in the previous section, a computer relies on various numbering systems. Understanding these systems will make it easier to work with your computer—you'll have a better grasp of what is happening and why. The main thing to remember about these different systems is that they are all methods of representing the same thing.

DECIMAL

The *decimal* system is the system people are most familiar with, as it is the first numbering system taught in school. It counts in base 10 using ten digits, 0, 1, 2, 3, 4, 5, 6, 7, 8, and 9, to represent numbers.

The position of each digit is important and contributes to the value of the number. The right-hand digit is the ones place, the second position (moving to the left) is the tens place, the third is the hundreds place, and so on. To determine a decimal number's value, you can multiply each digit by its position and then add the individual sums together. For example, the decimal number 1234 equals

$$(1 \times 4) + (10 \times 3) + (100 \times 2) + (1000 \times 1)$$
$$= \quad 4 \quad + \quad 30 \quad + \quad 200 \quad + \quad 1000$$

BINARY

The *binary* system uses only two digits, 0 and 1, which represent the only possible states of a bit—off or on. Counting in binary is relatively straightforward, although it is rather different from the traditional decimal-numbering scheme.

In the binary system, the weight of each position doubles each time you move a position to the left, instead of increasing by a factor of ten as in the decimal system. To convert the binary number 1011 into decimal, for example, you would perform the following calculation:

$$(1 \times 2^0) + (1 \times 2^1) + (0 \times 2^2) + (1 \times 2^3)$$
$$= \quad 1 \quad + \quad 2 \quad + \quad 0 \quad + \quad 8$$
$$= 11$$

Table E.4 shows the place values of the first eight places in the binary system in its top row. The bottom row shows the binary equivalent of decimal 11.

The binary system represents the exact state of the bits in a byte well, but it is inconvenient when all you want to know is the value of the byte and don't care about the status of its individual bits. In cases like this, it is often easier to work with the hexadecimal (or sometimes octal) system.

HEXADECIMAL

The third major numbering scheme used when working with computers is the *hexadecimal* system. This is often abbreviated to hex, or even to the single letter H. Sometimes even the H is omitted, and you have to guess from the context that the number is expressed in hexadecimal.

The hexadecimal digits A–F are always uppercased.

The hexadecimal system counts in base 16, using the digits 0 to 9 and A to F in the sequence: 0, 1, 2, 3, 4, 5, 6, 7, 8, 9, A, B, C, D, E, and F. The decimal and binary equivalents for this sequence are shown in Table E.5. In a hexadecimal number each digit's value is 16 times greater than the digit immediately to its right.

For example, to convert the hex number FF to decimal, remembering that F in hex is equivalent to 15 in the decimal system, perform the following calculation:

$$
\begin{aligned}
&\quad (15 \times 16^0) \ + \ (15 \times 16^1) \\
&= \quad\quad 15 \quad\quad + \quad\quad 240 \\
&= \quad\quad 255
\end{aligned}
$$

Hexadecimal notation is a convenient way to express byte values because a single hexadecimal digit is equivalent to four binary digits. Since there are eight binary digits in a byte, the value of a byte can be expressed as two hex digits.

Table E.4: Decimal 11 in the Binary System

PLACE VALUES	128	64	32	16	8	4	2	1
BINARY DIGITS	0	0	0	0	1	0	1	1

Table E.5: A Comparison of Decimal, Binary, and Hexadecimal Numbers

DECIMAL	BINARY	HEXADECIMAL	DECIMAL	BINARY	HEXADECIMAL
0	0	0	8	1000	8
1	1	1	9	1001	9
2	10	2	10	1010	A
3	11	3	11	1011	B
4	100	4	12	1100	C
5	101	5	13	1101	D
6	110	6	14	1110	E
7	111	7	15	1111	F

INDEX

A

B

C

E

Selections from The SYBEX Library

DOS

The ABC's of DOS 4
Alan R. Miller
250pp. Ref. 583-2

This step-by-step introduction to using DOS 4 is written especially for beginners. Filled with simple examples, *The ABC's of DOS 4* covers the basics of hardware, software, disks, the system editor EDLIN, DOS commands, and more.

ABC's of MS-DOS (Second Edition)
Alan R. Miller
233pp. Ref. 493-3

This handy guide to MS-DOS is all many PC users need to manage their computer files, organize floppy and hard disks, use EDLIN, and keep their computers organized. Additional information is given about utilities like Sidekick, and there is a DOS command and program summary. The second edition is fully updated for Version 3.3.

Mastering DOS (Second Edition)
Judd Robbins
700pp. Ref. 555-7

"The most useful DOS book." This seven-part, in-depth tutorial addresses the needs of users at all levels. Topics range from running applications, to managing files and directories, configuring the system, batch file programming, and techniques for system developers.

MS-DOS Handbook (Third Edition)
Richard Allen King
362pp. Ref. 492-5

This classic has been fully expanded and revised to include the latest features of MS-DOS Version 3.3. Two reference books in one, this title has separate sections for programmer and user. Multi-DOS partitons, 3 1/2disk format, batch file call and return feature, and comprehensive coverage of MS-DOS commands are included.

MS-DOS Power User's Guide, Volume I (Second Edition)
Jonathan Kamin
482pp. Ref. 473-9

A fully revised, expanded edition of our best-selling guide to high-performance DOS techniques and utilities--with details on Version 3.3. Configuration, I/O, directory structures, hard disks, RAM disks, batch file programming, the ANSI.SYS device driver, more.

MS-DOS Power User's Guide, Volume II
Martin Waterhouse/Jonathan Kamin
418pp, Ref. 411-9

A second volume of high-performance techniques and utilities, with expanded coverage of DOS 3.3, and new material on video modes, Token-Ring and PC Network support, micro-mainframe links, extended and expanded memory, multi-tasking systems, and more.

DOS User's Desktop Companion
Judd Robbins
969 pp. Ref. 505-0 Softcover
459-3 Hardcover

This comprehensive reference covers DOS commands, batch files, memory enhancements, printing, communications and more information on optimizing each user's DOS environment. Written with step-by-step instructions and plenty of examples, this volume covers all versions through 3.3.

MS-DOS Advanced Programming
Michael J. Young
490pp. Ref. 578-6

Practical techniques for maximizing performance in MS-DOS software by making best use of system resources. Topics include functions, interrupts, devices, multitasking, memory residency and more, with examples in C and assembler.

Essential PC-DOS
(Second Edition)
Myril Clement Shaw/
Susan Soltis Shaw
332pp. Ref. 413-5

An authoritative guide to PC-DOS, including version 3.2. Designed to make experts out of beginners, it explores everything from disk management to batch file programming. Includes an 85-page command summary.

The IBM PC-DOS Handbook
(Third Edition)
Richard Allen King
359pp. Ref. 512-3

A guide to the inner workings of PC-DOS 3.2, for intermediate to advanced users and programmers of the IBM PC series. Topics include disk, screen and port control, batch files, networks, compatibility, and more.

DOS Instant Reference
SYBEX Prompter Series
Greg Harvey/Kay Yarborough Nelson
220pp. Ref. 477-1; 4 3/4x8

A complete fingertip reference for fast, easy on-line help:command summaries, syntax, usage and error messages. Organized by function--system commands, file commands, disk management, directories, batch files, I/O, networking, programming, and more.

OTHER OPERATING SYSTEMS AND ENVIRONMENTS

Essential OS/2
Judd Robbins
367pp. Ref. 478-X

This introduction to OS/2 for new and prospective users offers clear explanations of multitasking, details key OS/2 commands and functions, and updates current DOS users to the new OS/2 world. Details are also given for users to run existing DOS programs under OS/2.

Programmer's Guide to OS/2
Michael J. Young
625pp. Ref. 464-X

This concise introduction gives a complete overview of program development under OS/2, with careful attention to new tools and features. Topics include MS-DOS compatibility, device drivers, services, graphics, windows, the LAN manager, and more.

Programmer's Guide to GEM
Phillip Balma/William Fitler
504pp. Ref. 297-3

GEM programming from the ground up, including the Resource Construction Set, ICON Editor, and Virtual Device Interface. Build a complete graphics application with objects, events, menus, windows, alerts and dialogs.

Understanding Hard Disk
Management
Jonathan Kamin
500pp. Ref. 561-1

Put your work, your office or your entire business literally at your fingertips, in a customized, automated MS-DOS work environment. Topics include RAM disks, extended and expanded memory, and more.

Programmer's Guide to
Windows
(Second Edition)
David Durant/Geta Carlson/Paul Yao
704pp. Ref. 496-8

The first edition of this programmer's guide was hailed as a classic. This new edition covers Windows 2 and Windows/386 in depth. Special emphasis is given to over fifty new routines to the Windows interface, and to preparation for OS/2 Presentation Manager compatibility.

Graphics Programming Under
Windows
Brian Myers/Chris Doner
646pp. Ref. 448-8

Straightforward discussion, abundant examples, and a concise reference guide to graphics commands make this book a must for Windows programmers. Topics range from how Windows works to programming for business, animation, CAD, and desktop publishing. For Version 2.

LANGUAGES

Mastering Turbo Pascal 5
Douglas Hergert
595pp. Ref. 529-8
This in-depth treatment of Turbo Pascal Versions 4 and 5 offers separate sections on the Turbo environment, the new debugger, the extensive capabilities of the language itself, and special techniques for graphics, date arithmetic, and recursion. Assumes some programming knowledge.

Advanced Techniques in Turbo Pascal
Charles C. Edwards
309pp. Ref. 350-3
This collection of system-oriented techniques and sample programs shows how to make the most of IBM PC capabilities using Turbo Pascal. Topics include screens, windows, directory management, the mouse interface, and communications.

Turbo BASIC Instant Reference SYBEX Prompter Series
Douglas Hergert
393pp. Ref. 485-2
This quick reference for programmers offers concise, alphabetical entries on every command--statement, metastatement, function, and operation--in the Turbo BASIC language with descriptions, syntax, and examples cross-referenced to related commands.

Introduction to Turbo BASIC
Douglas Hergert
523pp. Ref. 441-0
A complete tutorial and guide to this now highly professional language: Turbo BASIC, including important Turbo extras such as parameter passing, structured loops, long integers, recursion, and 8087 compatibility for high-speed numerical operation.

Advanced Techniques in Turbo Prolog
Carl Townsend
398pp. Ref. 428-3
A goldmine of techniques and predicates for control procedures, string operations, list processing, database operations, BIOS-level support, program development, expert systems, natural language processing, and much more.

Introduction to Turbo Prolog
Carl Townsend
315pp. Ref. 359-7
This comprehensive tutorial includes sample applications for expert systems, natural language interfaces, and simulation. Covers every aspect of Prolog: facts, objects and predicates, rules, recursion, databases, and much more.

Turbo Pascal Toolbox (Second Edition)
Frank Dutton
425pp. Ref. 602-2
This collection of tested, efficient Turbo Pascal building blocks gives a boost to intermediate-level programmers, while teaching effective programming by example. Topics include accessing DOS, menus, bit maps, screen handling, and much more.

Introduction to Pascal: Including Turbo Pascal (Second Edition)
Rodnay Zaks
464pp. Ref. 533-6
This best-selling tutorial builds complete mastery of Pascal--from basic structured programming concepts, to advanced I/O, data structures, file operations, sets, pointers and lists, and more. Both ISO Standard and Turbo Pascal.

Introduction to Pascal (Including UCSD Pascal)
Rodnay Zaks
420pp. Ref. 066-0
This edition of our best-selling tutorial on Pascal programming gives special attention to the UCSD Pascal implementation for small computers. Covers everything

from basic concepts to advanced data structures and more.

Celestial BASIC: Astronomy on Your Computer
Eric Burgess
300pp. Ref. 087-3
A complete home planetarium. This collection of BASIC programs for astronomical calculations enables armchair astronomers to observe and identify on screen the configurations and motions of sun, moon, planets and stars.

Mastering Turbo C
Stan Kelly-Bootle
578pp. Ref. 462-3
No prior knowledge of C or structured programming is required for this introductory course on the Turbo C language and development environment by this well-known author. A logical progression of tutorials and useful sample programs build a thorough understanding of Turbo C.

Systems Programming in Turbo C
Michael J. Young
365pp. Ref. 467-4
An introduction to advanced programming with Borland's Turbo C, and a goldmine of ready-made routines for the system programmer's library: DOS and BIOS interfacing, interrupt handling, windows, graphics, expanded memory, UNIX utilities, and more.

Understanding C
Bruce H. Hunter
320pp. Ref. 123-3
A programmer's introduction to C, with special attention to implementations for microcomputers--both CP/M and MS-DOS. Topics include data types, storage management, pointers, random I/O, function libraries, compilers and more.

Mastering C
Craig Bolon
437pp. Ref. 326-0
This in-depth guide stresses planning, testing, efficiency and portability in C applications. Topics include data types, storage classes, arrays, pointers, data structures, control statements, I/O and the C function library.

Data Handling Utilities in Microsoft C
Robert A. Radcliffe/Thomas J. Raab
519pp. Ref. 444-5
A C library for commercial programmers, with techniques and utilities for data entry, validation, display and storage. Focuses on creating and manipulating custom logical data types: dates, dollars, phone numbers, much more.

COMMUNICATIONS

Mastering Crosstalk XVI
Peter W. Gofton
187pp. Ref. 388-0
Recoup the cost of this book in a matter of hours with ready-made routines that speed up and automate your on-line database sessions. Tutorials cover every aspect of installing, running and customizing Crosstalk XVI.

HARDWARE

The RS-232 Solution
Joe Campbell
194pp. Ref. 140-3
A complete how-to guide to trouble-free RS-232-C interfacing from scratch. In-depth coverage of concepts, techniques and testing devices, and case studies deriving cables for a variety of common computers, printers and modems.

Mastering Serial Communications
Peter W. Gofton
289pp. Ref. 180-2
The software side of communications, with details on the IBM PC's serial programming, the XMODEM and Kermit protocols, non-ASCII data transfer, interrupt-level programming and more. Sample programs in C, assembly language and BASIC.

Microprocessor Interfacing Techniques (Third Edition)
Austin Lesea/Rodnay Zaks
456pp. Ref. 029-6

This handbook is for engineers and hobbyists alike, covering every aspect of interfacing microprocessors with peripheral devices. Topics include assembling a CPU, basic I/O, analog circuitry, and bus standards.

From Chips to Systems: An Introduction to Microcomputers (Second Edition)
Rodnay Zaks/Alexander Wolfe
580pp. Ref. 377-5

The best-selling introduction to microcomputer hardware--now fully updated, revised, and illustrated. Such recent advances as 32-bit processors and RISC architecture are introduced and explained for the first time in a beginning text.

Mastering Digital Device Control
William G. Houghton
366pp. Ref. 346-5

Complete principles of system design using single-chip microcontrollers, with numerous examples. Topics include expanding memory and I/O, interfacing with multi-chip CPUs, clocks, display devices, analog measurements, and much more.

SPREADSHEETS AND INTEGRATED SOFTWARE

The ABC's of 1-2-3 (Second Edition)
Chris Gilbert/Laurie Williams
245pp. Ref. 355-4

Online Today recommends it as "an easy and comfortable way to get started with the program." An essential tutorial for novices, it will remain on your desk as a valuable source of ongoing reference and support. For Release 2.

Mastering 1-2-3 (Second Edition)
Carolyn Jorgensen
702pp. Ref. 528-X

Get the most from 1-2-3 Release 2 with this step-by-step guide emphasizing advanced features and practical uses. Topics include data sharing, macros, spreadsheet security, expanded memory, and graphics enhancements.

Lotus 1-2-3 Desktop Companion (SYBEX Ready Reference Series)
Greg Harvey
976pp. Ref. 501-8

A full-time consultant, right on your desk. Hundreds of self-contained entries cover every 1-2-3 feature, organized by topic, indexed and cross-referenced, and supplemented by tips, macros and working examples. For Release 2.

Advanced Techniques in Lotus 1-2-3
Peter Antoniak/E. Michael Lunsford
367pp. Ref. 556-5

This guide for experienced users focuses on advanced functions, and techniques for designing menu-driven applications using macros and the Release 2 command language. Interfacing techniques and add-on products are also considered.

Lotus 1-2-3 Tips and Tricks
Gene Weisskopf
396pp. Ref. 454-2

A rare collection of timesavers and tricks for longtime Lotus users. Topics include macros, range names, spreadsheet design, hardware considerations, DOS operations, efficient data analysis, printing, data interchange, applications development, and more.

Lotus 1-2-3 Instant Reference SYBEX Prompter Series
Greg Harvey/Kay Yarborough Nelson
296pp. Ref. 475-5; 4 3/4x8

Organized information at a glance. When you don't have time to hunt through hundreds of pages of manuals, turn here for a quick reminder: the right key sequence, a brief explanation of a command, or the correct syntax for a specialized function.

Mastering Lotus HAL
Mary V. Campbell

342pp. Ref. 422-4

A complete guide to using HAL "natural language" requests to communicate with 1-2-3—for new and experienced users. Covers all the basics, plus advanced HAL features such as worksheet linking and auditing, macro recording, and more.

Mastering Symphony (Fourth Edition)
Douglas Cobb

857pp. Ref. 494-1

Thoroughly revised to cover all aspects of the major upgrade of Symphony Version 2, this Fourth Edition of Doug Cobb's classic is still "the Symphony bible" to this complex but even more powerful package. All the new features are discussed and placed in context with prior versions so that both new and previous users will benefit from Cobb's insights.

The ABC's of Quattro
Alan Simpson/Douglas J. Wolf

286pp. Ref. 560-3

Especially for users new to spreadsheets, this is an introduction to the basic concepts and a guide to instant productivity through editing and using spreadsheet formulas and functions. Includes how to print out graphs and data for presentation. For Quattro 1.1.

Mastering Quattro
Alan Simpson

576pp. Ref. 514-X

This tutorial covers not only all of Quattro's classic spreadsheet features, but also its added capabilities including extended graphing, modifiable menus, and the macro debugging environment. Simpson brings out how to use all of Quattro's new-generation-spreadsheet capabilities.

Mastering Framework II
Douglas Hergert/Jonathan Kamin

509pp. Ref. 390-2

This business-minded tutorial includes a complete introduction to idea processing, "frames," and software integration, along with its comprehensive treatment of word

processing, spreadsheet, and database management with Framework.

The ABC's of Excel on the IBM PC
Douglas Hergert

326pp. Ref. 567-0

This book is a brisk and friendly introduction to the most important features of Microsoft Excel for PC's. This beginner's book discusses worksheets, charts, database operations, and macros, all with hands-on examples. Written for all versions through Version 2.

Mastering Excel on the IBM PC
Carl Townsend

628pp. Ref. 403-8

A complete Excel handbook with step-by-step tutorials, sample applications and an extensive reference section. Topics include worksheet fundamentals, formulas and windows, graphics, database techniques, special features, macros and more.

Mastering Enable
Keith D. Bishop

517pp. Ref. 440-2

A comprehensive, practical, hands-on guide to Enable 2.0—integrated word processing, spreadsheet, database management, graphics, and communications—from basic concepts to custom menus, macros and the Enable Procedural Language.

Mastering Q & A (Second Edition)
Greg Harvey

540pp. Ref. 452-6

This hands-on tutorial explores the Q & A Write, File, and Report modules, and the Intelligent Assistant. English-language command processor, macro creation, interfacing with other software, and more, using practical business examples.

Mastering SuperCalc 4
Greg Harvey

311pp. Ref. 419-4

A guided tour of this spreadsheet, database and graphics package shows how and why it adds up to a powerful business planning tool. Step-by-step lessons and real-life examples cover every aspect of the program.

Understanding Javelin PLUS
John R. Levine
Margaret Levine Young
Jordan M. Young
558pp. Ref. 358-9
This detailed guide to Javelin's latest release includes a concise introduction to business modeling, from profit-and-loss analysis to manufacturing studies. Readers build sample models and produce multiple reports and graphs, to master Javelin's unique features.

DATABASE MANAGEMENT

Mastering Paradox (Third Edition)
Alan Simpson
663pp. Ref. 490-9
Paradox is given authoritative, comprehensive explanation in Simpson's up-to-date new edition which goes from database basics to command-file programming with PAL. Topics include multiuser networking, the Personal Programmer Application Generator, the Data-Entry Toolkit, and more.

The ABC's of dBASE IV
Robert Cowart
300pp. Ref. 531-X
This superb tutorial introduces beginners to the concept of databases and practical dBASE IV applications featuring the new menu-driven interface, the new report writer, and Query by Example.

Understanding dBASE IV (Special Edition)
Alan Simpson
880pp. Ref. 509-3
This Special Edition is the best introduction to dBASE IV, written by 1 million-reader-strong dBASE expert Alan Simpson. First it gives basic skills for creating and manipulating efficient databases. Then the author explains how to

make reports, manage multiple databases, and build applications. Includes Fast Track speed notes.

dBASE III PLUS Programmer's Reference Guide (SYBEX Ready Reference Series)
Alan Simpson
1056pp. Ref. 508-5
Programmers will save untold hours and effort using this comprehensive, well-organized dBASE encyclopedia. Complete technical details on commands and functions, plus scores of often-needed algorithms.

The ABC's of dBASE III PLUS
Robert Cowart
264pp. Ref. 379-1
The most efficient way to get beginners up and running with dBASE. Every 'how' and 'why' of database management is demonstrated through tutorials and practical dBASE III PLUS applications.

Mastering dBASE III PLUS: A Structured Approach
Carl Townsend
342pp. Ref. 372-4
In-depth treatment of structured programming for custom dBASE solutions. An ideal study and reference guide for applications developers, new and experienced users with an interest in efficient programming.

Also:
Mastering dBASE III: A Structured Approach
Carl Townsend
338pp. Ref. 301-5

Understanding dBASE III PLUS
Alan Simpson
415pp. Ref. 349-X
A solid sourcebook of training and ongoing support. Everything from creating a first database to command file programming is presented in working examples, with tips and techniques you won't find anywhere else.

Also:

Understanding dBASE III
Alan Simpson
300pp. Ref. 267-1

Understanding dBASE II
Alan Simpson
260pp. Ref. 147-0

**Advanced Techniques
in dBASE III PLUS**
Alan Simpson
454pp. Ref. 369-4
A full course in database design and
structured programming, with routines for
inventory control, accounts receivable,
system management, and integrated
databases.

**Simpson's dBASE Tips and
Tricks (For dBASE III PLUS)**
Alan Simpson
420pp. Ref. 383-X
A unique library of techniques and programs shows how creative use of built-in
features can solve all your needs--without
expensive add-on products or external languages. Spreadsheet functions, graphics,
and much more.

Expert dBASE III PLUS
Judd Robbins/Ken Braly
423pp. Ref. 404-6
Experienced dBASE programmers learn
scores of advanced techniques for maximizing performance and efficiency in program design, development and testing,
database design, indexing, input and output, using compilers, and much more.

**dBASE Instant Reference
SYBEX Prompter Series**
Alan Simpson
471pp. Ref. 484-4; 4 3/4x8
Comprehensive information at a glance: a
brief explanation of syntax and usage for
every dBASE command, with step-by-
step instructions and exact keystroke
sequences. Commands are grouped by
function in twenty precise categories.

Understanding R:BASE
Alan Simpson/Karen Watterson
609pp. Ref.503-4
This is the definitive R:BASE tutorial, for
use with either OS/2 or DOS. Hands-on
lessons cover every aspect of the software, from creating and using a database, to custom systems. Includes Fast
Track speed notes.

Also:

Understanding R:BASE 5000
Alan Simpson
413pp. Ref. 302-3

Understanding Oracle
James T. Perry/Joseph G. Lateer
634pp. Ref. 534-4
A comprehensive guide to the Oracle
database management system for admin-
istrators, users, and applications developers. Covers everything in Version 5
from database basics to multi-user systems, performance, and development
tools including SQL*Forms, SQL*Report,
and SQL*Calc. Includes Fast Track
speed notes.

GENERAL UTILITIES

**The ABC's of the IBM PC
(Second Edition)**
Joan Lasselle/Carol Ramsay
167pp. Ref. 370-8
Hands-on experience—without technical
detail—for first-time users. Step-by-step
tutorials show how to use essential commands, handle disks, use applications
programs, and harness the PC's special
capabilities.

COMPUTER-AIDED
DESIGN AND
DRAFTING

**The ABC's of AutoCAD
(Second Edition)**
Alan R. Miller
375pp. Ref. 584-0

This brief but effective introduction to AutoCAD quickly gets users drafting and designing with this complex CADD package. The essential operations and capabilities of AutoCAD are neatly detailed, using a proven, step-by-step method that is tailored to the results-oriented beginner.

Mastering AutoCAD (Third Edition)
George Omura
825pp. Ref. 574-3
Now in its third edition, this tutorial guide to computer-aided design and drafting with AutoCAD is perfect for newcomers to CADD, as well as AutoCAD users seeking greater proficiency. An architectural project serves as an example throughout.

Advanced Techniques in AutoCAD (Second Edition)
Robert M. Thomas
425pp. Ref. 593-X
Develop custom applications using screen menus, command macros, and AutoLISP programming--no prior programming experience required. Topics include customizing the AutoCAD environment, advanced data extraction techniques, and much more.

FOR SCIENTISTS AND ENGINEERS

1-2-3 for Scientists and Engineers
William J. Orvis
341pp. Ref. 407-0
Fast, elegant solutions to common problems in science and engineering, using Lotus 1-2-3. Tables and plotting, curve fitting, statistics, derivatives, integrals and differentials, solving systems of equations, and more.

BASIC Programs for Scientists and Engineers
Alan R. Miller
318pp. Ref. 073-3
The algorithms presented in this book are programmed in standard BASIC code which should be usable with almost any implementation of BASIC. Includes statistical calculations, matrix algebra, curve fitting, integration, and more.

Turbo BASIC Programs for Scientists and Engineers
Alan R. Miller
276pp. Ref. 429-1
This practical text develops commonly-needed algorithms for scientific and engineering applications, and programs them in Turbo BASIC. Simultaneous solution, curve fitting, nonlinear equations, numerical integration and more.

Turbo Pascal Programs for Scientists and Engineers
Alan R. Miller
332pp. Ref. 424-0
The author develops commonly-needed algorithms for science and engineering, then programs them in Turbo Pascal. Includes algorithms for statistics, simultaneous solutions, curve fitting, integration, and nonlinear equations.

FORTRAN Programs for Scientists and Engineers (Second Edition)
Alan R. Miller
280pp. Ref. 571-9
In this collection of widely used scientific algorithms--for statistics, vector and matrix operations, curve fitting, and more--the author stresses effective use of little-known and powerful features of FORTRAN.

WORD PROCESSING

The ABC's of WordPerfect 5
Alan R. Neibauer
283pp. Ref. 504-2
This introduction explains the basics of desktop publishing with WordPerfect 5: editing, layout, formatting, printing, sorting, merging, and more. Readers are shown how to use WordPerfect 5's new features to produce great-looking reports.

SYBEX Computer Books are different.

Here is why . . .

At SYBEX, each book is designed with you in mind. Every manuscript is carefully selected and supervised by our editors, who are themselves computer experts. We publish the best authors, whose technical expertise is matched by an ability to write clearly and to communicate effectively. Programs are thoroughly tested for accuracy by our technical staff. Our computerized production department goes to great lengths to make sure that each book is well-designed.

In the pursuit of timeliness, SYBEX has achieved many publishing firsts. SYBEX was among the first to integrate personal computers used by authors and staff into the publishing process. SYBEX was the first to publish books on the CP/M operating system, microprocessor interfacing techniques, word processing, and many more topics.

Expertise in computers and dedication to the highest quality product have made SYBEX a world leader in computer book publishing. Translated into fourteen languages, SYBEX books have helped millions of people around the world to get the most from their computers. We hope we have helped you, too.

For a complete catalog of our publications:

SYBEX, Inc. 2021 Challenger Drive, #100, Alameda, CA 94501
Tel: (415) 523-8233/(800) 227-2346   Telex: 336311
Fax: (415) 523-2373

SYBEX®

TO JOIN THE SYBEX MAILING LIST OR ORDER BOOKS
PLEASE COMPLETE THIS FORM

NAME _____ COMPANY _____

STREET _____ CITY _____

STATE _____ ZIP _____

☐ PLEASE MAIL ME MORE INFORMATION ABOUT **SYBEX** TITLES

ORDER FORM (There is no obligation to order)

PLEASE SEND ME THE FOLLOWING:

TITLE	QTY	PRICE
_____	____	____
_____	____	____
_____	____	____
_____	____	____

TOTAL BOOK ORDER   ____ $____

CUSTOMER SIGNATURE _____

SHIPPING AND HANDLING PLEASE ADD $2.00 PER BOOK VIA UPS   ____

FOR OVERSEAS SURFACE ADD $5.25 PER BOOK PLUS $4.40 REGISTRATION FEE   ____

FOR OVERSEAS AIRMAIL ADD $18.25 PER BOOK PLUS $4.40 REGISTRATION FEE   ____

CALIFORNIA RESIDENTS PLEASE ADD APPLICABLE SALES TAX   ____

TOTAL AMOUNT PAYABLE   ____

☐ CHECK ENCLOSED   ☐ VISA
☐ MASTERCARD   ☐ AMERICAN EXPRESS

ACCOUNT NUMBER _____

EXPIR. DATE _____ DAYTIME PHONE _____

CHECK AREA OF COMPUTER INTEREST:

☐ BUSINESS SOFTWARE

☐ TECHNICAL PROGRAMMING

☐ OTHER: _____

THE FACTOR THAT WAS MOST IMPORTANT IN YOUR SELECTION:

☐ THE SYBEX NAME

☐ QUALITY

☐ PRICE

☐ EXTRA FEATURES

☐ COMPREHENSIVENESS

☐ CLEAR WRITING

☐ OTHER _____

OTHER COMPUTER TITLES YOU WOULD LIKE TO SEE IN PRINT:

_____

_____

OCCUPATION

☐ PROGRAMMER   ☐ TEACHER

☐ SENIOR EXECUTIVE   ☐ HOMEMAKER

☐ COMPUTER CONSULTANT   ☐ RETIRED

☐ SUPERVISOR   ☐ STUDENT

☐ MIDDLE MANAGEMENT   ☐ OTHER:

☐ ENGINEER/TECHNICAL   _____

☐ CLERICAL/SERVICE

☐ BUSINESS OWNER/SELF EMPLOYED

CHECK YOUR LEVEL OF COMPUTER USE   OTHER COMMENTS:

☐ NEW TO COMPUTERS

☐ INFREQUENT COMPUTER USER

☐ FREQUENT USER OF ONE SOFTWARE

   PACKAGE:

   NAME _____

☐ FREQUENT USER OF MANY SOFTWARE

   PACKAGES

☐ PROFESSIONAL PROGRAMMER

PLEASE FOLD, SEAL, AND MAIL TO SYBEX

SYBEX, INC.
2021 CHALLENGER DR. #100
ALAMEDA, CALIFORNIA USA
                 94501

SEAL